China in Oceania

Foundations in Asia Pacific Studies

Editors:

Malcolm Cooper, Vice President, International Cooperation and Research at Ritsumeikan Asia Pacific University.

Jerry Eades, Dean of Asia Pacific Studies at Ritsumeikan Asia Pacific University.

The Asia Pacific Region is establishing itself as the new center of the world economy in the 21st Century, reflected by a growing political and cultural influence. This series documents its rise and examines its structure through accessible accounts from leading social science experts and perspectives from inside and outside the region. Invaluable to students and researchers alike, this series will form a basis for our knowledge of the region and the changes taking place within it.

VOLUME 1
China in Oceania: Reshaping the Pacific?
Edited by Terence Wesley-Smith and Edgar A. Porter

VOLUME 2
Wind over Water: Rethinking Migration in an East Asian Setting
Edited by David W. Haines, Keiko Yamanaka, and Shinji Yamashita

VOLUME 3
Tourism in the Asia Pacific Region: Past, Present, and Future Trends
Edited by Malcolm Cooper, Jeremy S. Eades, and Patricia Erfurt-Cooper

China in Oceania

Reshaping the Pacific?

EDITED BY
Terence Wesley-Smith
AND
Edgar A. Porter

Berghahn Books
New York • Oxford

First published in 2010 by

Berghahn Books

www.berghahnbooks.com

Library of Congress Cataloging-in-Publication Data

China in Oceania : reshaping the Pacific? / edited by Terence Wesley-Smith and
Edgar A. Porter.
    p. cm. — (Foundations in Asia Pacific studies ; v. 1)
    Includes bibliographical references and index.
    ISBN 978-1-84545-632-0 (pbk. : alk. paper)
    1. Oceania—Relations—China. 2. China—Relations—Oceania. I. Wesley-Smith,
Terence. II. Porter, Edgar A.
    DU68.C6C45 2010
    303.48′251095—dc22

              2010003700

British Library Cataloguing in Publication Data

A catalogue record for this book is available from the British Library

Printed in the United States on acid-free paper.

ISBN: 978-1-84545-632-0 Paperback

✄ Contents

𝄢 Figures

Maps

Tables

Illustrations

✦ Acknowledgments

Most of the chapters in this volume started life as papers presented at the conference "China in Oceania: Towards a New Regional Order?" held at Ritsumeikan Asia Pacific University, Beppu, Japan, 26–27 March 2007. The chapters by Bill Willmott (Chapter 5) and Hank Nelson (Chapter 6) were solicited later. The conference was co-convened by Edgar A. Porter and Terence Wesley-Smith and co-sponsored by the Institute of International Strategic Studies at Ritsumeikan Asia Pacific University, and the Center for Pacific Islands Studies at the University of Hawai`i at Manoa. Additional funding was provided by the Islands of Globalization Project at East-West Center's Pacific Islands Development Program, Ritsumeikan University in Kyoto, and the Research Division of Ritsumeikan Asia Pacific University. The editors are grateful for the generous support received from these institutions, and for the cheerful cooperation of the contributors in the preparation of the manuscript. They would also like to thank Professor Jeremy Eades (Ritsumeikan Asia Pacific University) and an anonymous external reader for their very valuable comments on earlier versions of the book.

The Pacific Islands and East Asia

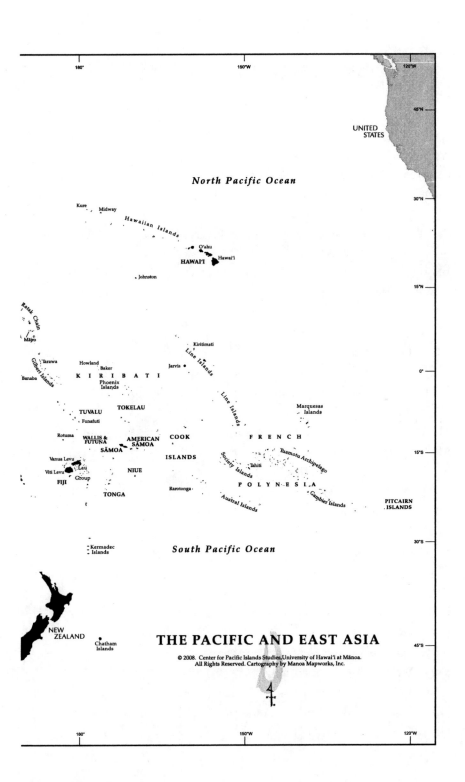

180° 150°W 120°W

UNITED
STATES

45°N

North Pacific Ocean

30°N

Kure · Midway

Hawaiian Islands

O'ahu
HAWAI'I Hawai'i

· Johnston

15°N

Ratak Chain

Majro

Kiritimati

Tarawa Howland Line Islands
Baker Jarvis ·

Gilbert Islands

Banaba K I R I B A T I
Phoenix
Islands

0°

Line Islands

Marquesas
Islands

TUVALU TOKELAU
· Funafuti

Rotuma WALLIS & AMERICAN COOK F R E N C H
FUTUNA SĀMOA
SĀMOA ISLANDS Tuamotu Archipelago

15°S

Vanua Levu Society Islands Tahiti
Viti Levu Lau NIUE P O L Y N E S I A
Group Gambier Islands
FIJI Rarotonga ·
TONGA Austral Islands PITCAIRN
ISLANDS

30°S

Kermadec South Pacific Ocean
Islands

NEW
ZEALAND Chatham
Islands

45°S

THE PACIFIC AND EAST ASIA

© 2008. Center for Pacific Islands Studies, University of Hawai'i at Mānoa.
All Rights Reserved. Cartography by Manoa Mapworks, Inc.

180° 150°W 120°W

Abbreviations

ASEAN, the Association of Southeast Asian Nations
AusAID, the Australian Government's Overseas Aid Program
EEZ, Exclusive Economic Zone
EPG, Eminent Persons' Group
ESCAP, the Executive Secretary of the United Nations Social and Economic
    Commission for Asia and the Pacific
FSM, the Federated States of Micronesia
FTA, Free Trade Agreement
GDP, Gross Domestic Product
GNI, Gross National Income
G8, Group of Eight
ICBC, the International Commercial Bank of China
ICDF, the International Cooperation and Development Fund
IMF, International Monetary Fund
MOU, Memorandum of Understanding
MCC, Metallurgical Group Corporation
MHLC, the Multilateral High Level Conference
ODA, Overseas Development Aid
OECD, Organization for Economic Co-operation and Development
PIF, Pacific Islands Forum
PNG, Papua New Guinea
PRC, the People's Republic of China
PSB the Pacific Savings Bank
RCDF, the Rural Constituency Development Fund
RMB, renminbi, the currency of the People's Republic of China
ROC, Republic of China/Taiwan
WTO World Trade Organization
UNCLOS, the UN Convention on the Law of the Sea
UNCTAD, the United Nations Conference on Trade and Development
UNDP, United Nations Development Program

INTRODUCTION

Oceania Matters

Edgar A. Porter and Terence Wesley-Smith

Introduction

In 1982 one of the editors of this volume visited the quiet campus of Brigham Young University-Hawai'i on the north shore of Oahu. Recently returned from a two-year stay as a "foreign expert" at a Chinese university, he was surprised to find a small group of young Chinese officials studying at this Mormon institution. It turned out that they had been sent by the Chinese Foreign Ministry to study the history, politics, and cultures of the Pacific Islands, and become experts on this isolated region of the world. In those early days of China's emergence as a global power, it seems, real-world politics trumped Beijing's remaining sensitivities regarding both religion and political ideology.

Today we tend to view China's vigorous role in the Pacific as a relatively new phenomenon, but this initiative was put in place only a few years after the end of the Cultural Revolution and before the outline of a new global strategy became obvious. As part of the radical changes initiated by Deng Xiaoping, China chose to take an active, if softer and more informed, stance toward the world. The vision was there: future leaders were placed in strategic locations and, while we do not know what roles the Hawai'i-trained foreign ministry officials play today, they are certainly part of a grand scheme that has changed the economic and geopolitical reality of Oceania. Governor of the London School of Economics Will Hutton identifies the mantra originating with Deng and still followed today: "China should not attempt to be a hegemon, it should never practice power politics and it should never pose a threat to its neighbors or to world peace" (Hutton 2007: 220). This is the image China strives to project to its global neighbors, and one that is now readily accepted in many Pacific Island states.

So, what is China up to in the vast but sparsely populated region of Oceania? As shown in the following chapters, there are answers, but not one answer. Certainly the diplomatic struggle between China and Taiwan for influence among the fourteen independent or self-governing island states is an important part of the calculus. Access to natural resources is also significant, with a current focus on fisheries, timber, oil, gas, and minerals, and a longer-term interest in the vast untapped wealth of the Pacific seabed. Beijing may also see opportunities to increase its political sway in a region of the world long considered an integral part of the Western sphere of influence, especially at a time when the United States and Great Britain have lowered their regional profiles. Whatever the particular mix of foreign policy motivations at work in Beijing, however, one thing is clear. As pointed out in this volume by former New Zealand ambassador to Beijing Michael Powles, China's presence will be long-lasting and patient. Indeed, it is just this realization that has caused the more established regional powers, including the United States, Australia, New Zealand, and Japan, to sit up and take notice. Many of the contributors to this collection discuss the implications of China's active presence for Western interests in Oceania.

It is important to see China's activities in the Pacific Islands not just in terms of a specific set of interests, but in the context of Beijing's recent efforts to develop a comprehensive foreign policy that is global in scope. China's policy toward Oceania is part of a much larger outreach to the developing world, a major work in progress that involves similar initiatives in Asia, Africa, Latin America, and the Middle East (Eisenman, Heginbotham, and Mitchell 2007a). Much of this introductory chapter is devoted to tracing the recent evolution of China's foreign policy by identifying its fundamental objectives, as well as the changing strategies and tools deployed to achieve those ends. Oceania is but the latest part of the world to see the writing on the wall, to confront the realities of China's emergence as a significant force in the global politics of the twenty-first century (Hutton 2007).

What of the view from the Pacific? A central purpose of this collection is to give voice to those from the region who view China's influence from a grounded and local perspective, and whose voices too often are drowned out by external observers with their own axes to grind and ready access to popular and scholarly media. We have found a general consensus that while there is concern about such an enormous and relatively unfamiliar power acquiring a significant stake in Pacific futures, there is also clear appreciation for China's recent efforts in the region. Those within official circles, for example, acknowledge the fact that China pledges not to interfere in domestic policy, comment on governance or other development issues, or attach conditions to transfers of aid and other resources. Speaking to a reporter about similar responses in Africa, Garth Shelton of South Africa's Wits University indicates that there is growing optimism about China: "If we deal with the United States or West European governments they would bring a list of 33 items requiring restructuring of your democracy, your human rights issues. China would arrive and say we accept you as you are. And that's a refreshing change" (Gracie 2006).

Pacific presidents and prime ministers also respond positively to the egalitarian qualities of contemporary Chinese diplomacy. Leaders of island states are treated with respect regardless of their nation's size, resource endowment, or system of government. Perhaps most important, China's growing regional presence allows Pacific leaders to contemplate alternatives to established networks of power and influence, and entrenched models of economic and political development.

Not surprisingly, the emergence of these Pacific alternatives is of concern to policy makers in Western centers of power accustomed to setting regional agendas. As discussed later in this chapter, and by several other contributors, some analysts argue that China's no-strings-attached foreign policy approach is already undermining Western efforts to enhance human rights and good governance in the developing world. At one level, this is a discussion about development theory and practice, and about the relevance of these ideas to the welfare of populations in the Pacific Islands and elsewhere. But at another, it is a high-stakes debate about China's ability to influence international rules, norms, and values—and ultimately about control of the international system itself.

Following professor of international relations Barry Buzan (2004: 143), we suggest in this chapter that the most important question to ask is not if China matters in global politics, because it clearly does, but rather "How and to whom does China matter?" Along with the other contributors, we will argue that the rise of China in Oceania certainly matters to established regional powers like Australia, New Zealand, and Japan, as well as to the sole global superpower, the United States. But it matters most immediately to the peoples of Oceania who, like others in the developing world, continue to face uncertain economic and political prospects.

China Matters

Less than a decade ago, a prominent international relations analyst, the late Gerald Segal, could argue that China's global power and influence were greatly overrated: "At best, China is a second-rank middle power that has mastered the art of diplomatic theater.... Only when we finally understand how little China matters will we be able to craft a sensible policy toward it" (Segal 1999: 11). Whatever its merits at the time, Segal's thesis would attract few endorsements today, especially from economists. Since the late 1990s China's economy has continued to grow much faster than the global economy as a whole. By 2006, China accounted for 5.5 percent of world Gross Domestic Product (GDP), up from the 3.5 percent cited by Segal, and was closing in on Germany for third place in world ranking. Using an alternative purchasing-power-parity measure, the World Bank estimates that China has increased its global share from 11.8 percent when Segal wrote to 15 percent today, placing it second only to the United States. Expansion in trade with the outside word is equally impressive. By 2005 China accounted for more than 7 percent of world merchandise exports and over 6 percent of imports, ranking third behind the United States and Germany in both categories.[1] And even if it is not yet a major locomotive of global economic growth like the United States or Japan, it may well play that role in the not-too-distant future. As senior Australian analyst Stuart Harris put it, China's economy "does matter, and its concerns and interests do have to be taken into account" by the rest of the world (Harris 2004: 70, 68–70).

For Segal, the question of whether or not China matters in world politics was also linked to its ability to reshape an international system heavily dominated by the United States. He was most dismissive of this possibility. China was a non–status quo power, Segal argued, that "matters most for the West because it can make mischief, either by threatening its neighbors, or assisting anti-Western forces further afield" (Segal 1999: 19). Here Segal may have been referring to China's heavy-handed approach to territorial disputes in Southeast Asia during the 1990s, although his comments appear to hark back to an earlier era when Beijing lent its support to radical movements worldwide. However, by the time Segal's *Foreign Affairs* piece was published in the late 1990s, a new approach to China's foreign policy was already apparent. This new strategy is global in scope, and pragmatically focused on core objectives to be achieved through a variety of "soft power" techniques. The approach has improved Beijing's global reputation and influence, especially among its immediate neighbors and in the developing world more generally. Even among developed countries, China's constructive role in key international political and economic institutions is increasingly (if grudgingly) acknowledged. According to Kurt Campbell of the Center for Strategic and International Studies, a Washington-based think tank with strong ties to government and private industry, "China has determined that in most circumstances—and at least for now—its needs are best met by seeking to shape the current global framework from inside the tent" (Campbell 2007: x).

Changing Foreign Policy

For much of China's long history its leaders have focused their energies on internal politics, despite periodic forays to secure or expand the country's periphery. Under the leadership of Mao Zedong after 1949, however, China developed a focus on other nations that had experienced the humiliations of Western colonialism and economic exploitation. In 1953 Premier Zhou Enlai articulated "five principles of peaceful coexistence" to guide relations with these nations, and the 1955 Bandung conference signaled the emergence of China as a leader of the Non-Aligned Movement, whose members resisted taking sides in an increasingly polarized world.[2] Through the late 1950s and 1960s China's leaders advocated socialist revolution and economic self-reliance in Asia, Africa, and Latin America, and provided political, material, and military support to revolutionary movements throughout the developing world (Mitchell and McGiffert 2007: 13–17).

In the aftermath of the Cultural Revolution China began to reform its internal and external relations, increasingly emphasizing pragmatic over ideological considerations. By 1972 it had reestablished relations with the United States and resumed its place at the United Nations. But the present foreign policy era really began in 1979, as the tenets of wealth creation through economic liberalization took center stage under the leadership of Deng Xiaoping. According to sociologist Doug Guthrie, changing patterns of foreign relations, especially in trade, are inextricably linked to internal change in China over the last three decades. The course of change, he argued, "has been a fundamentally global one.... Chinese leaders have leveraged the process of global integration to transform China from within" (Guthrie 2006: 331).

By 1980 China had joined the World Bank and International Monetary Fund, two bedrock institutions in the Western-dominated international financial order. China's eventual entry into the World Trade Organization (WTO) in December 2001 represented an internal victory of reform-minded leaders over hard-liners with a continuing commitment to communist principles. The long resistance of the United States to China's WTO entry reflected ongoing concerns about human rights issues and authoritarian governance practices. But anxiety about China's growing ability to disturb established economic relations within the United States and elsewhere in the world undoubtedly added weight to the opposition in Washington, D.C. (Guthrie 2006: 25–26).

China's fundamental foreign policy objectives have remained constant in recent years, although its strategies to achieve those goals have changed dramatically. As summarized by the RAND Corporation's Eric Heginbotham (2007: 203), one of China's core objectives is to preserve a peaceful international environment. This allows Beijing to pursue economic growth and focus on pressing internal issues without the distraction of conflict with other countries, especially those on its borders.[3] With its roots in Zhou Enlai's philosophies of the early 1950s, the notion of China's peaceful rise counters any tendency to challenge the United States or other powers, and helps explain Beijing's current preference for working "inside the tent" of existing international institutions. A major exception to this emphasis on peace and stability is Beijing's belligerent stand on the issue of independence for Taiwan, which it still regards as an integral part of the People's Republic of China. However, even in this most sensitive of areas, Beijing has worked hard in recent years to avoid escalating the military and political standoff across the Taiwan Straits.

Another key objective for Beijing is to avoid encirclement or isolation, a sentiment that has deep roots in China's history of engagement with imperialist powers such as the United States, Great Britain, and Japan, as well as its sometimes volatile relationships with neighboring states, including Russia. In its current form, the objective largely reflects a determination to offset any attempts by the United States (and to a lesser extent Japan) to contain or limit China's economic and political rise, especially in Asia and other resource-rich parts of the world. Many recent foreign-policy initiatives, including strategic partnerships with key regional states and increased involvement in regional organizations, serve to further this counter-containment goal.

An increasingly important foreign policy objective involves securing and maintaining reliable access to the raw materials and markets necessary to support China's continued economic expansion. China's phenomenal record of wealth creation in recent decades rests in large part on the development of a coastally based, export-oriented economy, which by 2006 was generating a GDP of US$2.67 trillion and foreign trade worth US $1.4 trillion. The demand for raw materials is not only rising rapidly, but in many cases fast outstripping domestic supplies.[4] The problem is most acute in the field of energy. Although China is a major producer of oil and gas, it is already importing substantial quantities of these items from overseas. Indeed, according to some estimates, by the year 2030 China will import as much oil as the United States (Harris 2004: 62–63).

On the other side of the trade equation, China exports much of what it manufactures to corporate partners in the United States and other developed countries, as well as to consumers in markets around the world. China's leaders have staked their future on rising standards of living associated with continued economic growth, and Beijing's foreign policy establishment works hard to make this possible.

A final core foreign policy objective for China is the creation of a more evenly balanced and decentralized international system. This emphasis on multipolarity has its roots in China's largely unsuccessful post–World War II attempts to carve out more space for a developing world caught between two ideological poles during the cold war. Although the collapse of the Soviet Union in 1989 raised the possibility of a more open system, there was no decisive shift toward multipolarity. Instead, the 1991 Gulf War quickly demonstrated the overwhelming military might of the United States, as well as its determination to remain the principal steward of global politics. Indeed, the invasion of Afghanistan and the Bush administration's "war on terror" reinforced rather than diminished the preeminent position of the United States in the global system.[5] China frequently advocates the democratization of international relations, but its commitment to a peaceful rise precludes any dramatic moves in this direction. For the moment at least, Beijing focuses on building numerous bilateral and multilateral initiatives that collectively serve to balance, rather than confront, United States hegemony (Heginbotham 2007: 198).

Soft Power

Although the fundamental objectives of China's foreign policy have been in place for nearly three decades, the way those objectives are prioritized has shifted in response to changing circumstances. Reliable access to raw materials has become much more important, while China's quest for a multipolar world has been tempered for now. Meanwhile, the idea of China's peaceful rise to power has come to the fore, not just as an objective in itself, but as a key instrument to help achieve other core foreign policy goals. Indeed, the most dramatic changes to Beijing's foreign policy in recent times have been in the strategies employed to achieve key objectives, rather than in the objectives themselves.

By the mid 1990s it was apparent that China's new, more pragmatic foreign policy was producing mixed results. Its willingness to use force in a series of territorial disputes in Southeast Asia served to raise tensions with neighboring states already uneasy about the economic implications of China's rise, and added momentum to a regional movement to close ranks against Beijing's increasing influence. The relationship with the United States had also reached a low ebb following the Tiananmen Square incident in 1989, new US arms sales to Taiwan in 1992, and ongoing attempts in the United States Congress to link human rights conditions to trade arrangements with China. In response to such developments, Beijing began to implement a more proactive foreign policy approach after about 1997.

According to Eric Heginbotham (2007: 205), Beijing's new approach is "smarter rather than more muscular" and contains a number of distinctive elements. First, it involves a new emphasis on multilateral organizations, especially at the regional level. The first such engagements were in Asia, starting in the mid 1990s with the Shanghai Cooperation Organization, which included neighboring Russia, Kazakhstan, Kyrgyzstan, Tajikstan, and Uzbekistan (Oresman 2007: 63). Perhaps more significant was a new commitment to improved relations with the Association of Southeast Asian Nations (ASEAN), which in November 2002 resulted in a historic agreement designed to ease tensions in the South China Sea, as well as the breakthrough China-ASEAN Free Trade Agreement (Glosny 2007). Since then, Beijing has signed numerous multilateral agreements dealing with trade and other issues in Latin America, the Caribbean, the Middle East, Africa, and Oceania.

Second, these multilateral arrangements have been complemented by a series of comprehensive bilateral relationships with key partner states around the world, including Brazil, Venezuela, Mexico, South Africa, Argentina, India, Indonesia, Nigeria, and Algeria. These "strategic partnerships" are designed to further specific political or economic goals. The relationship with India, for example, is aimed primarily at countering United States containment efforts in South Asia, while attention to Nigeria reflects that country's rich natural resource endowments (Lal 2007; Eisenman 2007: 33–43).

A third strand of China's new-look policy promotes overseas investments. Although China is best known as a destination for foreign direct investment, outflows of funds to other countries have surged in recent years, exceeding US$16 billion by 2006. Some observers note that China's foreign investment remains relatively small, even compared to other developing countries (Morck, Yeung, and Zhao 2007: 2–3). Others argue that not all of what is promised is actually delivered (Kurlantzick 2007: 87). Behind the bland statistics, however, lies a national investment approach that is as much political as it is economic in nature. Chinese companies are offered a range of government incentives to invest overseas, particularly in key industries such as energy, and Kurlantzick (2007: 90) describes "a frantic shopping spree" for oil and gas fields and related companies over the last five years. If Beijing seeks to control the production of commodities that are vital to China's economic well-being, it also emphasizes investment as a way of cementing relationships with overseas partners.

The most significant changes in China's foreign policy in recent years have involved style as well as substance. Nations may be singled out for attention because of their potential to meet Beijing's short- or long-term goals, but the likelihood of success is enhanced by the manner in which leaders are approached and relations nurtured. There has been a concerted attempt to reassure potential partners of Beijing's commitment to the peaceful rise ideal, to more symmetrical forms of international relations characterized by cooperation rather than coercion, and to "win-win" outcomes. Bilateral or multilateral agreements are typically multi-dimensional, involving trade concessions, investment or loan packages, and sometimes development assistance. Potential partners are not necessarily asked to choose sides in situations where third-party interests—such as those of the United States or Japan—are at stake.

Perhaps as important, especially in smaller or poorer countries, leaders in Beijing articulate a classical view of state sovereignty, one that makes no judgments about the internal affairs of partner states and rejects overt attempts to use external relations to leverage internal political or economic change. This is an aspect of China's soft power that often impresses leaders of developing countries and influences their willingness to entertain expanded levels of cooperation. It is also the aspect that raises eyebrows in Western capitals, where relations with developing countries are increasingly structured around issues of transparency, good governance, and respect for human rights. As Heginbotham (2007: 208) concludes: "Perhaps the most challenging aspect of China's rise in the near and middle term ... will be managing its impact on evolving global norms, rather than on stability (where its interests largely, but not entirely, coincide with those of the United States)."

A Regional Emphasis

Often overlooked in the debate about China's rise is the importance of its regional dimensions. Much of Beijing's foreign policy focus in recent years has been on the developing world, and on those states categorized as "transitional" by the United

Nations.[6] Between 1999 and 2003 China's trade with developing countries grew 88 percent faster than that with developed states (Eisenman, Heginbotham, and Mitchell 2007b: xv). That its diplomacy is "taking the developing world by storm" is evidenced by a plethora of recent investment and trade agreements, construction projects, and multilateral initiatives in Africa, Latin America, and the Middle East, and throughout Asia (Heginbotham 2007: 189). And it is at the regional level that a rising China is having its largest and most immediate impacts.

Given its core objectives, China's increased attention to developing and transitional states is hardly surprising. Beijing's primary external interest has always been in the neighboring countries of Central Asia, where strategic, great power, and economic concerns coincide. What has changed in recent years is its level of success in these states, where Beijing's new emphasis on mutual benefits and good-faith leadership has paid handsome dividends (Oresman 2007). Perhaps even more remarkable are Beijing's dramatically improved relations with its neighbors in Southeast Asia, where significant security, political, and economic interests are at stake. These diplomatic gains have resulted largely from similar proactive efforts to reduce mistrust and address regional concerns (Glosny 2007).

Unlike its activities in Asia, China's recent forays into Africa, Latin America, and the Middle East are largely unprecedented—and all the more dramatic as a result. Trade between China and Africa increased by 700 percent during the 1990s, and it doubled again in the four years after the first China-Africa Forum in 2000. Today, China is Africa's third most important trading partner after the United States and France, numerous Chinese companies are doing business on the continent, and there is intense Chinese diplomatic activity (Servant 2005; Eisenman 2007). The predominantly economic nature of Beijing's interest in Latin America is reflected in a significant increase in trade. Between 1999 and 2004 Latin American and Caribbean exports to China increased sevenfold, imports more than tripled, and resource-related Chinese investments surged (Jenkins and Peters 2006; Teng 2007). Meanwhile, China has been aggressively pursuing energy supplies and markets for its products in the Middle East. Rapidly expanding imports of oil and exports of manufactured goods generated trade valued at US$36.7 billion by 2004—about the same as the value of trade between the United States and the Arab world. Furthermore, the volume of trade continues to grow at more than 40 percent annually (Yufeng 2007: 113, 118).[7]

China's intense new interest in the developing world is highly significant for several reasons. First, it is now a central focus of Beijing's external efforts and thus reflects the essential nature and objectives of China's evolving foreign policy. Second, China's regional activities have major economic and political consequences, not only for the countries immediately involved, but for other global actors and, ultimately, for the international community as a whole—whether Beijing intends those secondary impacts or not (Campbell 2007; Eisenman, Heginbotham, and Mitchell 2007a).

Today, these "knock-on" dynamics are most apparent in Central, East, and Southeast Asia (Freedman 2004: 35–36). Beijing has made major diplomatic strides in these parts of the world in recent years, and its potential for regional leadership is increasingly acknowledged. China's success in Asia has obvious implications for other powers actively involved there, most notably the United States and Japan. Although regional leadership is a more distant prospect for China in Africa, Latin America, and the Arab world, the potential to bump up against the strategic, economic, and political interests of other world powers is obvious. That there has been remarkably little great power tension in these potential flashpoints is largely attributable to Beijing's current conciliatory approach to bilateral and multilateral relations.

Finally, and most important, the recent extension of China's global reach has profound implications for an increasing number of people in developing countries. However, few analysts have examined the regional dimensions of Beijing's new foreign policy in any depth, let alone investigated China's evolving relationship with the developing world as a whole. A notable exception here is *China and the Developing World,* edited by Joshua Eisenman, Eric Heginbotham, and Derek Mitchell (2007b).[8] But even the authors in this collection tend to examine the material through Western lenses, asking questions mostly about great power interests and potential challenges to the status quo in international politics. Most of the existing literature is concerned with what China's rise might mean for the global interests of the United States, rather than for the welfare of the people who inhabit affected parts of the developing world—and represent fully three fourths of humanity as well as a disproportionate share of its poor and disempowered.

Authors who comment on these aspects of China's new-found influence tend to hedge their bets, acknowledging a generally positive reception for China's overtures, but also noting some potential future difficulties. In a recent book-length analysis, journalist Joshua Kurlantzick (2007) celebrates the success of China's global "charm offensive," comparing it unfavorably with Washington's waning soft power efforts.[9] But he also warns that China's growing power could eventually serve to erode "labor and environmental standards in other countries ... and undermine efforts by Western governments and international financial institutions to demand better governance ... from aid recipients" (Kurlantzick 2007: 171). Such arguments draw our attention to negative future possibilities—but they also tend to assume the virtues of the status quo in the political economy of development.

Trends in global development leave no room for complacency. At the turn of the millennium, and after a half-century of massive Western-led development efforts around the globe, United Nations Secretary-General Kofi Anan (2000) could report that "[t]he gross disparities of wealth in today's world, the miserable conditions in which well over a billion people live, the prevalence of endemic conflict in some regions, and the rapid degradation of the natural environment:

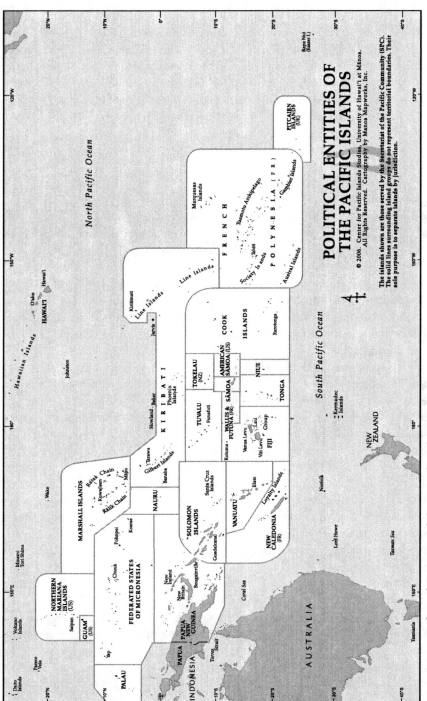

POLITICAL ENTITIES OF THE PACIFIC ISLANDS

© 2006. Center for Pacific Islands Studies, University of Hawai'i at Mānoa. All Rights Reserved. Cartography by Manoa Mapworks, Inc.

The islands shown are those served by the Secretariat of the Pacific Community (SPC). The solid lines surrounding island groups do not represent territorial boundaries. Their sole purpose is to separate islands by jurisdiction.

Map I.1 • Political Entities of the Pacific Islands

all these combine to make the present model of development unsustainable, unless remedial measures are taken by common agreement." There has been some progress toward the achievement of the so-called Millennium Development Goals initiated by Anan, including efforts to reduce the incidence of global poverty. However, it is worth noting that the biggest gains in the war against poverty have been achieved in countries—particularly China—not always noted for their strict adherence to the advice of Western development agencies.[10]

Oceania Matters

Georgetown University's Robert Sutter and Michael Green describe *China and the Developing World* as the first comprehensive treatment of this important topic since the conclusion of the cold war (Eisenman, Heginbotham, and Mitchell 2007b: frontispiece). The work includes six chapters examining China's relations with Africa, Central Asia, Latin America, the Middle East, South Asia, and Southeast Asia, as well as introductory and concluding analysis. Yet there is not a single mention of the Pacific Islands region or of individual island states, and no acknowledgment of this absence. Meanwhile, Joshua Kurlantzick (2007) does little better with just three passing references to the "remote Pacific" in his 300-page treatment of China's global influence.

It is appropriate to question why Oceania, which includes more than twenty separate political entities and encompasses almost a third of the surface of the globe, remains underrepresented in media and scholarly coverage of contemporary world events (see Map I.2). A large part of the explanation has to do with the size of the island entities involved (see Table I.1). Papua New Guinea is the giant of the region, but with a population of less than seven million and land area of about 179,000 square miles it is still relatively small by global standards. All other Pacific Island entities have populations of less than one million, often inhabiting widely scattered archipelagoes of tiny islands. Associated with small size is a popular assumption that island places lack resources of significant interest to the outside world. Indeed, if the Pacific Islands region exists at all in the popular imagination it is as a tourist destination, a benign tropical playground of pleasure and escape.

Oceania does contain significant natural resources. The region's remaining stands of tropical timber are much in demand on global markets, and Papua New Guinea is already a major producer of copper, gold, nickel, oil, and natural gas. The combined 200 mile exclusive economic zones of the region represent more than 11.6 million square miles (30 million square kilometers) of sea space—30 percent of all such zones worldwide—dramatically extending the resource profile of island microstates (see Map I.2). To date this has meant an ownership stake in the world's largest tuna resource and the multibillion dollar industry it supports.

Table I.1 • Key Indicators, Selected Pacific Island Nations*

	Population (2008, est.)	Land Area (sq. miles)	GNI** per capita (US$, 2005)	Aid per capita (US$, 2002)
Cook Islands	15,537	92	10,201	491
FSM***	110,443	271	2,300	702
Fiji	839,324	7,055	3,170	41
Kiribati	97,231	313	1,294	203
Marshall Islands	53,236	70	2,930	823
Nauru	10,163	8	5,828	——
Niue	1,549	100	——	——
Palau	20,279	171	7,670	986
Papua New Guinea	6,473,910	178,704	816	36
Samoa	179,645	1,133	2,020	214
Solomon Islands	517,455	10,954	620	57
Tonga	102,724	251	2,062	217
Tuvalu	9,729	10	2,516	260
Vanuatu	233,026	4,707	1,560	133

*Independent and self-governing members of the Pacific Islands Forum
**Gross National Income
***FSM, Federated States of Micronesia

Sources: World Bank, World Development Indicators Online
　　　PC, Secretariat of the Pacific Community
　　　Jayaraman and Choong 2006: 334.

Probably more important in the longer term, however, are the enormous deposits of manganese, copper, and cobalt that are known to exist on the Pacific seabed, particularly in the vicinity of the Clarion-Clipperton fracture zone, as well as those that are yet to be identified elsewhere in the region. It is only a matter of time before market and technological factors combine to make the large-scale exploitation of these resources feasible—with significant implications for some Pacific Island states and the regional economy as a whole.

Nevertheless, strategic rather than economic considerations have tended to determine the nature and extent of external interest in the region over the centuries. Oceania's strategic value is usually perceived as a function of its location relative to other, more dynamic, regions of economic or political activity.[11] As a result, external involvement has often been driven not by a compelling need to access the resources of a particular territory, but by a defensive desire to exclude others from what is often condescendingly described as America's "backyard," Australia's "patch," or New Zealand's "neighborhood."

The idea of strategic denial featured prominently in the early colonial history of the Pacific, as expansionist European powers like Great Britain, France, Germany, and the Netherlands established large colonial spheres of influence in

Map I.2 • 200 Mile Exclusive Economic Zones of the Pacific

order to protect smaller nodes of real economic or political interest. Similarly, the massive military deployments of the Pacific War were designed not just to liberate island populations from Japanese occupation, but to protect the security and economic interests of places like Australia, New Zealand, and the United States. The pattern was repeated during the cold war, as a group of allies, including the United States, France, Australia, and New Zealand, worked diligently to exclude the Soviet Union or any threatening surrogates from establishing footholds in this vast buffer zone of Western influence. These efforts relied on large transfers of development assistance, and today per capita aid flows to Pacific Island nations remain among the highest in the world (see Tables I.1 and I.2).

Oceania's low profile in global politics owes as much to its tacit status as an "American lake" as to its marginal importance in the global economy. Furthermore, at least until recently, the sorts of pressing political and humanitarian issues afflicting many other parts of the developing world were conspicuously absent in the Pacific. The process of decolonization was generally peaceful and, despite disadvantages of small size and lack of resources, most of the newly formed island states have been relatively stable in the post-independence period.

However, some serious political problems have emerged in more recent years (see e.g. Henderson and Watson 2005). Fiji, for example, has experienced four coups since 1987, the latest in December 2006, and the Solomon Islands has yet to fully recover from violent clashes between militant groups that by mid 2000 had brought most state functions to a standstill. The secessionist conflict on the island of Bougainville, politically part of Papua New Guinea and the site of a giant copper and gold mine, was more serious in humanitarian terms. In the decade after the crisis erupted in 1988, an estimated 20,000 people lost their lives either in armed clashes between official forces and factions of the Bougainville Revolutionary Army, or as result of deprivations associated with the government-imposed blockade of the island.[12]

Table I.2 • Aid Donors to Oceania, 2006*

Donor	Amount US$m	Share %
Australia	480	42.6
United States	187	16.6
New Zealand	113	10.1
France	112	9.9
EC	78	6.9
Japan	76	6.8

*The table reflects Organization for Economic Co-operation and Development (OECD) statistics, which do not include information about China

Source: OECD International Development Statistics

Despite increasingly alarmist talk in Australia and New Zealand of a Pacific "arc of instability," these regional crises have attracted relatively little international attention. No extra-regional powers have rallied to the aid of dissident factions in any of the regional conflicts, and efforts in support of besieged governments have come almost exclusively from within the region. Although Commonwealth connections have been activated after each of the Fiji coups, and United Nations observers were involved in peacekeeping activities in Bougainville, these interventions have been of relatively minor importance. And it is interesting to note that the most significant interventionist effort to date—the Australian-led Regional Assistance Mission to the Solomon Islands launched in 2003—was justified with reference to a perceived threat to regional security. At the time analysts suggested that the Solomon Islands constituted a "failed state" that might provide a safe haven for international terrorists and threaten the interests of neighboring states, particularly Australia—even though no such subversive activity had been identified (Wesley-Smith 2008).

China and the Pacific Islands

Although seen as marginal by many commentators, Oceania has obviously not escaped the attention of some "nontraditional" external powers, including China. Indeed, University of the South Pacific Professor Emeritus Ron Crocombe identified what he calls "a spectacular transition" underway in the region: "For the past 200 years, external influences, whether cultural, economic, political or other, have come overwhelmingly from Western sources. That is now in the process of shifting to predominantly Asian sources" (Crocombe 2007). Crocombe discussed the growing regional involvement of Japan, Indonesia, Malaysia, Korea, and the Philippines, and described China as the "expansionist power of the Asia-Pacific this century" (2007: 249). Other analysts have addressed various aspects of China's new relationship with Oceania, although most are primarily concerned about the implications for Western interests in the region.[13] *China in Oceania* is the first book-length collection to address the topic in a systematic way—and the first publication to include a range of Pacific Island perspectives on the evolving relationship.

As several contributors to this volume discuss, China has a long history of interaction with Oceania. Chinese traders were active in the region in the nineteenth century, and significant numbers of contract laborers and small business operators followed later. Motivated mainly by cold war–related political and strategic concerns, Beijing began to establish official ties with newly independent Pacific Island states in the mid 1970s (Godley 1983). Today Chinese officials have regular interactions with representatives of all of the independent or self-governing island nations, and Beijing maintains formal diplomatic relations with

Papua New Guinea, Samoa, Tonga, Cook Islands, Fiji, Vanuatu, and the Federated States of Micronesia. China has also developed working relations with major
regional organizations including the Pacific Islands Forum.

China's interest and involvement in Oceania have increased significantly over
the last decade. In an address at the annual meeting of the Pacific Islands Forum in
October 2000, China's Vice Foreign Minister Yang Jiechi noted that the value of
trade with the region had almost doubled in each of the previous two years, and
that the number of Chinese-funded infrastructure projects was also expanding
rapidly. He announced the establishment of the China–Pacific Islands Forum Cooperation Fund, the opening of a Pacific Islands Forum Trade Office in Beijing,
and predicted a "lasting, stable and ever growing relationship" with the region
(Yang 2000). By 2006 the value of trade had reached US$743 million, more than
four times the total in 1999. In the same year Beijing announced plans to raise
substantially the level of its engagement with the region.

At the first China–Pacific Island Countries Economic Development and Cooperation Forum in Fiji in April 2006, Chinese Premier Wen Jiabao pledged to
make available preferential loans worth US$376 million over three years, estab-
lish a fund to encourage Chinese companies to invest in the region, cancel or
extend debts maturing in 2005, and remove tariffs on imports from the least
developed island nations (see Appendix for Wen's statement and a response from
Papua New Guinea Prime Minister Michael Somare).[14] In a recent report for
the Sydney-based Lowy Institute for International Policy, Fergus Hanson (2008)
demonstrates that China's aid program in Oceania is large and growing rapidly.
Indeed, he suggests that if all pledged aid is actually delivered, China is now one
of the largest aid donors to the independent and self-governing Pacific Island
states, second only to Australia (see Tables I.2 and I.3).[15]

Beijing's new Oceania initiative shares many of the hallmarks of its recent
engagement with other parts of the developing world. First, it includes comprehensive bilateral relations with a number of regional states, some of which are
discussed in detail later in this volume. There is a particular emphasis on relations with Fiji, perhaps because of its pivotal role as the focus of much regional
commerce and diplomatic activity (Chapter 7). Samoa, arguably China's oldest

Table I.3 • China's Pledged Aid to Selected Pacific Island Nations,
2005–2007*

US$millions		
2005	**2006**	**2007**
33	78	293

*Cook Islands, Federated States of Micronesia, Fiji, Niue, Papua New Guinea, Samoa, Tonga, and
Vanuatu.

Source: Hanson 2008: 11

and most faithful ally in the region, also seems to be singled out for favorable treatment (Chapter 9). Although Tonga recognized China relatively recently, a number of business deals—particularly one allowing China access to Tonga-controlled satellite orbits—appear to make it worthy of special attention (Chapter 10). Relations with Papua New Guinea have proved rather more volatile, but its vast array of natural resources makes it a natural trading partner for China (Chapter 6). Second, China's bilateral agreements in the Pacific Islands region are multifaceted and typically include trade concessions, investments, and concessionary loans, as well as aid and technical assistance.

Finally, there is a new emphasis on multilateral relations. The April 2006 summit in Fiji was a first for the region, and with plans for a follow-up meeting in 2010. But it reflects the form and substance of similar events elsewhere, including the China-Africa Forum on Cooperation series launched in 2000, and the China-Caribbean Economic and Trade Cooperation Forum held for the first time in Jamaica in February 2005. It is also worth noting that these multilateral initiatives are specifically designed not to replicate or replace the existing architecture of regional cooperation. Indeed, Beijing has been careful also to work within established Pacific regional organizations in recent years, and to avoid any direct challenges to existing patterns of leadership. China has been a dialogue partner of the most important regional organization, the Pacific Islands Forum, since the dialogue mechanism was created in 1989. In general, it has used this annual venue to establish its credentials as an interested party in regional affairs, and to offer relatively modest material support for the operation of regional bodies, including the Forum Secretariat, the Forum Fisheries Agency, and the South Pacific Regional Environment Program. However, Beijing has not demonstrated any leadership ambitions at the forum.[16] Perhaps in part to assuage Australian fears that a rising China will derail ongoing attempts to enhance regional cooperation and encourage good governance, Beijing has recently pledged support for the Pacific Plan, a major blueprint for such efforts. It has also agreed to participate in meetings designed to coordinate the efforts of regional aid donors, and in February 2008 China signed the Kavieng Declaration on Aid Effectiveness, which provides some guidelines for donor countries involved in Papua New Guinea (Hanson 2008: 15).

Chapters

In the chapters that follow, the authors explore motivations for and implications of China's (and Taiwan's) expanded presence in Oceania. Some present broad regional overviews, while others examine more specific issues. Half of the chapters offer studies focused on the experiences of particular Pacific Island nations with China and/or Taiwan.

In Chapter 1 of this volume, Terence Wesley-Smith, a professor of Pacific Islands studies at the University of Hawai'i at Manoa, provides a broad overview of some strategic, political, and economic dimensions of Beijing's heightened interest in Oceania. He challenges the often disingenuous threat discourse pervading the existing literature and argues that China's rise offers island states opportunities not available under established structures of power. Former Director of the New Zealand Asia Institute at Auckland University and current Professor of International Politics at the University of Bristol Yonjin Zhang arrives at a similar conclusion, but goes even further (Chapter 2). He argues that how island states can capitalize on new opportunities for economic development "remains one of the most formidable challenges in the construction of a new regional order in the Pacific," adding that "the shaping of the emerging regional order is firmly in the hands of Pacific Island countries." Zhang dismisses the notion that China has a well-defined strategy to fill a leadership vacuum associated with the United States' neglect of the region. He sees Beijing's Pacific initiatives as consistent with its general approach to the developing world, and argues that, if anything, China has become a regional power "by default."

In Chapter 3, Michael Powles, who has long personal and professional ties to the islands region and has served as New Zealand's ambassador to Beijing, takes a close look at some of the factors affecting China's expanding relationship with Oceania. He identifies access to minerals and rivalry with Taiwan as Beijing's two main interests in the region, and notes that "both these goals are pursued against a background of self-recognition that China is now a major Asia Pacific power." Along with Wesley-Smith and Zhang, Powles finds no evidence that the Pacific is being singled out for special attention, but he has mixed feelings about the implications of this new presence for island states. He argues that there are certain issues—such as possible great power competition, and escalating China-Taiwan conflict—over which islanders have little control. On the other hand, Powles is optimistic that "with skill and possibly some luck," island states will be able to retain control of the tuna and mineral wealth of the ocean as exploitation of these resources increases.

Unlike many authors in this volume, Kobayashi Izumi, a professor of international studies at Osaka-Gakuin University, makes little reference to the roles of Australia, New Zealand, and the United States in the changing politics of the region (Chapter 4). In perhaps the first English-language treatment of the topic, Kobayashi focuses instead on Japan's interests in Oceania and how they are impacted by China's heightened presence. He explains the mounting sense of unease in Japan about China's rise in the wider Asia-Pacific region, and describes the significant economic and political interests at stake. Kobayashi discusses the intricacies of Japan's policy making regarding overseas development assistance and argues that the sharp rise in funds to Oceania announced at the Fourth Japan Pacific Islands Forum summit in May 2006 was clearly related to China's high-profile overtures to the region just one month before. However, he is generally critical of the way Japan's overseas aid program operates, and is not confident that the additional money will help Tokyo retain its present level of influence in a rapidly changing Oceania.

Commentators often note the increased presence of Chinese migrants in Oceania, as well as the resentment they provoke in some island places. However, these authors do not always take care to differentiate between different types of Chinese communities in the islands, or explain the often complex relationship between those communities and government officials in Beijing. In Chapter 5, sociologist Bill Willmott of the University of Canterbury outlines the long history of Chinese migration to the region. He identifies four waves of migration into Oceania, each with its own distinctive characteristics and significance for island communities today. Willmott argues that although Chinese communities can have an impact on local politics, their activities have very little to do with the policies of the Chinese government. Australian National University's Hank Nelson, a historian, takes up similar themes in his discussion of Chinese communities in Papua New Guinea, which hosts the largest number of ethnic Chinese in the region (Chapter 6). He notes that Chinese now outnumber Australians in this former Australian territory by a ratio of two to one, although they do not constitute a single homogenous community. Nelson discusses how some Chinese have become quite influential in business, politics, and the media in Papua New Guinea.

The next five chapters in the volume discuss the involvement of China and Taiwan with particular island countries. In the first case study, in Chapter 7, University of the South Pacific political scientist Sandra Tarte examines China's relations with Fiji, a regional hub and "natural focal point" for both China and Taiwan's activities in Oceania. Fiji was the first Pacific Island state to establish diplomatic relations with China in the 1970s, and Tarte describes how the relationship has intensified in recent years to reflect China's new interest in the region, as well as Fiji's efforts to "look north" in the face of post-coup sanctions imposed by its traditional Western allies. She notes that although aid commitments have done much to promote closer political ties, so far China's contributions to Fiji's development efforts appear to be limited. Tarte also discusses Fiji's active but "unofficial" ties with Taiwan, and the resulting friction in the relationship with Beijing.

In Chapter 8, Tarcisius Tara Kabutaulaka, a professor with the Center for Pacific Islands Studies at the University of Hawai`i, looks at Taiwan's long-standing relationship with the Solomon Islands, which for some commentators epitomizes the dangers of Taipei's "checkbook diplomacy" in the region. In this detailed account, Kabutaulaka examines the decision in the early 1980s to recognize Taiwan rather than China, and the expectations associated with that choice. He notes that the anticipated economic development benefits have largely failed to materialize and examines the key role of Taiwanese funds during the economic and political crises affecting the country from 1999 to 2003. In perhaps the only published analysis of its kind, Kabutaulaka examines how Taiwanese money helps support "a complex network of patron-client relationships that weaves all the way from the very local level to the international arena." He also argues that it is only a matter of time before members of the local business community begin to lobby for enhanced relations with China, which in many ways is a more natural trading partner for the Solomon Islands than Taiwan.

Chapter 9 deals with China's relations with Samoa, which, like those with Fiji, date back to the 1970s. Political scientist Iati Iati, a lecturer in politics at the University of Canterbury, argues that Samoa is one of China's most reliable allies in the region and notes the almost complete absence of ties with Taiwan. He discusses how the Samoan government has effectively used the relationship with China to further its own development agenda, and notes the significant infrastructural and other benefits that have accrued as a result. Iati observes that so far Beijing has demanded little in return for its support, and wonders whether there will be an eventual day of reckoning.

Recent graduate of Ritsumeikan Asia Pacific University Dr. Palenitina Langa'oi discusses China's relations with the Kingdom of Tonga in Chapter 10. She focuses first on the factors affecting the 1998 decision to recognize China and terminate twenty-six years of diplomatic relations with Taiwan. Langa'oi finds that the preferences of particular members of the royal family, shaped largely by their personal business interests, provided much of the momentum for the switch. However, she also identifies a desire to escape pressure for political reform from traditional donors as a significant contributing factor, a situation exacerbated by Tonga's heavy dependence on aid. Later in the chapter, Langa'oi describes mounting local resentment against Chinese residents and the targeting of Chinese-owned businesses in the 2006 rioting that devastated the capital city of Nuku'alofa. She notes the irony in the fact that China is funding much of the reconstruction of Nuku'alofa, and discusses how increasing Chinese influence is affecting Tongan culture and society in significant ways.

Finally, in Chapter 11, political scientist and long-time observer of Palau Takashi Mita examines in some detail recent trends in Palau's relations with Taiwan. The relationship between the two is long-standing and multifaceted. In addition to significant transfers of aid and loans, Taiwanese companies have made substantial investments in Palau, mainly in support of a tourist industry that hosts many Taiwanese visitors. Indeed, Taiwan selected Palau to host its first summit meeting with regional allies in 2006 (see Appendix for the communiqué emerging from this meeting, and a subsequent gathering in the Marshall Islands). Mita traces the circumstances surrounding the decision to recognize Taiwan in 1999 and the subsequent development of the relationship. However, he also notes a growing interest in China among certain Palauan leaders, perhaps spurred by a Chinese proposal to develop a large scale resort in Melekeok State.

Themes

Although contributors to *China in Oceania* do not necessarily interpret China-related regional developments in exactly the same way, some key themes emerge from the collection as a whole. First, there is general agreement that Beijing's recent activities in Oceania represent a relatively minor part of a larger foreign policy effort, a global initiative driven largely by pragmatic rather than ideological concerns. Second, the authors agree that whereas China has a significant interest in the natural resources of Oceania, this is not sufficient to explain all aspects of its regional engagement. Third, contributors argue that rivalry with Taiwan remains an important preoccupation in Beijing and an important driver of regional activities. However, they also note a level of constraint in China's Taiwan-related responses, suggesting that Beijing seeks to avoid the emergence of major fissures between its regional allies and supporters of Taipei. Fourth, authors document the generally positive response of Pacific leaders to the style and substance of China's new level of engagement, despite public unease in some island places about the increased presence of Chinese workers or business owners. Finally, these observers recognize that China's new, more robust role in the region has implications for other, more established, regional powers. But they do not detect the direct challenge to Western leadership that other analysts have proposed. For the most part, contributors to *China in Oceania* seem cautiously optimistic that China can play a generally constructive role in regional development.

Oceania was among the last places on earth to be settled by humans, endure the impact of European colonialism, and feel the winds of change in the era of decolonization. It is also among the last of the world's regions to experience the economic and political shock waves associated with China's spectacular rise to power. The dynamics of China's rise, as well as the logic guiding Beijing's relations with the rest of the world, make this encounter all but inevitable. China's growing presence in Oceania matters to the more established regional powers because it challenges existing patterns of influence and complicates ongoing efforts to secure strategic and other interests in the region. But it matters most immediately to the island states themselves, who now confront a wider range of economic and political options than before. The authors in this collection demonstrate clearly that Pacific Islanders are not hapless observers in an ongoing drama of great power politics. Instead they are actively attempting to shape the emerging regional order to suit their own needs and aspirations. To what extent they will manage to succeed remains to be seen.

Notes

1. It is worth noting that despite scoring significantly lower than China on these measures, both Canada and Russia are members of the exclusive Group of Eight (G8), which ostensibly brings together the world's major economic powers.
2. The five principles were mutual respect for territorial integrity and sovereignty, non-aggression, non-interference in the internal affairs of other states, equality and mutual benefit in international relations, and peaceful coexistence.
3. China shares borders with fourteen neighboring nations.
4. Today China accounts for about half the global production of cement, a third of its steel, a fifth of its aluminum, and about a quarter of its copper. It is now the world's second largest consumer of primary energy after the United States.
5. Even the ongoing debacle of the war in Iraq has not shaken the foundations of the United States' role in the world, despite attendant death and destruction, vast financial and military costs, fragmentation of the "coalition of the willing," and widespread anti-American sentiment.
6. "Transitional states" include those emerging from the breakup of the former Soviet Union.
7. The Sino-Arab Cooperation Forum was established in 2004, facilitating regular interactions between foreign ministers and businessmen. In addition, China has established language schools in the region, and offers the services of a neutral Middle East peace envoy.
8. Earlier works on the topic include Harris (1985), Harris and Worden (1986), and Kim (1989).
9. Political Scientist Joseph Nye (2004) coined the term "soft power" to refer to a state's ability to shape the preferences of other states without having to resort to "carrots or sticks."
10. According to the World Bank, the number of people living in poverty in China fell by more than 400 million in the twenty years to 2001.
11. To many outsiders, the Pacific appears as a vast, largely empty space to be traversed to get to somewhere more important (Ward 1999). Of course, this empty quality has sometimes been regarded as an asset by external powers intent on testing nuclear weapons or disposing of hazardous waste.
12. Forced by militant action to cease production in 1989, the Panguna mine remains closed today. However, the terms of the remarkable 2001 Arawa Peace Agreement allow Bougainville considerable autonomy from Papua New Guinea and a future referendum on full independence.
13. See for example D'Arcy 2007a, 2007b; Henderson 2001; Henderson and Reilly 2003; Dobell 2007; Hegarty 2007; Herr 2007; Shie 2007; and Windybank 2005.
14. Taiwan also brought its Pacific allies together for regional forums in 2006 and 2008. See Appendix for the communiqués emerging from these meetings.
15. The two tables are not comparable. Table I.2 is based on OECD statistics, which do not include information about China as an aid donor, and Table I.3 reports pledged rather than delivered aid. However, it is reasonable to conclude with Hanson (2008: 11) that China's aid is now "significantly more than New Zealand's aid budget but much less than Australia's."

16. China's only strident statements in post-forum dialogue sessions over the years have concerned Taiwan's attempts to obtain full dialogue status at the forum.

References

Anan, Kofi. 2000. *We the Peoples: Executive Summary.* Secretary-General Statement to the United Nations General Assembly. Accessed 4 August 2008 at http://www.un.org/millennium/sg/report/summ.htm

Buzan, Barry. 2004. "Conclusions: How and To Whom Does China Matter?" In *Does China Matter? A Reassessment,* ed. Barry Buzan and Rosemary Foot, 143–164. London and New York: Routledge.

Campbell, Kurt. 2007. "Foreword." In *China and the Developing World: Beijing's Strategy for the Twenty-First Century,* ed. Joshua Eisenman, Eric Heinbotham, and Derek Mitchell, ix–xii. New York and London: M.E. Sharpe.

Crocombe, Ron. 2007. *Asia in the Pacific Islands: Replacing the West.* Suva, Fiji: Institute of Pacific Studies, University of the South Pacific.

D'Arcy, Paul. 2007a. *China in the Pacific: Some Policy Considerations for Australia and New Zealand.* Discussion Paper 2007/4. Canberra: Australian National University, State, Society and Governance in Melanesia.

———, ed.. 2007b. *Chinese in the Pacific: Where to Now?* CSCSD Occasional Paper, no. 1, May. Canberra: Centre for the Study of the Chinese Southern Diaspora, Research School of Pacific and Asian Studies, Australian National University.

Dobell, Graeme. 2007. "China and Taiwan in the South Pacific: Diplomatic Chess versus Political Rugby." In *Chinese in the Pacific: Where to Now?* ed. Paul D'Arcy. CSCSD Occasional Paper, no. 1, May. Canberra: Centre for the Study of the Chinese Southern Diaspora, Research School of Pacific and Asian Studies, Australian National University.

Eisenman, Joshua. 2007. "China's Post–Cold War Strategy in Africa: Examining Beijing's Methods and Objectives." In *China and the Developing World: Beijing's Strategy for the Twenty-First Century,* ed. Joshua Eisenman, Eric Heinbotham, and Derek Mitchell, 29–59. New York and London: M.E. Sharpe.

Eisenman, Joshua, Eric Heginbotham, and Derek Mitchell. 2007a. "Introduction." In *China and the Developing World: Beijing's Strategy for the Twenty-First Century,* ed. Joshua Eisenman, Eric Heinbotham, and Derek Mitchell, xii–xxiii. New York and London: M.E. Sharpe.

Eisenman, Joshua, Eric Heinbotham, and Derek Mitchell, eds. 2007b. *China and the Developing World: Beijing's Strategy for the Twenty-First Century.* New York and London: M.E. Sharpe.

Freedman, Lawrence. 2004. "China as a Global Strategic Actor." In *Does China Matter? A Reassessment,* ed. Barry Buzan and Rosemary Foot, 21–36. London and New York: Routledge.

Glosny, Michael. 2007. "Stabilizing the Backyard: Recent Developments in China's Policy Toward Southeast Asia." In *China and the Developing World: Beijing's Strategy for the Twenty-First Century,* ed. Joshua Eisenman, Eric Heinbotham, and Derek Mitchell, 150–186. New York and London: M.E. Sharpe.

Godley, Michael. 1983. "China: The Waking Giant." In *Foreign Forces in Pacific Politics,* ed. Ahmed Ali, Ron Crocombe, and Ronald Gordon, 130–142. Suva, Fiji: Institute of Pacific Studies, University of the South Pacific.

Gracie, Carrie. 2006. "China's Rise Leaves West Wondering." In BBC News, 16 August. Accessed 14 May 2008 at http://news.bbc.co.uk/2/hi/asia-pacific/4797903.stm

Guthrie, Doug. 2006. *China and Globalization: The Social, Economic, and Political Transformation of Chinese Society.* New York: Routledge.

Hanson, Fergus. 2008. *The Dragon Looks South.* Analysis. Sydney, Australia: Lowy Institute for International Policy.

Harris, Lillian. 1985. *China's Foreign Policy Toward the Third World.* New York: Praeger.

Harris, Lillian, and Robert Worden, eds. 1986. *China and the Third World: Champion or Challenger?* Dover: Auburn House.

Harris, Stuart. 2004. "China in the Global Economy." In *Does China Matter? A Reassessment,* ed. Barry Buzan and Rosemary Foot, 54–70. London and New York: Routledge.

Hegarty, David. 2007. "China in the South Pacific." *Working Paper 2007/2.* Canberra: Australian National University, State, Society and Governance in Melanesia.

Heginbotham, Eric. 2007. "Evaluating China's Strategy Toward the Developing World." In *China and the Developing World: Beijing's Strategy for the Twenty-First Century,* ed. Joshua Eisenman, Eric Heinbotham, and Derek Mitchell, 189–216. New York and London: M.E. Sharpe.

Henderson, John. 2001. "China, Taiwan and the Changing Strategic Significance of Oceania." In *Contemporary Challenges in the Pacific: Toward a New Consensus,* vol. 1, special issue of *Revue Juridique Polynesienne,* ed. Stephen Levine and Tyves-Louis Sage, 143–155.

Henderson, John, and Benjamin Reilly. 2003. "Dragon in Paradise: China's Rising Star in Oceania." *The National Interest* 72 (summer): 94–104.

Henderson, John, and Greg Watson, eds. 2005. *Securing a Peaceful Pacific.* Christchurch, New Zealand: Canterbury University Press.

Herr, Richard. 2007. "Sovereignty and Responsibility: Some Issues in Chinese/Taiwanese Rivalry in the Pacific." *Fijian Studies* 4 (2): 111–125.

Hutton, Will. 2007. *The Writing on the Wall: China and the West in the 21ˢᵗ Century.* London: Little Brown.

Jayaraman, T. K., and Chee-Keong Choong. 2006. "Aid and Economic Growth in Pacific Island Countries: An Empirical Study of Aid Effectiveness in Fiji." *Perspectives on Global Development and Technology* 5 (4): 329–350.

Jenkins, Rhys, and Enrique Dussel Peters. 2006. *The Impact of China on Latin America and the Caribbean.* Brighton, UK: Institute of Development Studies, Asian Drivers Programme.

Kim, Samuel. 1989. *The Third World in Chinese World Policy.* Princeton: Princeton University Press.

Kurlantzick, Joshua. 2007. *Charm Offensive: How China's Soft Power is Transforming the World.* New Haven and London: Yale University Press.

Lal, Rollie. 2007. "China's Relations with South Asia." In *China and the Developing World: Beijing's Strategy for the Twenty-First Century,* ed. Joshua Eisenman, Eric Heinbotham, and Derek Mitchell, 133–149. New York and London: M.E. Sharpe.

Mitchell, Derek, and Carola McGiffert. 2007. "Expanding the 'Strategic Periphery': A History of China's Interaction with the Developing World." In *China and the Developing World: Beijing's Strategy for the Twenty-First Century,* ed. Joshua Eisenman, Eric Heinbotham, and Derek Mitchell, 3–25. New York and London: M.E. Sharpe.

Morck, Randall, Bernard Yeung, and Minyuan Zhao. 2007. "Perspectives on China's Outward Foreign Direct Investment." Unpublished paper.

Nye, Joseph. 2004. *Soft Power: The Means to Success in World Politics.* New York: Public Affairs.

Oresman, Matthew. 2007. "Repaving the Silk Road: China's Emergence in Central Asia." In *China and the Developing World: Beijing's Strategy for the Twenty-First Century,* ed. Joshua Eisenman, Eric Heinbotham, and Derek Mitchell, 60–83. New York and London: M.E. Sharpe.

Segal, Gerald. 1999. "Does China Matter?" *Foreign Affairs* 78 (5) (September/October). Reproduced in *Does China Matter? A Reassessment,* ed. Barry Buzan and Rosemary Foot, 11–20. London and New York: Routledge (2004).

Servant, Jean-Christophe. 2005. "China's Trade Safari in Africa." *Le Monde Diplomatique* (May). Accessed 15 May 2008 at http://mondediplo.com/2005/05/11chinafrica

Shie, Tamara Renee. 2007. "Rising Chinese Influence in the South Pacific." *Asian Survey* 47 (2): 307–326.

Teng Chung-chian. 2007. "Hegemony or Partnership: China's Strategy and Diplomacy Toward Latin America." In *China and the Developing World: Beijing's Strategy for the Twenty-First Century,* ed. Joshua Eisenman, Eric Heinbotham, and Derek Mitchell, 84–112. New York and London: M.E. Sharpe.

Ward, R. Gerard. 1999. *Widening Worlds, Shrinking Worlds? The Reshaping of Oceania.* Canberra: Australian National University, Centre for the Contemporary Pacific.

Wesley-Smith, Terence. 2008. "Altered States: Regional Intervention and the Politics of State Failure in Oceania." In *Intervention and State-Building in the Pacific: The Political Legitimacy of 'Co-operative Intervention,'* ed. Greg Fry and Tarcisius Kabutaulaka, 37–53. Manchester: Manchester University Press.

Windybank, Susan. 2005. "The China Syndrome." *Policy* 21 (2): 28–33.

Yang Jiechi. 2000. "Statement by Vice Foreign Minister Yang Jiechie at the Post-Forum Dialogue," 31st Pacific Islands Forum, Tarawa, Kiribati, 30 October. Accessed 5 June 2008 at *Pacific Islands Report* <http://archives.pirereport.org>

Yufeng, Mao. 2007. "China's Interests and Strategy in the Middle East and the Arab World." In *China and the Developing World: Beijing's Strategy for the Twenty-First Century,* ed. Joshua Eisenman, Eric Heinbotham, and Derek Mitchell, 113–132. New York and London: M.E. Sharpe.

CHAPTER 1

China's Pacific Engagement

Terence Wesley-Smith

A New Page in Regional History

In January 2007 Fiji coup leader and self-appointed Prime Minister Frank Baini-marama announced he would send senior officials to China to discuss enhanced relations. He did so in the face of sanctions imposed by Australia, New Zealand, and the United States, Fiji's traditional aid and security partners (Associated Press 2007). Ironically, Commodore Bainimarama's actions echoed the sentiments of the man he deposed in the military takeover. In April 2006 Prime Minister Laise-nia Qarase described a meeting between island leaders and Chinese Premier Wen Jiabao as marking a "new page in regional history." China, he argued, "defines a new and compelling reality, politically and economically" for the island countries (Qarase 2006). This chapter explores some strategic, political, and economic dimensions of this new regional reality. It challenges the sometimes disingenuous threat discourse pervading the existing literature on the topic and argues that China's rise offers Pacific Island states opportunities not available under established structures of power and influence.

China's heightened profile has not been greeted enthusiastically by other powers active in Oceania. Japan's unease is clear, and a substantial increase in aid announced in May 2006 seemed intended to counter Beijing's growing sway in the region (Associated Press 2006). Other actors appear ambivalent. In language reminiscent of the cold war, United States officials talk about the crucial need to keep island states "firmly on our side," although it is not clear who is considered opposed (Davies 2007). New Zealand Minister for Defense and Pacific Islands Affairs Phil Goff described China's presence as a "growing reality" but urged Beijing to work in partnership with other donors and "pay proper heed to the interests of the Pacific" (Nadkarni 2006: 4). Similarly, Australia is concerned about China's role in the region but reluctant to criticize an increasingly significant trade partner. Some commentators are not so circumspect. Political scientists John Henderson and Benjamin Reilly argue bluntly that China is in the process of "incorporating the Pacific islands into its broader quest to become a major Asia-Pacific power" at the expense of the United States, Japan, and other Western allies (Henderson and Reilly 2003: 94). Susan Windybank of the Centre for Independent Studies, an influential Australian think tank, concurs, maintaining that Oceania may become a "testing ground for China's growing power, and ability to shore up allegiances in a region hitherto considered an 'American lake'" (Windybank 2005: 29).

This talk of changing configurations of power in Oceania reflects a larger debate about the nature and implications of China's increased global activism. The nation's recent economic transformation has been spectacular, making a more prominent global role all but inevitable. It is less clear what China's rise means for the international system itself, and particularly for the unprecedented influence that the United States has enjoyed, especially since the collapse of the Soviet Union. According to Doug Guthrie, a sociology professor at New York University, the question is no longer whether China will play a major role in the world. Rather, "it is only a question of what role China will play"—and how the United States responds to this challenge to its global dominance (Guthrie 2006: 4). Some even predict a new cold war, this one fought out not in Europe but "among Pacific atolls that were last in the news when the Marines stormed them in World War II" (Kaplan 2005: 1).

This is not the first time that Pacific Island societies have faced the impositions and opportunities associated with great power competition. Strategic rivalry between expanding European powers was an important dynamic in the nineteenth-century colonization of the islands, and both world wars had destructive Pacific dimensions. Cold war tensions structured the process of decolonization in the region as well as the nature of postcolonial relations between island states and metropolitan powers. Nor has the end of the cold war enhanced the autonomy of the small, aid-dependent states of Oceania. Indeed, this has been an era of increased pressure from traditional allies, particularly Australia, to undertake extensive market-driven economic and political reforms, initiatives that island leaders have sometimes regarded as intrusive, disruptive, and even hostile. It is perhaps not surprising that most island leaders—including Commodore Bainimarama—have pragmatically welcomed the arrival of what a *Time* magazine cover story (22 January 2007) calls "The Chinese Century," and the new options it appears to present.

China Goes Global

The internal transformation of the world's most populous nation over the last twenty-five years has been dramatic indeed. Since 1979, when China's leadership began to implement radical reforms, the economy has expanded extremely rapidly. GDP rose by an average of more than 10 percent per annum in the 1980s and more than 12 percent per annum in the 1990s. China now has the fourth largest economy in the world, although analysts argue that conventional measures grossly underestimate its relative strength and purchasing power (Guthrie 2006: 3–5). This economic surge is unprecedented in modern times, easily surpassing the growth performances of Japan and South Korea in the decades after World War II (Fishman 2005: 12). Furthermore, it continues apace.

The social consequences of economic change have been profound for China's population of more than 1.3 billion. Existing political and legal institutions are rapidly giving way to new ones, and family networks and cultural values have come under severe strain. Urban landscapes have been transformed virtually overnight as millions of hopeful citizens head for booming cities and coastal provinces in what may be the greatest rural exodus in human history. China's "floating population" of rural-to-urban migrants is now estimated to exceed 100 million. Meanwhile, income and other inequalities are rising rapidly across regions and economic sectors, and between rural and urban workers (Guthrie 2006: 202–213).

The velocity and intensity of change in China has produced widespread social unrest. Official statistics indicate dramatic annual increases in public protests in recent decades, and National Defense University researcher Phillip Saunders notes that in 2004 there were more than 74,000 "mass group incidents" involving 3.7 million people (Tanner 2004: 138; Saunders 2006: 3). It is beyond the scope of this chapter to analyze these destabilizing trends in any depth. However, it is worth noting that many, including the Chinese leadership, see internal instability as one of the greatest challenges facing the country in the foreseeable future. It is also worth noting that political leaders seek to counter unrest through continued economic growth. In 2003 outgoing Premier Zhu argued that development was "the key to resolving all problems" facing China. "We must," he urged, "maintain a comparatively high growth rate in our national economy" (quoted in Tanner 2004: 145).

Economic development is the major factor propelling China onto the world's stage. Rapid growth has been largely market-driven, with foreign investment and global trade as essential components in a meteoric rise to increased wealth and power. Reliable supplies of raw materials of all sorts are increasingly important, with the search for oil and natural gas providing the single most important focus for Beijing's international trade policy. Already the world's second largest energy consumer, China's needs are rapidly outstripping domestic supplies of coal and oil. By 2020 an estimated 60 percent of the country's oil supplies will come from overseas—up from less than 8 percent in 1995 (*People's Daily* 2003). Chinese firms also face growing competition at home and are increasingly looking to export markets—often in developing countries—to enhance business performance. Growing trade has meant more emphasis on bilateral relations with an increasing number of trading partners and heightened interest in international organizations, such as the World Trade Organization, that regulate global trade and commerce.

The need for resources and markets largely explains China's increased presence in the Middle East, Africa, Latin America, the Caribbean, and Central Asia in recent years. Chinese business leaders often target resource-rich areas that have yet to be developed, or that rivals avoid for political or other reasons. In Africa, for example, China has invested heavily in the neglected oil industries of Sudan, Nigeria, and Angola and the mining industries of Zambia, Congo, and Zimbabwe, and is now selling competitively priced consumer goods across the continent. The value of trade with Africa doubled between 2003 and 2004, and jumped by a further 50 percent in 2005 (Lyman 2005). The volume of China's oil imports from the Middle East increased eightfold between 1992 and 2002, and the country now obtains more than 50 percent of its oil needs from that region (Liangxiang 2005).

If there is a compelling interest in a "stable international and regional environment in which China can modernize its economy and improve its relative power position," strategic issues are also increasingly important in Beijing's view of the world (Saunders 2006: 3). Foremost among these are US efforts—real or anticipated—to offset China's rising influence, especially in the Asia Pacific region, in order to preserve its own preeminent global role, as well as fears that Japan might one day remilitarize and adopt a more aggressive regional posture. Of central concern is the issue of Taiwan, which Beijing regards as a renegade province that must eventually be reintegrated. China's leaders do not take kindly to efforts to support Taipei's ongoing bid for recognition as an independent state. As a rising power, China has a strategic interest in cultivating strong relations with other states in order to minimize potential threats while enhancing its standing and influence in the global community.

Strategic interests sometimes coincide with economic ones in China's foreign policy. For example, the country has a compelling strategic interest in the sea routes that service its burgeoning international trade, some of which—like the Malacca Straits—are vulnerable to disruption by pirates, terrorists, or hostile powers. Often, however, strategic and economic interests form separate components of foreign policy in different parts of the world. In some cases, the two foreign policy tracks may conflict with each other. For most of the last decade economic considerations appear to have trumped strategic ones as Beijing works to avoid confrontation with the United States, Japan, and Taiwan in favor of enhanced trade and investment relations with those states.

Citing significant increases in military spending in recent years, some analysts see this willingness to compromise as a temporary phenomenon, one that will pass once China has accumulated the wherewithal to adopt a more assertive posture. In this view, China is currently "punching below its weight" in international politics, awaiting the right time to mount a significant challenge to the status quo in global politics (Weinstein 2005).

China in Oceania

The island states of Oceania play a small but increasingly significant role in China's efforts to further its economic and strategic interests. The modern relationships between these two parts of the world date back to the Chinese labor migrations of the late nineteenth century and, as sociologist Bill Wilmott notes, only Tuvalu, Tokelau, and Niue have no history of Chinese settlement (Chapter 5 in this volume). China has maintained an important official presence in the region since the mid 1970s, when it first established diplomatic relations with Fiji, Western Samoa, and newly independent Papua New Guinea. Since then, Beijing has established formal or informal relations with all of the independent and self-governing states and with major regional organizations, including the Pacific Islands Forum. While some aspects of the relationship have remained constant, new economic and strategic elements have emerged in recent years. The China–Pacific Island Countries Economic and Cooperation Forum, held in Fiji in April 2006, marked a ratcheting-up of China's interest and signaled significant increases in trade, investment, aid, and technical cooperation with Oceania. In his address to the forum, Chinese Premier Wen Jiabao emphasized a long-term commitment: "China has proved and will continue to prove itself to be a sincere, trustworthy and reliable friend and partner of the Pacific Island countries forever" (Wen 2006; see Appendix for the full text of his comments).

Philip Saunders identifies commercial interests, the search for economic inputs, efforts to expand political influence, and the need to offset US challenges as the "key drivers of increased Chinese global activism" (Saunders 2006: 6–10). Elements of all four motives are apparent in China's activities in Oceania, although one, the search for political influence, is particularly significant. Some see a second, rivalry with the United States and its allies, as increasingly important.

China is interested in pursuing commercial opportunities in Oceania, and total trade between China and the forum island countries has increased by more than 200 percent since 2002, reaching an estimated value of US$1 billion by the end of 2006 (Somare 2006; see Appendix for the full text of his comments). Although the present balance of trade favors China and benefits certain Chinese companies, the overall commercial relationship is vastly more important to the island states than it is to China. Despite recent increases, trade with Oceania still only represents less than one tenth of 1 percent of the total value of China's global trade. A similar point could be made regarding tourism, which is expected to grow quite significantly now that ten Pacific countries have received Approved Destination status from China's tourism authority.[1] Although of great interest to the island states, this growth in tourist traffic is unlikely to be of much concern to foreign policy planners in Beijing.

Oceania is more important to China as a source of key natural resource inputs for its burgeoning economy. China already imports significant quantities of timber and fish from Pacific Island countries, including Solomon Islands and Papua New Guinea. It has a particular interest in Papua New Guinea's vast energy and mineral resources. Officials of China's biggest oil company, China National Petroleum, have discussed the possibility of building a plant to produce liquefied natural gas in Papua New Guinea, a prospect that may have improved since early 2007 when Exxon Mobil finally scrapped its plans to pipe huge quantities of natural gas to Australia (Macdonald-Smith 2005, 2007). In March 2005, a major government-owned construction and operating company, Chinese Metallurgical Construction (Group) Corporation, purchased a majority interest in the Ramu nickel and cobalt mining project in Madang. Construction of the US$800 million complex commenced in late 2006. When complete, the mine is expected to produce 32,800 tonnes of nickel annually, all of which will be exported to support China's booming stainless steel industry (Callick 2007; Ramu Nickel Limited 2005). In 2006, the Papua New Guinea government signed an agreement to allow China Exploration and Engineering Bureau to explore further opportunities to develop gold, copper, chromites, magnesium, or other mineral resources (*The National* 2006).[2]

Although commercial motives and the quest for reliable access to particular natural resources may explain some of China's heightened interest in Oceania, they cannot explain all of it. For the last two decades, China's primary objective in the region has been to build political influence among the island states in support of Beijing's interests in international forums such as the United Nations. This remains the case today. Indeed, political motives probably best explain the large number of Chinese diplomats posted to the region, the "visit diplomacy" that brings large numbers of island leaders on goodwill trips to Beijing every year, as well as the high-profile aid projects that have built sports complexes and other public facilities in island countries over the last two decades. Along with similar efforts in the Caribbean and smaller countries in Africa, China hopes to mute international criticism of its record on human rights, advance its economic goals in organizations like the World Trade Organization, and block Japan's aspirations to play a more active international role. Of key importance in the Pacific Islands are China's ongoing efforts to isolate Taiwan.

The competition between the two Chinas for influence in Oceania dates back to the 1970s, after US President Richard Nixon's visit to Beijing and loss of UN membership pushed Taiwan to seek diplomatic recognition wherever it could (Harwit 2000: 465–467). Although Taipei's efforts yielded significant results among the smaller states of Africa, Central America, the Caribbean, and the Pacific, China's growing political and economic influence has taken its toll in recent years. Since 2003, Taiwan has lost six of its thirty diplomatic allies (and the Vatican may follow soon), although it retains informal trade and other ties with many more (Lai 2006).

Taiwan remains relatively successful in Oceania. Although Tonga switched its allegiance to China in 1998, the Marshall Islands came over to the Taiwan camp the same year. Nauru recognized China in 2002 but returned to Taiwan less than two years later. Perhaps Taipei's greatest diplomatic victory came in 2003, when China lost its long-standing formal ties to Kiribati—and its satellite tracking facility there (Herr 2007: 6–10). Today, six Pacific Island states (Kiribati, Solomon Islands, Palau, the Marshall Islands, Tuvalu, and Nauru) recognize Taiwan, while a further seven (Papua New Guinea, Samoa, Tonga, the Cook Islands, Fiji, Vanuatu, and the Federated States of Micronesia) have formal relations with China.

It seems unlikely that Taiwan will be able to maintain for much longer its largely aid-based efforts—what many call "checkbook diplomacy"—in the face of China's considerably deeper pockets and rising political influence. I-chung Lai, a board member of a Taipei-based public policy research institute, suggests that Taiwan's bilateral international assistance is increasingly focused on particular strategic and economic objectives, and notes a new emphasis on multilateral initiatives (Lai 2007: 2). In September 2006, the first Taiwan–Pacific Allies Summit was held in Palau. Delegates identified nine areas for economic, technical, and cultural cooperation and agreed to hold a second summit in the Marshall Islands in September 2007 (see Appendix for forum communiqués). Nevertheless, the escalating rivalry with Taiwan for influence in the region continues to attract much critical attention from observers. According to senior Australian journalist Graeme Dobell, for example, "The diplomatic competition between China and Taiwan is destabilizing island states … making Pacific politics more corrupt and more violent" (Dobell 2007). These assertions will be considered below.

In addition to interests in commerce, access to resources, and political influence, China's foreign policy in Oceania has always had a powerful strategic component. Indeed, it was China's intense antagonism toward the Soviet Union that spurred its early involvement in the region. It was no coincidence that the first major approaches to island states occurred shortly after the Soviets established relations with Fiji, and policy statements thereafter reflected a determination to restrict Russian influence and maritime expansion (Godley 1983: 131, 139). It is worth noting that during the cold war China's interests were closely aligned with other external actors such as the United States, Australia, and New Zealand, whose policies were also geared to denying the Soviet Union access to Oceania. Now the tables have turned, and it is the growing suspicion between China and the Western powers that increasingly influences the strategic environment in Oceania.

Threat Discourse

Much of the small but growing corpus of literature on China's changing role in Oceania is suspicious of Beijing's motives and critical of its influence on island societies (see, e.g., Henderson and Reilly 2003; Henderson 2001; Windybank 2005; Dobell 2007). The writers often emphasize what they see as negative local impacts before going on to question China's long-term goals in the region. However, it is apparent that the condition of island states and the welfare of Pacific Islanders are, at best, of secondary concern in these analyses. The real purpose of these works is to suggest a threat to the strategic status quo, a challenge to "the US as the prime mover in the area" (Linter 2007: 2). The Pacific material echoes dominant themes in analyses of China's role elsewhere in the world, and is often derivative of this literature.

Upstaged since 2001 by events in the Middle East and the US "war on terror" under President George W. Bush, talk of China as a "credible threat" to the United States has recently reemerged. Citing significant increases in defense spending, a 2006 US Department of Defense review noted that China is the only world power capable of competing militarily with the United States and offsetting "traditional US military advantages" (US Department of Defense 2006a: 29). In its report to Congress later in the same year, the department reiterated these claims and berated the Chinese leadership for not adequately explaining "the purposes or desired end-states of their military expansion" (US Department of Defense 2006b: 1). Then, in January 2007, a Chinese missile test that reportedly destroyed one of the country's own orbiting satellites sparked diplomatic protests from some countries, including the United States, Japan, and Australia, and extensive media speculation about a new arms race in space (see, e.g., Watson 2007). Council on Foreign Relations member Elizabeth Economy took the opportunity to accuse China of exerting "an unsettling and often negative impact on the world" and described its leaders as "not ready for prime time." She went on to argue that "if this is the reality of China's rise, then the United States has work to do" (Economy 2007).

A good part of this work would take place in the Asia Pacific region where many of China's immediate economic, strategic, and political interests lie. It would likely amount to a policy of containment, with efforts to strengthen long-standing alliances with key players like Japan, Australia, and South Korea, and consolidate relations with newer strategic partners like Thailand, Singapore, and India. The immediate purpose would be to head off attempts by China to build new architecture for regional cooperation that excludes the United States. And, as US Secretary of State Condoleezza Rice put it before her own rise to power in the Bush administration, this makes it inconceivable for strategic competitors like China "to use force because American military power is a compelling factor in their equations" (Rice 2000: 4). Most analysts—even the hawks—recognize that the enormous disparity in military capability between the two powers is likely to continue for decades to come, and that this makes conventional military confrontation unlikely any time soon.[3] Instead, according to veteran American author and journalist Robert Kaplan, China would employ an asymmetric approach, as terrorists do, using submarines and missile systems to launch largely symbolic strikes against US military installations and warships (Kaplan 2005: 7).

The "credible threat" thesis provides the starting point for much writing on China's role in Oceania. Henderson and Reilly (2003: 95), for example, have no doubt that China's long-term goal is to "replace the United States as the preeminent power in the Pacific Ocean." Windybank repeats this theme in the context

of Australian interests when she suggests that if present trends continue, "the island states in a region for which the Australian government has taken responsibility would owe their allegiance to a country outside the US system of regional
alliances" (Windybank 2005: 29). These authors assume, rather than demonstrate,
that China represents a long-term threat to Western global interests, and that the
threat will include a military dimension. They do not consider alternative scenarios, which cite China's heavy investment in the global economy, and its complex
financial entanglements with rival powers, including the United States, Japan,
and Australia, among the factors likely to favor compromise and cooperation over
confrontation, even in the longer term. Strategic analyst Thomas Barnett, for example, describes a Pentagon establishment that, though intent on framing the rise
of China as an annex to the cold war, ignores the growing volume of trade between the two countries, China's huge dependence on direct investment from the
United States, Europe, and Japan, and the increasing reliance of the United States
on loans from China to finance its budget deficit.[4] Barnett sees a country "finally
joining the world, not setting itself up for confrontation" (Barnett 2004: 68).

Even if we accept that China does represent a credible threat, it is not clear how
Oceania might feature in the strategic planning of the potential protagonists. The
writers cite China's future naval power as important in this regard. They are also
quick to remind us how Japan used some of the islands in the western part of the
region (the "second island chain") to launch its expansionist plans in World War
II. These arguments are of questionable relevance, not least because China's blue
water capability remains a very distant prospect. At the moment, the country's
strategic interests are heavily focused on the straits of Taiwan and on securing
reliable supplies of energy—increasingly from the Middle East—to fuel its rapid
economic expansion. None of the island states lie close to the strategic sea lanes
that service the bulk of China's trade in energy and raw materials or, for that matter, to other important trans-Pacific commercial or military sea routes.

The islands north of the equator are usually assumed to be strategically much
more important than those to the south. Certainly, strategic concerns provided
the primary rationale for the United States as it negotiated detailed compacts of
free association with the emerging states of Micronesia in the 1980s. However,
in a 2002 report to Congress, the US General Accounting Office argued that the
Federated States of Micronesia and Marshall Islands no longer play any role in
US strategy in the Asia Pacific region. The single exception, the report noted, is
Kwajalein Atoll in the Marshall Islands, which the United States continues to use
to conduct missile tests and space-tracking operations (US General Accounting
office 2002). Other parts of Oceania that might provide attractive staging options
for US military deployments in the event of any conflict with China over Taiwan,
like Guam or the Commonwealth of the Northern Marianas, are already firmly
under US control—and, in the case of Guam, heavily militarized. Kaplan men-
tions the strategic significance of the Republic of Palau in his conflict scenario,
but it is interesting to note that the United States has made no attempt to build

military facilities there despite its ability to do so under the terms of the 1994 Compact of Free Association. Rather more convincing is Kaplan's argument that China could in the future use island territory or sea space to "lob missiles … at moving ships" of the US Navy. But he fails to mention which Pacific atolls he sees as likely candidates for such deployments (Kaplan 2005: 1).

Writers like Reilly, Henderson, and Windybank offer no proof that China is actually engaged in any military-related activities in Oceania, or has any plans to do so. Indeed, there is no published evidence of any attempts to establish port facilities or negotiate military bases anywhere in the vast reaches of Oceania. The single possible exception is the Chinese satellite tracking facility established in the Republic of Kiribati in 1997, which some suspect was also used to monitor US activities at the Kwajalein missile testing range in the neighboring Marshall Islands. However, the authors offer no evidence to support their claims that the facility was used for anything other than its stated function, let alone that it played "an important role in the development of China's space warfare program." And, even if this modest facility did in fact play such a role, does that really justify a claim that the region as a whole has significant "strategic value" to China (Henderson and Reilly 2003: 100)? It is worth noting that the tracking station was dismantled after a new Kiribati government switched its allegiance to Taiwan in November 2003. Admittedly, China left under protest, but the fact that it withdrew at all seems inconsistent with the assessment that this facility was key to Beijing's strategic planning. Beijing has offered modest military training and supply programs to some Pacific states. However, no arms shipments have been involved, and these initiatives can be seen as part of a routine program of technical training and capacity building.

Perhaps aware of the weakness of "hard power" threat scenarios, Susan Windybank proposes that it is actually the *lack* of strategic significance that makes Oceania interesting to an expansionist China: "Paradoxically, the very fact that the Southwest Pacific is considered a strategic backwater may make it more attractive as a testing ground for China's growing power and ability to shore up allegiances in a region hitherto considered an 'American lake'" (Windybank 2005: 29). It is difficult to know how to respond to this sort of argument, which could be applied indiscriminately to any part of the globe. What Windybank suggests here is a perfect world for China threat aficionados, one where all corners of the earth have major significance for strategic planners. At best, this seems like a shaky basis for serious policy planning and analysis.

Dragon Talk

Unlike their benevolent image in Chinese mythology, dragons have a generally negative reputation in the Western imagination. The title of Henderson and

Reilly's 2003 article, "Dragon in Paradise," carries the latter connotation. These authors argue that China's "rising star" in Oceania has been facilitated by certain regional vulnerabilities. They suggest further that Beijing has simultaneously exploited and encouraged corruption and instability in the region and somehow will hinder the economic and political development of island states. It is worth examining these allegations in more depth.

Analysts such as Henderson, Reilly, Windybank, and Dobell cite a variety of domestic characteristics that ostensibly make the island states particularly vulnerable to China's (and Taiwan's) soft power overtures. However, they fail to explain how these factors—which include small size, modest means, and the disproportionate influence of individual leaders—have actually facilitated China's regional rise. The idea that small size is important could have merit, if this suggests lack of state capacity to make informed decisions or resist external pressure. However, some Pacific states, like Papua New Guinea and Fiji, have relatively sophisticated foreign affairs establishments, and the smaller states routinely obtain relevant information and advice from allied powers like Australia, New Zealand, and the United States, or share information in regional organizations like the Pacific Islands Forum.

It is also misleading to suggest that all island states are "cash-strapped" or "impoverished" and therefore, by implication, willing to accept whatever financial deals come along. Money laundering through offshore banking facilities in the region has attracted international attention, and in the year 2000 the Cook Islands, the Marshall Islands, Nauru, and Niue were listed as Non-Cooperating Countries by the OECD's Financial Action Task Force. However, by 2005 all of these countries had been delisted after implementing more stringent regulations (FATF 2007). There are also well-documented cases of island governments or individual leaders becoming involved in dubious overseas business or investment schemes, sometimes in the face of pressing fiscal concerns. The imprudent deals accelerating once-rich Nauru's descent into bankruptcy, or Tuvalu's unfortunate experience with a Texas real estate scam, are notable examples (Finin 2002: 6–7). However, these are exceptional situations, and most financial transactions undertaken by Pacific Island states in recent decades have been aboveboard and beyond reproach.

It is appropriate to note the large impact that individual leaders can have on decision-making processes in small island states. The role of the king and other members of the Tongan royal family, who occupy the pinnacle of a highly centralized political system, is an obvious example here. But it is also worth remembering that the small-scale, face-to-face nature of politics often provides a major disincentive to maverick action in island societies. Most island leaders do not act in this fashion, and those that do often pay a high price. Members of the Tongan royal family who have engaged in self-serving business deals with overseas interests have come under extreme pressure from a well-organized domestic reform movement in recent years. Vanuatu's Prime Minister Serge Vohor lost office less than a month after he signed an agreement with Taiwan in 2004, apparently without the consent of his Council of Ministers. Similarly, Papua New Guinea Prime Minister Bill Skate's "egregious" 1998 attempt to switch allegiance to Taiwan in return for a large financial package collapsed when his government lost power within a few weeks (Windybank 2005: 31).

It is easy to get the impression from this literature that all island leaders are corrupt, malleable, self-serving, and impulsive. Some Pacific leaders might well be described in this way, but the same could be said about individual leaders in any country or region in the world. Not only does the Pacific Islands region as a whole compare well with other parts of the developing world in terms of corruption, but these issues are much more apparent in some island states than others (Larmour 2005: 15, Table 2). Furthermore, the general argument that Pacific Island states are "cheap to buy" needs further scrutiny. Henderson and Reilly, for example, contend that "a relatively small outlay can buy significant political influence" in the "region's smallest, poorest, and weakest countries" (2003: 101). If that is the case, then why was China unwilling to trump Taiwan's relatively modest offer to Kiribati in 2003, especially given the supposed strategic significance of that relationship? And if island allegiances are so easy to buy, then why have traditional allies like Australia and New Zealand not enjoyed more success in the region in recent years? There are many, like influential Australian analyst Helen Hughes, who argue strongly that US$50 billion worth of "development assistance" since 1970 has not produced anything like the desired results (Hughes 2003).

Although none of the authors state directly that China had a hand in precipitating recent political crises in places like Fiji, Papua New Guinea, or the Solomon Islands, they do imply that Beijing has at least taken advantage of the resultant instability. For example, after discussing various flash points along Oceania's so-called "arc of crisis," Henderson and Reilly argue that "it is no accident that China's increased involvement coincides with growing regional instability. The very weakness of Pacific Island states makes them valuable as a strategic resource for China" (Henderson and Reilly 2003: 98). However, they do not elaborate on the proposed relationship between instability and involvement. Few of the cited examples of Chinese activities relate to the countries most affected by crisis, and those that do involve events and relationships that could be adequately explained in other ways.

Probably the most compelling case of strategic meddling involves the crisis-torn Solomon Islands. Here, external aid money did become a significant part of the dynamics of the internal crisis that erupted in the late 1990s. But the principal actor in this case was Taiwan, not China (see Chapter 8). It is also clear that the China-Taiwan competition for influence became a major issue in the domestic politics of Kiribati in 2003, and that opposed political factions were offered financial support in the run-up to elections. However, Kiribati is one of the most stable political entities in the region, and the fact that the new government was able to terminate the relationship with China suggests state strength rather than state weakness.

These authors also fail to distinguish adequately between China's foreign policy toward Oceania and the increasing number of people of Chinese ancestry living and working in island states. Henderson and Reilly, for example, devote a whole section of their article to the social tensions associated with Chinese workers and small business owners in Fiji, Tonga, Solomon Islands, and Papua New Guinea, as well as some issues associated with Chinese "boat people" in Guam, Papua New Guinea, and New Caledonia. They justify this inclusion by arguing that, although this type of migration is not part of any government policy, "China can be a vocal advocate of the rights of ethnic Chinese in the Pacific, particularly when they are under threat" (Henderson and Reilly 2003: 99). Although that may well be the case, it would seem to have little to do with China's new foreign policy toward the region. Indeed, local resentment toward Chinese migrants may actually complicate Beijing's attempts to build alliances with island states. If there is an issue here, it has more to do with the immigration policies of island governments (and passport sales, in some cases) than with the intent of policy makers in Beijing, malevolent or not.

Much of the unease about Chinese commercial practice in Oceania has focused on the increasing prominence of small retailers, but there is also growing concern about the effects of large-scale natural resource investments. Since this type of activity is relatively new in the region, much of the current suspicion reflects the sometimes negative experience with large Chinese corporations in other parts of the world. The early record at the Ramu nickel mine, to date the largest Chinese-owned project in Oceania, is not reassuring. The project has been controversial from the start, mainly because of the likely impact of the underwater dumping of tailings on the marine ecology of Astrolabe Bay (MPI 2005). There has also been concern about poor labor conditions at the mine construction site, and in February 2007 Papua New Guinea Labour Secretary David Tibu threatened to close the operation unless things improved (Matbob 2007). A ten-year tax holiday and other unusual concessions to the mining company have been justified on the grounds that this major project has been delayed for many years and otherwise might not have gone ahead (Jack 2006; see Chapter 6).

Large-scale mining in Papua New Guinea has long been associated with concerns about environmental damage and almost constant disputes about how benefits are shared. It remains to be seen whether this Chinese venture will fare any better than Western companies like Conzinc Riotinto of Australia did at the giant Panguna mine in Bougainville, which was closed down by hostile landowners in 1989, or Broken Hill Propriety has at the Ok Tedi complex in the Star Mountains, where a 1996 lawsuit successfully claimed compensation on behalf of 30,000 indigenous residents affected by the massive discharge of untreated tailings into the Fly River system.[5]

Washington Consensus versus Beijing Consensus

Washington's stance is often cited as an important factor in understanding China's new role in Oceania. According to some commentators, United States neglect or preoccupation has made the region particularly vulnerable to what Windybank (2005) calls "The China Syndrome." Henderson and Reilly, for example, note that US links to the region have been "significantly downgraded" since the end of the cold war, and Windybank sees China busy "cultivating new friends and allies across the Asia Pacific region" while the United States is preoccupied with terrorism and the Middle East (Henderson and Reilly 2003: 94; Windybank 2005: 28). This is a mantra common to analyses of other regions such as Africa and Southeast Asia.

Since the end of the cold war the United States has closed its small consular post in the Solomon Islands and reduced some of its aid program outreach, and it no longer maintains a separate Pacific Islands office in the State Department. In March 2007 a senior State Department official admitted that "the nations of the Pacific have not always received either adequate diplomatic attention or development assistance" and promised a reversal of the trend (Davies 2007). It is worth noting, however, that Washington continues to loom large in the states and territories of Micronesia. Furthermore, its presence south of the equator was never particularly robust even at the height of the cold war. If the reductions of the 1990s created any sort of diplomatic vacuum, it has been more that adequately filled by the increased activities of allied powers like Australia, New Zealand, Japan, and the European Union.

It would be a mistake to assume that these countries always back the United States' position on China. Indeed, some commentators identify a growing conflict between the material benefits associated with Australia's deepening relationship with Beijing and the broad security concerns it shares with the United States (Jennings 2005).[6] However, for the moment it is safe to assume that in Oceania at least, US and allied interests roughly coincide. And these countries have hardly neglected the region. Aid levels to Oceania from US-aligned sources are higher than ever, most island students seeking overseas opportunities still travel to these countries to pursue higher education and training, and the vast majority of person-to-person diplomatic exchanges continue to involve traditional partners.

If anything, China's increasing influence in Oceania owes more to Western involvement than to Western neglect. Since the early 1990s aid donors and financial institutions have made concerted efforts to persuade island leaders to implement comprehensive economic and political reforms. Increasingly leveraged by aid conditionality, the regional reform agenda is based on a set of neoliberal economic ideas commonly referred to as the Washington Consensus. Some observers are skeptical about the wisdom of this global exhortation to "stabilize, privatize, and liberalize" but recognize the difficulties of resisting it (Rodrik 2006:

1). According to Australian scholar Stewart Firth, Pacific Islands governments have no alternative but to embrace such policies: "The international pressures are too great to do otherwise, and the capacity of international financial institutions to compel obedience too large" (Firth 2000: 186, 2007; Slatter 2006a, 2006b). The rise of China, which attaches few conditions to its financial or technical assistance, appears to provide island leaders with other options. At issue in Oceania, then, is not the US presence as such, but the influence of a set of economic ideas originating in Washington-based financial institutions.

Oceania's reform agenda owes its immediate origins to two critical World Bank reports of the early 1990s and the urgings of influential analysts in Australia and New Zealand (World Bank 1991, 1993; Slatter 2006b: 27). The main contours of the new orthodoxy appeared in a 1993 report published by Australia's National Centre for Development Studies, which warned that the island states faced a bleak future unless they enhanced their competitiveness in the global economy (Cole 1993). The following year, Australia began to use its aid "as a carrot and stick to ensure Pacific Islands governments reduce the size of their civil services, privatize, [and] encourage private investment" (Firth 2000: 185). Since then, all of the major aid agencies and lending institutions active in the region, as well as the region's premier multilateral organization, the Pacific Islands Forum, have adopted this "reform-speak" (Slatter 2006b: 27). More recently, the agenda has broadened to include "good governance," not only because of concerns about political instability in the region, but because qualities of accountability, efficiency, and transparency have come to be seen by international agencies as prerequisites to successful economic reform. Indeed, these ideas are now enshrined in the Pacific Plan for Strengthening Regional Cooperation and Integration, an important road map for Pacific futures recently adopted by the Pacific Islands Forum.[7]

This is not the place for a detailed review of Oceania's reform agenda. However, it is worth noting that, although publicly supportive, island leaders are often privately doubtful about the intent and likely outcomes of the agenda. Some reform-inspired initiatives, such as those designed to prepare Vanuatu for accession to the World Trade Organization, have been resisted or rejected, while others have been vigorously protested by trade unions, church groups, and a wide variety of nongovernmental organizations (Slatter 2006b: 27–31). Initiatives designed to overhaul existing land tenure systems have been particularly contentious, while some critics note that far-reaching regional trade agreements have been implemented with no public debate and little apparent concern for likely social and cultural impacts (Kelsey 2004, 2005). University of the South Pacific regional politics specialist Elise Huffer has argued that the Pacific Plan pays only lip service to fundamental island values and worldviews (Huffer 2006). Others have warned that further integration into the global economy is likely to exacerbate rather than alleviate growing levels of poverty in the region (World Council of Churches 2001).

Pacific Islanders have good reason to be concerned. In a 2005 report, the World Bank itself noted the conspicuous lack of success during the 1990s of similar reform efforts in sub-Saharan Africa, Latin America, East Asia, Russia, and Turkey, as well as in the new republics of the former Soviet Union (World Bank 2005).[8] Indeed, according to Harvard University economist Dani Rodrik, "nobody really believes in the Washington Consensus anymore" (Rodrik 2006: 2).

Under these circumstances it is perhaps understandable that the alternative development message brought to the region by Chinese Premier Wen in April 2006 was warmly received, despite its own apparent contradictions. In a thinly veiled critique of Western approaches to development, Wen noted an increasingly imbalanced global system characterized by widening gaps between North and South, rich and poor. He pointed out that both China and the Pacific Islands were developing countries, and offered a "new model for South-South cooperation." He promised an approach based on peaceful coexistence, equality, and respect for the social systems, sovereignty, and independence of Pacific Island countries. Perhaps most telling, he said that China stood ready "to provide assistance without any political strings attached" (Wen 2006).

Wen might also have pointed out that China's phenomenal record of economic growth belies the very essence of the Washington Consensus. Although heavily invested in market forces, China's economy has taken off "with high levels of trade protection, lack of privatization, extensive industrial policies, and lax fiscal and financial policies" (Rodrik 2006: 4). Nor does today's China stand as an exemplar of good governance practice as it is usually understood by the global financial institutions and development agencies. As Guthrie notes, "the stunning success of China turns some key assumptions of economic theory on their head" (Guthrie 2006: 9). According to Tsinghua University Professor Joshua Cooper Ramo, "China is marking a path for other nations ... who are trying to figure out not simply how to develop their countries, but also how to fit into the international order in a way that allows them to be truly independent, to protect their way of life and political choices in a world with a single massively powerful center of gravity" (2004: 3). Nevertheless, skeptical island leaders may wonder about China's growing domestic discontent, as well as Beijing's dubious track record on issues like global warming and fisheries management that are of immediate concern in Oceania. Many (although probably not Commodore Bainimarama) are also proud of the region's democratic institutions and concerned about China's lack of commitment in that regard.

China's Pacific Century

China is making its new, more robust presence felt around the globe, including in Oceania. However, there is no evidence to suggest that Pacific Island states are being singled out for special attention. Indeed, it is clear that other regions, including the Middle East, certain parts of Asia, and Africa are of much greater and more immediate interest to policy makers in Beijing. Under certain circumstances, most likely involving a military confrontation with Taiwan, the Pacific Islands region (or rather, certain western parts of it) could assume more importance as the combatants and their allies—most notably the United States—jockey for strategic advantage. Meanwhile, the medium-term transition of the People's Liberation Army Navy to "green water" capability has few implications for Oceania. The ability to operate effectively along the "second island chain," which includes Guam, the Northern Marianas, and Palau, would have a more definite impact on the balance of military power in the region. It is unlikely, though, that China will acquire this "blue water" capacity before mid century, and it may take longer than that.

Most of China's recent activities in the region can be explained with reference to a general and growing economic appetite for trade and natural resources, as well as a more pointed political interest in garnering support for Beijing's agenda in multilateral institutions. As such, China's immediate interests are not much different from those of other powers active in the region, such as the United States, Japan, New Zealand, and Australia. The major difference is that these powers are well established in Oceania, while China is not. Most other influential actors have engaged with Pacific Islands societies for more than a century, initially as colonists. Some, particularly Australia, still appear to believe they have a right, if not a duty, "to speak for the inhabitants of this region, to represent them to themselves and to others, to lead, and to manage them," and they often act accordingly (Fry 1997: 306). Significant numbers of Pacific Islanders have migrated to these countries since the 1960s and, especially in New Zealand, now represent a significant force in domestic politics. At the very least, then, China's arrival challenges existing assumptions about leadership roles and responsibilities in the region.

China's rise disturbs a situation where a small number of allied powers exercise an enormous amount of regional influence. Although the United States, France, Australia, New Zealand, and Japan have distinct foreign policies toward Oceania, they share a fundamental strategic interest in the region. Their influence is maintained in part through comprehensive bilateral relations with individual island states. Indeed, since 2003 Australia has added to its already significant aid and diplomatic presence by launching major interventionist programs to combat instability in Solomon Islands, Papua New Guinea, and Nauru. Also important in the longer term are recent Australian-led initiatives designed to strengthen multilateral organizations and promote a coordinated approach to regional development. These efforts have yielded significant results with the adoption of a common reform agenda and, more recently, with the promulgation of the Pacific Plan. China stands apart from this consortium of interested donors, a "silent partner" offering support and resources but asking little beyond recognition of the one China policy (Dobell 2007: 4).

Existing regional powers have no option but to accept that, barring significant economic or military setbacks, China is in Oceania to stay. They can do little more than allied leaders have already done, which is to urge Beijing to play a constructive role in regional affairs—in other words, to play by the rules they themselves have established and enforced for many decades. From their perspective, the best outcome would be for China to align itself with existing reform efforts, much as a rising Japan did in the 1990s. This would be more likely to occur if island leaders were firmly committed to the reform agenda, instead of seeing it as largely externally imposed. Under these circumstances, China will probably continue to assert its own version of constructive engagement, one informed by a rather different set of economic, political, and strategic interests. It could be the allied powers, rather than China, that ultimately have to compromise in order to maintain their influence in Oceania. All of these regional actors have their own growing economic entanglements with China—and compelling reasons to avoid confrontation.

Much of the debate surrounding China's rise in Oceania invokes the welfare and interests of island communities. Writers often assume a common interest in matters like "development" or economic growth, state institutions of a particular type, and regional stability. That may be true at a certain level of generality, and among certain regional actors. But island communities tend to reject economic policies when they threaten existing stakes in land or natural resources, often resist state impositions in favor of local autonomy, and understand that stability sometimes masks situations of inequality or even oppression. And, as global experience with the Washington Consensus demonstrates, even where there is apparent agreement about development values there is still much room for debate about how such objectives can be achieved. If there are choices to be made about objectives, or how to achieve them, then they should be made by those who have a long-term stake in the outcomes. At least for the moment, China appears to broaden the menu of options for these island states, whose leaders are well accustomed to operating in a world controlled by great powers.

Notes

A longer version of this chapter was published as *China in Oceania: New Forces in Pacific Politics*. Honolulu: East-West Center, Pacific Islands Policy Paper #2 (2007).

1. The countries with this status are the Cook Islands, the Federated States of Micronesia, Fiji, Tonga, Niue, Vanuatu, Samoa, Papua New Guinea, French Polynesia, and New Caledonia.
2. It will be interesting to see if Chinese firms also express interest in the mineral resources of the Solomon Islands, New Caledonia, and Fiji.

3. US defense spending is nearly seven times that of China, and represents more than 40 percent of all global military expenditures.
4. China is one of the largest buyers of treasury bonds, which help fund the United States' $4.6 trillion budget deficit.
5. The 1996 out-of-court settlement obliged the company to build dams to prevent further damage to the river system, and provide trust funds worth more and $150 million for affected villagers along the Ok Tedi and Fly Rivers.
6. US officials worry that Australia's increased economic dependence on China could compromise Canberra's position on the Taiwan issue (Kremmer 2005).
7. The plan's overall objective is to "enhance and stimulate economic growth, sustainable development, good governance and security for Pacific countries through regionalism" (Pacific Plan 2006).
8. Ramo (2004: 4) describes the Washington Consensus as "a hallmark of end-of-history arrogance; it left a trail of destroyed economies and bad feelings around the globe."

References

Associated Press. 2006. "Japan Lavishes Aid on Pacific Islands." *Taipei Times,* 28 May. Accessed 2 November 2007 at www.taipeitimes.com/News/world/archives/2006/05/28/2003310408.
———. 2007. "Fiji's Coup-Installed Government to Send Delegation to Asia to Build Ties." *International Herald Tribune,* 22 January. Accessed 15 November 2007 at www.iht.com/articles/ap/2007/01/23/asia/AS-GEN-Fiji-Coup.php.
Barnett, Thomas P. M. 2004. *The Pentagon's New Map: War and Peace in the Twenty-First Century.* New York: Berkley Books.
Callick, Rowan. 2007. "Chinese Mine Treating PNG Workers Like Slaves." *The Australian,* 9 February: 10
Cole, Rodney, ed. 1993. *Pacific 2010: Challenging the Future.* Pacific Policy Paper, no. 9. Canberra: National Centre for Development Studies, Australian National University.
Davies, Glyn. 2007. "US Policy Toward South Pacific Island Nations, including Australia and New Zealand." Statement before the Subcommittee on Asia, the Pacific, and the Global Environment House Committee on Foreign Affairs. Washington, D.C., 15 March.
Dobell, Graeme. 2007. "China and Taiwan in the South Pacific: Diplomatic Chess versus Political Rugby." In *Chinese in the Pacific: Where to Now?* ed. Paul D`Arcy. CSCSD Occasional Paper, no. 1, May. Canberra: Centre for the Study of the Chinese Southern Diaspora, Research School of Pacific and Asian Studies, Australian National University. Accessed 16 November 2007 at rspas.anu.edu.au/cscsd/occasional_papers/index.php?issue=01.
Economy, Elizabeth. 2007. "China's Missile Message." *The Washington Post.* 25 January, A25.
FATF (Financial Action Task Force). 2007. "Non-Cooperative Countries and Territories: Timeline." Accessed 3 December 2007 at www.fatf-gafi.org.
Finin, Gerard A. 2002. *Small is Viable: The Global Ebbs and Flows of a Pacific Atoll Nation.* East-West Center Working Papers, Pacific Islands Development Series, no. 15 (April). Honolulu: East-West Center. Accessed 24 October 2007 at www.eastwestcenter.org.

Firth, Stewart. 2000. "The Pacific Islands and the Globalization Agenda." *The Contemporary Pacific* 12 (1): 178–219.

———. 2007. "Pacific Islands Trade, Labor, and Security in an Era of Globalization." *The Contemporary Pacific* 19 (1): 111–135.

Fishman, Ted C. 2005. *China Inc.: How the Rise of the Next Superpower Challenges America and the World.* New York: Scribner.

Fry, Greg. 1997. "Framing the Islands: Knowledge and Power in Changing Australian Images of the South Pacific." *The Contemporary Pacific* 9 (2): 305–344.

Godley, Michael. 1983. "China: The Waking Giant." In *Foreign Forces in Pacific Politics,* ed. Ron Crocombe, Te`o Fairbairn, and Yash Ghai et al., 130–149. Suva, Fiji: Institute of Pacific Studies, University of the South Pacific.

Guthrie, Doug. 2006. *China and Globalization: The Social, Economic, and Political Transformation of Chinese Society.* New York: Routledge.

Harwit, Eric. 2000. "Taiwan's Foreign Economic Relations with Developing Nations: A Case Study of Its Ties with Palau." *The Contemporary Pacific* 12 (2): 465–479.

Henderson, John. 2001. "China, Taiwan and the Changing Strategic Significance of Oceania." In *Contemporary Challenges in the Pacific: Toward a New Consensus,* vol. 1, special issue of *Revue Juridique Polynesienne,* ed. Stephen Levine and Tyves-Louis Sage, 143–155.

Henderson, John and Benjamin Reilly. 2003. "Dragon in Paradise: China's Rising Star in Oceania." *The National Interest* 72 (summer): 94–104.

Herr, Richard. 2007. "Sovereignty and Responsibility: Some Issues in Chinese/Taiwanese Rivalry in the Pacific." *Fijian Studies* 4 (2): 111–125.

Huffer, Elise. 2006. "Regionalism and Cultural Identity: Putting the Pacific Back into the Plan." In *Globalisation and Governance in the Pacific Islands,* Studies in State and Society in the Pacific, no. 1, ed. Stewart Firth. Canberra: Australia National University E Press.

Hughes, Helen. 2003. *Aid has Failed the Pacific.* Issue Analysis, no. 33. Sydney: The Centre for Independent Studies.

Jack, Gideon. 2006. "Chinese Firm Gets Go Ahead for PNG Nickel Project." *The National,* 11 August: 3.

Jennings, Peter. 2005. *Getting China Right: Australia's Policy Options for Dealing With China,* Strategic Insights, no. 19. Canberra: Australian Strategic Policy Institute.

Kaplan, Robert D. 2005. "How We Would Fight China." *Atlantic Monthly,* June. Accessed 24 October 2007 at http://www.theatlantic.com/doc/200506/kaplan.

Kelsey, Jane. 2004. *Big Brothers Behaving Badly: The Implications for the Pacific Islands of the Pacific Agreement on Closer Economic Relations (PACER).* Suva, Fiji: Pacific Network on Globalisation.

———. 2005. *A People's Guide to the Pacific's Economic Partnership Agreement, Negotiations between the Pacific Islands and the European Union pursuant to the Cotonou Agreement 2000.* Suva, Fiji: World Council of Churches Office in the Pacific. Accessed 2 April 2008 at www.arena.org.nz/REPA.pdf.

Kremmer, Janaki. 2005. "China Casts Long Shadow of US-Australian Ties." *Christian Science Monitor,* 15 July. Accessed 11 August 2009 at http://www.csmonitor.com/2005/0715/p07s01-woap.html

Lai I-chung. 2007. "Taiwan Examines Its Policies of Diplomacy." *China Brief* 6 (20) (4 October). Washington, D.C.: The Jamestown Foundation. Accessed 11 August 2009 at http://www.jamestown.org/programs/chinabrief/single/?tx_ttnews[tt_news]=3988 &tx_ttnews[backPid]=196&no_cache=1

Larmour, Peter. 2005. *Corruption and Accountability in the Pacific Islands*. Policy and Governance Discussion Paper, no. 05-10. Canberra: Australian National University, Asia Pacific School of Economics and Government, 27 April.

Liangxiang, Jin. 2005. "Energy First: China and the Middle East." *Middle East Quarterly* (spring). Accessed 14 January 2008 at www.meforum.org/article/694.

Linter, Bertil. 2007. "America's China Worries—Part III." *YaleGlobal*, 13 February. Accessed 3 March 2008 at yaleglobal.yale.edu/article.print?id=8751.

Lyman, Princeton. 2005. "China's Rising Role in Africa." Presentation to the US-China Commission, 21 July. Accessed 5 March 2008 at www.cfr.org/publication/8436/chinas_rising_role_in_africa.html.

Macdonald-Smith, Angela. 2005. "China is in Talks to Buy Papua New Guinea Gas." *International Herald Tribune*, 5 December: 15.

———. 2007. "Oil Search, Exxon Drop Papua New Guinea Gas Pipeline." *Bloomberg. com*, 1 February. Accessed 5 October 2008 at www.bloomberg.com.

Matbob, Patrick. 2007. "Developer Scrambles to Improve Conditions." *Islands Business* (March): 34–35.

MIP (Mineral Policy Institute). 2005. "Ramu Nickel Mine: Ocean Dumping Mine Source of Controversy." Accessed at www.mpi.org.au/regions/pacific/png/ramu.

Nadkarni, Dev. 2006. "Goff Tells China, Taiwan Pacific Interests First." *Islands Business* (May): 13.

The National. 2006. "China to Explore PNG for Minerals." 18 January: 18.

Pacific Plan. 2006. *The Pacific Plan for Strengthening Regional Cooperation and Integration*. Suva, Fiji: Pacific Islands Forum Secretariat. Accessed 23 January 2008 at www .pacificplan.org/tiki-page.php?pageName=Pacific+Plan+Documents.

People's Daily Online. 2003. "China to Face Challenges in Energy in Next 20 Years." 16 December. Accessed 15 March 2007 at us.tom.com/english/4856.htm.

Qarase, Laisenia. 2006. Remarks at the Opening of Ministerial Conference on Trade and Development. Fiji Government Online Portal, 5 April. Accessed 15 March 2007 at www.fiji.gov.fj/publish/page_6532.shtml.

Ramo, Joshua Cooper. 2004. *The Beijing Consensus*. London: The Foreign Policy Centre.

Ramu Nickel Limited. 2005. *Ramu Nickel/Cobalt Project*. Accessed 23 January 2008 at www.highlandspacific.com/projects/pdfsProjects/Ramu_Nickel_Cobalt_Project .pdf.

Rice, Condoleezza. 2000. "Campaign 2000: Promoting the National Interest." *Foreign Affairs* (January/February). Accessed 11 August 2009 at http://www.foreignaffairs.com/articles/55630/condoleezza-rice/campaign-2000-promoting-the-national-interest

Rodrik, Dani. 2006. "Goodbye Washington Consensus, Hello Washington Confusion? A Review of the World Bank's Economic Growth in the 1990s: Learning from a Decade of Reform." *Journal of Economic Literature* 44 (4): 983-987.

Saunders, Phillip C. 2006. *China's Global Activism: Strategy, Drivers, and Tools*. Occasional Paper, no. 4. Washington, D.C.: Institute for National Strategic Studies, National Defense University.

Slatter, Claire. 2006a. "Neo-Liberalism and the Disciplining of Pacific Islands States—The Dual Challenges of a Global Economic Creed and a Changed Geopolitical Order." In *Pacific Futures,* ed. Michael Powles, 91–110. Canberra: Pandanus Books.

———. 2006b. "Treading Water in Rapids? Non-Governmental Organisations and Resistance to Neo-Liberalism in Pacific Island States." In *Globalisation and Governance in the Pacific Islands,* Studies in State and Society in the Pacific, no. 1, ed. Stewart Firth, 23–42. Canberra: Australia National University E Press.

Somare, Michael. 2006. Speech, China-Pacific Island Countries Economic Cooperation Development Forum, Nadi, Fiji, 5–6 April. Accessed 25 April 2007 at www.forumsec .org/pages.cfm/speeches-2006.

Tanner, Murray Scot. 2004. "China Rethinks Unrest." *The Washington Quarterly* 27 (3): 137–156.

Time. 2007. "China: Dawn of New Dynasty." 22 January, cover story.

US Department of Defense. 2006a. *2006 Quadrennial Defense Review Report.* Washington, D.C.: US Department of Defense.

———. 2006b. *Annual Report to Congress: Military Power of the People's Republic of China 2006.* Washington, D.C.: Department of Defense, Office of the Secretary of Defense.

US General Accounting Office. 2002. *Foreign Relations: Kwajalein Atoll is the Key US Defense Interest in Two Micronesian Nations.* Washington, D.C.: US General Accounting Office.

Watson, Rob. 2007. "China Test Sparks Space Arms Fears." *BBC News,* 19 January. Accessed at news.bbc.co.uk/go/pr/fr/-/2/hi/asia-pacific/6278867.stm.

Weinstein, Michael A. 2005. "China's Geostrategy: Playing a Waiting Game." *Power and Interest News Report,* 7 January. Accessed at 12 January 2008 www.pinr.com/report .php.

Wen Jiabao. 2006. "Win-win Cooperation for Common Development." Keynote speech, China-Pacific Island Countries Economic Development and Cooperation Forum, Nadi, Fiji, 5 April. Accessed 25 April 2007 at news.xinhuanet.com/english/2006- 04/05/content_4385969.htm.

Windybank, Susan. "The China Syndrome." *Policy* 21 (2): 28–33.

World Bank. 1991. *Toward Higher Growth in the Pacific Islands Economies: Lessons from the 1980s.* Vol. 1, *Regional Overview;* vol. 2, *Country Surveys.* Washington, D.C.: World Bank.

———. 1993. *Pacific Island Economies: Toward Efficient and Sustainable Growth.* Vol. 1, *Overview,* 8 March. Washington, D.C.: World Bank.

———. 2005. *Economic Growth in the 1990s: Learning from a Decade of Reform.* Washington, D.C.: World Bank.

World Council of Churches. 2001. *The Island of Hope: An Alternative to Economic Globalization.* Dossier no. 7. N.p.: World Council of Churches. Accessed 3 June 2008 at www.oikoumene.org/index.php?id=2648.

CHAPTER 2

A Regional Power by Default

Yongjin Zhang

It has been widely, and rightly, observed that in the last decade China has engaged in more assertive diplomacy in the Pacific. It has substantially increased its presence in the regional economy through aid, trade, and investment, and steadily built up its broader interests in the region. China has, in fact, become a significant, if not yet dominant, power in the new regional order in the Pacific. Why has there been such an upsurge of the Chinese influence in the Pacific? What is the meaning and purpose of growing Chinese power? Does China have a grand strategy to seek regional dominance at the expense of other traditional powers? How can we best understand and evaluate the implications of China's growing presence in the region?

A number of claims have been made in recent analyses regarding the rising influence of China in the Pacific. John Henderson and Benjamin Reilly (2003: 94–95), for example, claim that the reduced commitment of the United States to Oceania and the rapid increase of Chinese influence have created a "shift of great power valence" that would "bear important long term consequences for the changing balance of international security," and that "China's long-term goal is to ultimately replace the United States as the preeminent power in the Pacific Ocean." Susan Windybank (2006), on the other hand, warns that China's Pacific strategy is changing the geopolitics of Australia's "special patch" and affecting the "arc of instability" in the Pacific. It is not just a coincidence, she observes, that China arrives as a significant regional player when the Pacific is experiencing growing instability. Similarly, Graeme Dobell (2007) asserts most recently that there is a "desperate contest" for diplomatic recognition between China and Taiwan in the South Pacific that is changing the face of politics across the region.[1]

It has also been suggested that China's recent aggressive diplomacy in the Pacific, and in Asia and Latin America as well, is in response to a post-9/11 power vacuum perceived since the United States became preoccupied by the global war on terror and with Iraq (Shie 2006). The prospect of a non-Western power dominating in the strategic backwater of the Pacific, traditionally regarded as an "American lake," poses an uncompromising challenge to the Western alliance in the region (Feizkhah 2001; Windybank 2005).

This chapter offers an alternative understanding of China's growing power and influence in the Pacific. Contrary to the conventional wisdom, it argues that there is not sufficient evidence to suggest that China has a clearly defined and well-coordinated strategy to fill a power vacuum in the Pacific. Setting my analysis of China's expanding influence in the Pacific in the broad context of China's global diplomacy in the South, I argue that the pattern of China's international behavior in the Pacific, such as its assertive diplomacy to counter Taiwan's quest for international recognition, its economic diplomacy, and its enhanced involvement with such regional organizations as the Pacific Islands Forum, is an integral part of its new diplomacy toward the global South. China's approach to the Pacific is no different from its broader diplomatic approach to other regions of the South such as Africa, Latin America, and Southeast Asia.

I further argue that the arrival of China as a regional power in the Pacific has to be evaluated in the context of the positioning and repositioning of other traditional powers in the region. With limited political, strategic, and financial investment in the South Pacific, China has in fact become a regional power by default. China's arrival as a significant player in the region is likely to shape the emergence of a regional order, although not by provoking a new game of traditional great power politics in the Pacific. While acknowledging destabilizing factors such as China and Taiwan's competition for international recognition, as well as the vulnerability of the Pacific Island states to the manipulations of "checkbook diplomacy" and its impact on corruption and governance, I argue that China's economic engagement with the region also provides serious alternatives and valuable opportunities for the Pacific Island countries in their endeavor to seek long-term sustainable economic growth and development. This aspect is largely neglected in the current analysis. How to capitalize on such opportunities for regional economic development remains one of the most formidable challenges in the construction of a new regional order in the Pacific. By extension of this logic, the shaping of the emerging regional order is firmly in the hands of Pacific Island countries.

Red Star in the Pacific

As far as China is concerned, fostering friendship and cooperation with the Pacific Island countries is not a diplomatic expediency but a strategic decision (Wen 2006). Chinese Premier Wen Jiabao's April 2006 visit to Fiji to attend the inaugural China–Pacific Island Countries Economic Development Cooperation Forum came thirty years after China made its first diplomatic forays into the Pacific. Over the last three decades, China has steadily built up its diplomatic presence in the region. In November 1975 China established diplomatic relations with Fiji and Samoa, followed by Papua New Guinea in 1976. In 1987, China signed Protocol 2 and Protocol 3 of the Treaty of Rarotonga, committing itself to honor the terms of the South Pacific Nuclear Free Zone. China's substantial engagement with regional multilateral diplomacy started when China became a dialogue partner of the South Pacific Forum (now Pacific Islands Forum) in 1989. In 1999, the China–Pacific Islands Forum Secretariat Cooperation Fund was established with an estimated start-up donation of US$3 million from China to be used for the promotion of bilateral trade, investment, tourism personnel training, and other cooperative projects. In April 2004, China joined the South Pacific Tourism Organization, becoming the first member from outside the region. The signing of the China–Pacific Island Countries Economic Cooperation and Development Guiding Framework in April 2006 stands as the culmination of this relationship as it has developed over the last thirty years.

The expansion of China's diplomatic presence and engagement in the Pacific is considerable but remains modest compared to the same period in many other regions, such as Latin America, Africa, and Southeast Asia. As of March 2007, China had diplomatic relations with only seven out of fourteen independent or freely associated Pacific Island countries (Papua New Guinea, Tonga, Samoa, Fiji, the Federated States of Micronesia, the Cook Islands, and Vanuatu).[2] As a number of studies indicate, the Pacific has been one of the most fiercely fought battlegrounds in the struggle between China and Taiwan for international recognition since the 1970s (Biddick 1989; Dobell 2007). Of twenty-six countries that still recognize Taipei today, six are in the Pacific. Countering Taiwan's diplomatic presence in the region is undoubtedly "a diplomatic expediency" that has until very recently dictated China's approach to the Pacific. China's aid, for instance, is criticized for being given generally "for political rather than economic purposes." Highly visible prestige projects—such as a new parliamentary complex in Vanuatu, the Foreign Ministry headquarters in Papua New Guinea, a multi-story government building in Samoa, and a sports stadium in Fiji for the 2003 South Pacific Games—"aimed at making a political statement rather than facilitating economic development" (Henderson 2001: 146).

The tug-of-war between China and Taiwan for international recognition, especially the "dollar diplomacy," seems to have magnified China's presence in the region, particularly with high-profile cases of Pacific Island countries attempting to switch or switching their allegiances between China and Taiwan. These include Vanuatu, Kiribati, Nauru, the Solomons, and Tonga. The positions of both China and Taiwan in the region are, however, firmly entrenched. If we look at the broader picture, the number of countries that recognize Taiwan has remained relatively static in the last two decades, varying between 26 and 29. These states are scattered mostly across Africa, Latin America, the Caribbean, and the Southwest Pacific. As has been observed, they "have only one thing in common: they are all either extremely small geographically, or economically impoverished. Most are actually both" (Taylor 2002: 127).[3]

Without corroborating figures from Chinese sources, it is impossible to verify the claim, which has now been repeated in many places, that "China has a stronger diplomatic presence in the South Pacific than any other country"—that Beijing has the largest number of diplomats, although not the most diplomatic missions, in the region (Australian Senate Foreign Affairs, Defence and Trade References Committee 2005: 163). Increasing Chinese influence in the region, however, is not just due to China coming to the Pacific, but is also enhanced by bringing the Pacific to China. "Visit diplomacy" is a good example. It was reported as early as June 2001 in *Time* magazine (South Pacific edition) that a string of Pacific Island leaders were "welcomed to Beijing and photographed in warm handclasps with President Jiang Zemin or Premier Zhu Rongji," and were hailed as "old friends of China" (Feizkhah 2001). Writing in 2003, Henderson and Reilly (2003: 95) lamented that "[i]t is now accepted routine that first official visit by a new head of government from the region is made to Beijing, not to Canberra, Washington or Wellington." There is also strong evidence to suggest that the "Look North (or East)" strategy of Pacific Island states is not only underwritten by trade and investment opportunities provided by China, but also by the appeal of China's successful economic development model.[4]

In recent years, China seems to have rapidly expanded its trade and investment in the Pacific. Official statistics indicate that China's total trade with Pacific Island countries jumped from US$530 million in 2004 to US$838 million in 2005, an increase of 58 percent, with US$324 million in exports and US$414 million in imports.[5] In 2005, China's trade with Papua New Guinea, its largest trading partner in the region, reached US$370 million (Wei 2006).

China also eyes the Pacific in search of resources for its rapid economic development. China is a major importer of timber from Papua New Guinea. On 31 March 2005, the China Metallurgical Construction (Group) Corporation signed an agreement with the Highland Pacific Group of Papua New Guinea for the development of the Ramu nickel and cobalt project, with promised Chinese investment of US$650 million. Chinese investment in the region is otherwise modest. According to the Chinese Ministry of Commerce, by the end of 2005 it had approved or recorded seventy companies, with US$110 million investment from the Chinese side.[6]

China also seems to have changed its approach to providing aid. In 2004, Tonga's sole electric power company received US$17 million in technical assistance from the Bank of China, and the Cook Islands government received US$4 million for various infrastructure projects (Shie 2006; Australian Senate Foreign Affairs, Defence and Trade References Committee 2005: 163). The three-year aid package that Premier Wen Jiabao announced in April 2006 includes not only Renminbi (RMB) 3 billion yuan (US$385 million) in preferential loans, but also debt cancellation and relief, training of 2,000 government officials and technical staff, and a zero tariff on the majority of exports to China from the least developed countries in the region that have diplomatic ties with China (Wen 2006).[7]

However, one thing about Chinese aid remains unchanged. It comes with no strings attached, apart from recognizing Beijing as the only legitimate government of China. This makes Chinese aid particularly attractive at a time when traditional donors to the South Pacific, countries such as Australia, New Zealand, and the European Union, as well as the International Monetary Fund and the World Bank, have increasingly made their aid conditional on measures designed to counter corruption and enhance good governance, accountability, and transparency. While such Chinese aid policies have increasingly attracted international criticism, Beijing insists that they spring from a commitment not to interfere in the internal affairs of other countries, a principle reinforced by its own experience at the receiving end of such interference.

The South in China's New Global Diplomacy

In recent years China has clearly shown much greater interest in the Pacific, making significantly larger investments, diplomatic and financial, and generally increasing its stakes. Chinese diplomacy in the region has become more active and more sophisticated. There is undoubtedly a new game in the region. What is China up to? Susan Windybank (2005: 33) argues that two strategic purposes underlie China's recent approach to the Pacific:

> Strategic issues often have economic faces. Rising Chinese activity in the region has a broader two-fold purpose: to sideline Taiwan and to undermine ties between Pacific Island nations and regional powers such as the United States, Australia and Japan. It should be seen as part of a longer-term political and strategic investment aimed at challenging the leadership of the United States in the greater Asia Pacific region.

To contest Taiwan's international legitimacy is certainly one strategic goal associated with China's expanded involvement in the Pacific. There is not sufficient evidence, however, to either refute or confirm the claim that Chinese diplomacy in the Pacific aims to undermine the relationships of Pacific Island countries with dominant powers in the region and challenge US leadership in the Asia Pacific in the longer term.

Several factors caution against such a claim. First, the Chinese leadership is confronted with formidable internal challenges, ranging from riots and protests to massive unemployment and environmental degradation. "Beijing's brand of authoritarian politics," according to Pei Minxin, "is spawning a dangerous mix of crony capitalism, rampant corruption, and widening inequality" (Pei 2006: 34). Looking inside the black box of Chinese politics, Susan Shirk (2007) argued most recently that there is a deep sense of insecurity among Chinese leaders. The troubling paradox here is that the more prosperous and developed China becomes, the more insecure and threatened they are. Not surprisingly, the immediate priority for the Chinese leadership is less about how this "fragile superpower" can project itself globally than about how it can effectively maintain stability in a society that is going through unprecedented social and economic transformations, and how the Chinese Communist Party can enhance its own legitimacy in the process.

Second, China has been increasingly seen as a status quo rather than revisionist power in the current international system (Johnston 2003; Taylor 2007). Although extremely uncomfortable with the US hegemony, China has grudgingly and tacitly accepted the unipolarity of the global order, which, Beijing has gradually realized, is not necessarily contrary to the primary goal of Chinese foreign policy: to foster a regional and global order conducive to China's continued economic growth and development. The rise of China's economic power has, for example, benefited immensely from the security environment provided by the United States in the Asia Pacific region. As the largest beneficiary of globalization, China now has too much at stake in the existing global systems of geopolitics, economics, rules, norms, and institutions. The call for China to play the role of "a responsible stakeholder" in the emerging global order is both an acknowledgement of the huge investment that China has in the current arrangements and the important part that China can play in preserving and promoting such arrangements (Christensen 2006).

Third, China's investment, political and financial, in the Pacific Islands region remains modest. For example, China's aid package to the Pacific Islands, announced in April 2006, may seem impressive, but it pales into insignificance when compared with Australian aid to the region. According to the Australian Government's Overseas Aid Program (AusAID), estimated Australian aid to the Pacific (excluding Papua New Guinea) in 2006–2007 was A$434.4 million, and the estimated Australian aid to Papua New Guinea was A$332.2 million, a total of A$766.6 million (AusAID 2006). It is also considerably less than that offered by Japan and the European Union.[8] Japan, for example, increased its offer of Official Development Assistance (ODA) to the Pacific Island Forum countries in May 2006 from 32 billion yen to 45 billion yen (US$415 million) for 2007–2009 (Fonua 2006: 1). As will be discussed later, on his way back to China from the Pacific, Premier Wen Jiabao offered a US$600 million aid package to Cambodia alone (Perlez 2006).[9] It should also be noted that the Chinese "have quietly turned to the US and Britain for help in devising foreign-aid policies" (Elliot 2007: 9).[10]

Nevertheless, it is notoriously difficult to read China's real strategic intention in the region because of the opaque nature of its political system, its secretive foreign policy-making process, and a general lack of information. The difficulty of the task increases as Chinese diplomacy becomes increasingly confident, employs a wider range of instruments, and expands its activities globally (Goldstein 2001). To go beyond an "educated guess" about China's strategic intention in the Pacific, it is perhaps useful and advisable to look at China's recent diplomatic activities in other regions of the South. This examination helps us understand whether China is doing something sinister or different in the Pacific compared to other parts of the developing world.

Africa provides a good comparative example in this instance, as it features significantly in China's global diplomacy. Following his trip to the Pacific in April, Premier Wen Jiabao visited seven African countries between 17 and 24 June 2006.[11] Barely two months earlier, Chinese President Hu Jintao had made a trip to three African countries: Nigeria, Morocco, and Kenya. The China-Africa Summit was held in November 2006 in Beijing and attended by forty-eight African heads of states and their representatives. This unusual flurry of diplomatic activity took place against the background of China's intensified political, economic, and diplomatic engagement with Africa in the past five years.

The China-Africa Cooperation Forum was initiated in 2000 to promote bilateral trade and investment, with China promising to provide financial aid and technical assistance. Since then, China's trade with Africa has increased more than five-fold. According to official Chinese statistics, it rose from US$10 billion in 2000 to US$55.5 billion in 2006, with US$ 26.7 billion in exports to Africa, and US$28.8 in imports from Africa. By the end of 2006, China's total investment in Africa amounted to US$6.6 billion (*Ethiopian Herald,* 7 February 2007: 6). On 9 January 2007, the China National Offshore Oil Corporation announced that it would buy a 45 percent stake in an offshore oil field in Nigeria for US$2.27 billion (Pan 2007).

China's aid to Africa was already substantial before the China-Africa Summit in November 2006. This includes forgiving more than US$1 billion in debt from African countries, investment in the African Human Resources Development Fund for training African personnel, sending more than 900 doctors to work across Africa, and improving infrastructure. In a controversial aid-for-oil deal with Angola, China offered US$2 billion in credit when an IMF loan was held up in 2004 because of suspected corruption within the Angolan government. These funds were used to build infrastructure destroyed during thirty years of civil war, including railroads, highways, bridges, hospitals, and port facilities, as well as to construct a fiber-optic network and to train Angolan telecommunications workers (Pan 2007).[12]

At the China-Africa Summit in Beijing in November 2006, China offered an even larger aid package to Africa for the 2007–2009 period. This includes US$5 billion in loans and credits, debt cancellation of over US$10 billion for the poorest African countries, building of sixty hospitals and malaria clinics, provision of free Chinese-made anti-malaria drugs, construction of 100 schools, and increased scholarships for African students. China has also offered to create a US$5 billion China-Africa Development Fund to encourage Chinese companies to invest in Africa (BBC News 2006).

China's aggressive African strategy has been subject to many criticisms (Servant 2005; Thompson 2005). Three principal explanations for this strategy have emerged. The first explanation comes exclusively from within China and contends that China's global diplomacy has gradually shifted from an obsession with great power relations to building political capital and economic relationships with the developing countries of the so-called South. This shift has become more clearly defined since Hu Jintao became president of China in 2002 (Bezlova 2006). The second regards Chinese initiatives to promote win-win common economic development with Africa as an integral part of Beijing's "charm diplomacy," which seeks to project an image of China as a gentle, kind, and caring rising power. The third explanation argues that China's voracious demand for energy and other raw materials to feed its booming economy has led it to seek energy and mineral supplies from the resource-rich African continent. China's forays into Africa are principally aimed at locking in supplies of these valuable resources.[13]

The same trade and investment pattern seems to have been repeated in Latin America since 2001, as China discovers Latin America in its hunt for resources and primary commodities. During his visit to Latin America in 2004, President Hu Jintao announced that China would invest US$100 billion in Latin America between 2005 and 2015. The investment projects highlighted include oil exploration and construction projects in Argentina, a nickel plant in Cuba, copper mining projects in Chile, and steel mill and oil exploration projects in Brazil. In November 2004, China announced a US$10 billion energy deal with Brazil (Dumbaugh and Sullivan 2005). The Chinese government is said to have "negotiated more than 400 trade and investment deals with Latin American countries in the last few years, investing more than $50 billion in the region" (Pan 2006).

China's trade with Latin America has expanded rapidly. Between 2000 and 2005, Latin America's exports to China grew at 39 percent per annum. By the end of 2005, China had become the second largest export market for Chile, Peru, and Cuba, and the third largest for Brazil. The region is now China's main supplier of copper, nickel, and iron, as well as soy, sugar, and fishmeal (Jubany and Poon 2006). China's trade with its largest trading partner in Latin America, Brazil, was worth US$8 billion in 2004 and is expected to rise to US$20 billion in 2007. Five Latin American countries—Argentina, Brazil, Chile, Peru, and Venezuela—have recognized China's market economy status.[14]

Cambodia in Southeast Asia provides another example of the global reach of China's diplomacy in the South. A few days after Premier Wen Jiabao promised to the Pacific Island countries an aid package including RMB 3 billion, he was in Phnom Penh to offer US$600 million in "no strings attached" loans to Cambodian Prime Minister Hun Sen for a number of infrastructure projects, including two major bridges near the Cambodian capital, a hydropower plant, and a fiber-optic network connecting Cambodia's telecommunications networks with those of Vietnam and Thailand (Perlez 2006). Writing in *Time* magazine in January

2007, Michael Elliot (2007: 6) describes the Chinese influence in Southeast Asia in the following words: "It is not aid from the US but trade with China—carried on new highways being built from Kunming in Yunnan province to Hanoi, Mandalay and Bangkok, or along a Mekong River whose channels are full of Chinese goods—that is transforming much of Southeast Asia."

Both Africa and Latin America, not to mention Southeast Asia, have a clear head start over the Pacific in developing extensive and dynamic political and economic ties with China. China's recent diplomatic overtures in the Pacific are no different from its active diplomacy, past and present, in these regions. To the extent that Beijing seeks energy security and access to natural resources to sustain China's economic growth, its diplomacy in the global South is undoubtedly an integral part of such a grand strategy (Malik 2006). So is China's charm diplomacy, characterized by skillful application of its soft power (Kurlantzick 2007).

This suggests, however, the rather limited strategic ambition of China as a rising power. That is probably why Washington remains "watchful but unalarmed" about China's activities in Latin America, often regarded as the backyard of the United States (Hakim 2006: 5). At the recent Eighth Pacific Islands Conference of Leaders, held at the State Department in Washington in May 2007, China was invited to a meeting of "core partners" that also included Australia, France, Germany, India, Japan, Korea, New Zealand, the United Kingdom, and the European Union, "to discuss regional issues and improve policy coordination" (US State Department 2007).

A recent report of the Australian Senate Foreign Affairs, Defence and Trade References Committee (2005: 182) recommends that "Australia work closely with China to encourage both countries to enter joint ventures designed to assist the development of the island states of the Southwest Pacific." Prime Minister John Howard seemed more ambivalent about China's arrival. On the one hand, he believed that China was "asserting her legitimate interests as a significant power" in the strategic backwater of the Pacific (ABC Radio 2006). On the other, he warned that if Australia walked away from its responsibilities as the regional power in the Pacific, the Pacific countries "will fall into the hands of the evil from other countries," and that there exists the danger of "these places being taken over by interests that are very hostile to Australia" (*Sunday Telegraph*, 31 December 2006: 7).

China and the New Regional Order in the Pacific

Power configurations in the Pacific are clearly undergoing a paradigm shift. The arrival of China as a significant player is impacting the emerging regional order. The question is not just how to interpret China's arrival as a regional power, but also how to understand the nature and purpose of Chinese power in the Pacific.

It is no more than alarmist to claim that "the increasing influence of China in the Pacific Islands has the potential to shift the long-term strategic balance of power in the Pacific away from the West" (Norris 2004: 4) or that the Pacific "is undergoing a geopolitical transition from American to Asian influence" (Henderson 2001: 143). These claims are problematic because they view the changing regional order largely in the context of traditional great power politics, and they deny the pivotal role of the Pacific Island states in shaping the emerging order. They are problematic also because they do not clearly acknowledge that the United States did not have much involvement south of the equator even at the height of the cold war, and they fail to explain the meaning and the purpose of the enhanced Australian role in the region as well as the importance of the continued commitments of European Union and Japan.

Chinese power, which is derived from its modest political, diplomatic, and financial investment, has become significant only when evaluated within the context of the positioning of other traditional powers in the Pacific. While China's arrival may necessitate further strategic adjustment and the reengagement of other traditional powers in the Pacific, it is very unlikely that this development will provoke a new round of strategic confrontation and competition for power and dominance between China and the United States. It is the challenges and opportunities provided by China's economic engagement with the Pacific that are shaping the emerging regional order.

There are three principal reasons why I argue China has become a significant power in the Pacific by default. First, Chinese power arrived in the Pacific against the background of the progressive and continual withdrawal from the region of two dominant traditional powers, the United States and Great Britain. Throughout the cold war years, the United States engaged the Pacific Island countries through a policy of "strategic denial" of Soviet attempts to establish a naval presence in the Pacific. It is true that even during the height of the cold war, United States aid to and interest in the Pacific south of the equator were minimal. The closing of the American consulate in the Solomon Islands after the end of the cold war, accompanied by the pull-out of aid offices in Fiji and Papua New Guinea and the cutback of scholarships and other assistance, help enhance the perception of United States withdrawal from the region. The reduction of the United States Pacific fleet by half further enforces such a perception (Henderson and Reilly 2003: 95, 101). Assistant Secretary of State Glyn Davies candidly admitted recently that "in the 1990s budget constraints and other priorities had meant that Pacific nations had not always received diplomatic attention or development assistance from the US." However, the United States is "seeking to expand our engagement and reverse any perception that the US has withdrawn from the Pacific" (Reuters, 15 March 2007). The United States labeled 2007 the "Year of the Pacific." At the Eighth Pacific Islands Conference of Leaders, held in Washington, D.C., in May 2007, Secretary of State Condoleezza Rice talked about the United States' special kinship with its Pacific neighbors and pledged to expand the US engagement with the Pacific and to "reaffirm the America's historical role in the Pacific" (Rice 2007). A series of public diplomacy initiatives were to be launched by the United States, including the establishment of a new regional office in Suva to oversee diplomatic activities in the Pacific, increased educational exchanges, and the introduction of new democracy grants (US State Department 2007).

The withdrawal of Great Britain is more complete. The British High Commission to Vanuatu in Port Vila was closed at the end of 2005. This was followed by the closure of the British High Commission in Tonga's capital Nuku'alofa in April 2006.[15] While visiting New Zealand in March 2006, Prime Minister Tony Blair did not mince words when he said that "Britain is no longer a player in the Pacific, nor does it want to be. It is the end of an era." Britain, he added, would have to rely on New Zealand as its eyes and ears in the region (Squires 2006).

Second, until recently, the major thrust of Chinese diplomacy in the region has been exclusively directed at the diplomatic rivalry with Taiwan. The increased diplomatic profile and other investment that China has put into the region are dictated by this consideration. They are not aimed at competing with other powers, such as Australia and the United States, for regional dominance. In other words, China has limited strategic ambitions in the region. China's increasing power and influence as well as responsibility in the Pacific may have been an unintended outcome of its intense diplomatic rivalry with Taiwan.

Third, many Pacific Island countries are so-called micro-states. Some of them are impoverished and among the least developed countries in the world. Internally divided, weakly governed, and heavily dependent upon aid, they are extremely vulnerable to the manipulations of external players. This is compounded by the region's uncertain economic future. As Stuart Harris put it to the Australian Senate Foreign Affairs, Defence and Trade References Committee (2005: 187), "You can disorient a government in the Pacific Islands with a very limited amount of money—just a few bribes to the right people at the top and you have undermined the whole governing system." This also means that that relatively small investment in these countries can have a significant impact and influence on the region, possibly resulting in major long-term payoffs for countries such as China.

Herein lies the irony of Chinese power in the Pacific. Beijing's expanding power is far from strong enough to shape the regional order; but it is sufficient to unsettle regional stability. China's growing power in the Pacific has not been accompanied by an expressed willingness to take more responsibility for regional affairs in the Pacific.

China is, however, a new kid on the block. It is playing a different game by different rules. The "dollar diplomacy" played competitively by both China and Taiwan is well documented, has helped entrench endemic corruption in the region, and poses a serious threat to efforts aimed at enhancing good governance and accountability (Windybank 2005; Dobell 2007). Why, then, have "most Pacific Island states ... viewed China's growing role in Oceania with favor rather than fear"? And in what sense is there "a particular congruence between China's broader foreign policy objectives and the interests of many Pacific Island nations"? (Henderson and Reilly 2003: 94–95). What encourages the Pacific Island countries to look north?

First, China provides an alternative to traditional donors for the Pacific Island countries. This is a welcome addition, particularly because Australia has increasingly been criticized for its "boomerang" aid and its behavior in the region is perceived as domineering (Aid Watch 2005). China also provides an option when financial packages offered by international organizations such as the Asian Development Bank, the World Bank, and the International Monetary Fund are increasingly conditioned on anti-corruption measures, good governance, and accountability.

Second, the aid package offered by China has no political strings attached (apart from recognizing Beijing as the legitimate government of China). It is not accompanied by large consultancy fees. With their proclaimed policy of no interference in the internal affairs of the recipient countries, the Chinese ask no questions about internal corruption, governance, and accountability. Chinese aid provides another source of technical assistance for capacity building. China's aid projects are often finished on time and within budget.

Third, the Chinese market also holds the key for Pacific Island countries to fulfill their trade and investment aspirations. As discussed above, Chinese investment in Africa and Latin America has grown exponentially in the last few years, largely to secure supplies of energy and raw materials for China's economic growth. In the aid package to the Pacific Island countries, the Chinese government promised to "set up a special fund to encourage Chinese companies to invest in the Pacific Island countries." According to Premier Wen Jiabao, "China has funding and expertise. The island countries are rich in natural resources. Herein lies some significant potential for bilateral cooperation" (*China Daily*, 6 April 2006).

But most important of all, China's engagement with the Pacific Island countries offers new opportunities for economic growth and development in the region. China can provide market access to these countries, particularly as growth-enhancing opportunities for trade and investment with traditional partners from the North, including Australia and New Zealand, remain limited. As mentioned earlier, China has already granted Approved Destination status to all seven Pacific Island countries that have diplomatic relations with China, increasing the potential of Chinese tourism in the region. It has offered zero-tariffs on most exports to China from the least developed countries in the region. "We look for new markets," the Prime Minister of Fiji stated after signing the aid package with Premier Wen Jiabao in April 2006, "where there is flexibility of entry and a readiness to meet the export needs of small, isolated island countries" (*People's Daily,* 6 April 2006).

Trade and investment are, of course, closely related. China is very much behind "a new silent revolution [that] is taking place in trade and economic cooperation among the developing nations."[16] The role of Chinese trade and investment in the rapid growth of intra-regional trade among developing nations in East and Southeast Asia is perhaps a familiar story. Recent studies of China's trade and investment activities in Africa have concluded that the high annual economic growth rates in sub-Saharan Africa—over 5 percent in recent years—is partly attributable to Chinese investment and trade with China.

In the World Bank–sponsored study *Africa's Silk Road: China and India's New Economic Frontier,* published in 2007, Harry Broadman emphasizes the pivotal role of China and India in the tripling of exports from Africa to Asia in the last five years. He notes in particular that skyrocketing Asian trade and investment in Africa is part of a global trend toward rapidly growing South-South commerce among developing nations. Noting the importance of policy reform in finding the way forward on both continents, Broadman (2007: 1) is firm in his view that "China and India's newfound interest in trade and investment with Africa— home of 300 million of the globe's poorest people and the world's most formidable development challenge—presents a significant opportunity for growth and integration of the sub-Saharan continent into the global economy."

I am not suggesting here that the China market will automatically work magic for the economic development of the Pacific Island countries. We also need to recognize that some Pacific Island countries are better positioned than others to cultivate the opportunities offered by the China market. But this situation is no different from that faced by sub-Saharan African states. The important point here is that the China market now offers a serious alternative and provides opportunities for Pacific Island countries to shape their economic development.

Conclusion

As China rises, it has become increasingly aggressive in applying its soft power globally. China's recent forays into the Pacific, its continued diplomatic rivalries with Taiwan, and its new aid offers have raised considerable concerns about Beijing's intentions in the strategic backwater of the Pacific, traditionally regarded as an "American lake" and Australia's "special patch." Looking more deeply, however, China's strategic, diplomatic, and economic investment in the Pacific remains rather limited in both absolute and relative terms. Examined in the broad context of Beijing's new global diplomacy, the pattern of China's assertive behavior in the Pacific is no different from its approach to other regions in the global South. Not only does Chinese power have limited reach, but the nature and the purpose of

Chinese power are not aimed at either domination of the region or great power competition as traditionally understood. Countering the conventional wisdom prevailing in the existing literature, I have argued that China has no special strategic ambitions in the Pacific.

The arrival of China as a new player in the Pacific, therefore, is unlikely to provoke a new round of geopolitical competition among great powers. In which way, then, is China's arrival likely to help shape the emerging regional order in the Pacific? As China becomes an additional and significant donor, Chinese aid will surely help promote the economic well-being of Pacific Island countries. At the same time, China's unrelenting diplomatic rivalry with Taiwan will continue to complicate and compromise regional political stability. But it is the opportunities and alternatives that China offers for the region to meet the formidable challenge of sustainable economic development and growth that may prove decisive in terms of Chinese influence in the emerging order. The China market, as mentioned above, has been instrumental in the rapid economic growth of sub-Saharan African states in the last five years. As the Pacific Island states seek long-term and sustainable economic growth as the foundation of a viable regional order, there is no reason why they cannot take advantage of the China market in a similar way. The challenge is how these small states, with varied resources and different development levels, can best explore the opportunities offered. The recent Chinese experience in economic development may prove inspirational for these island states to fulfill their aspirations in economic development—not so much in terms of following the China model, but in the prospect of economic prosperity. If such prospects are not taken up seriously and China market opportunities not explored to the full by Pacific Island states, China's arrival may simply prove to be a non-factor in the emerging regional order in the Pacific.

Notes

An earlier version of this chapter appeared in the *Australian Journal of International Affairs* 61(3), 2007, 367–381.

1. Both Windybank and Dobell have incorporated discussions of Chinese diasporas, old and new, in their examination of China's Pacific strategy. Here I have chosen to focus on the strategic and economic policies of the Chinese state.
2. Taiwan's diplomatic partners are the Marshall Islands, Palau, the Solomon Islands, Nauru, Kiribati, and Tuvalu.
3. Henderson and Reilly made a similar observation. Of the six Pacific Island countries that recognize Taiwan, three are among the world's micro-states, with populations under 20,000. These are Palau (15,000), Tuvalu (10,000), and Nauru (6,000)
4. For an elaboration of arguments about China's economic development model, see Joshua Cooper Ramo's (2004) *The Beijing Consensus*.

5. These figures include trade with Pacific Island countries that have no diplomatic relations with China, such as the Marshall Islands.

6. Henderson and Reilly (2003: 103) claim that "[o]ver 3000 Chinese state and private entities have established themselves in the region, with investment worth some $800 million." This claim is repeated in the Australian Senate Foreign Affairs, Defence and Trade Reference Committee report (2005: 175). The figures may include any small business opened by new migrants and settlers from China such as restaurants, small retail stores. They are not indicative of China's actual economic involvement in the region.

7. China also promises to provide free anti-malaria medicines to island countries in the next three years, to approve Papua New Guinea, Samoa and the Federated States of Micronesia as destinations for Chinese tourists, and to provide assistance in building an earthquake or tsunami early warning and monitoring network.

8. It is difficult to calculate how much Official Development Assistance (ODA) the European Union provides to the South Pacific annually. The figure of US$104 million budgeted for 2007 (*International Herald Tribune*, 3 August 2006) does not include bilateral ODA offered by European countries. According to the French ambassador to New Zealand, for example, France provides NZ$30 million bilateral ODA to South Pacific countries (excluding French Territories in the Pacific) in addition to its contribution to the European Development Fund, the source of the EU ODA (Jean-Michel Marlaud 2006).

9. Another comparison is also instructive. Between 2002 and 2006, China committed US$230 million to assistance in the reconstruction of Afghanistan.

10. In my personal interviews in Beijing in December 2006, I learned that China had started consultations with Australia and New Zealand about coordinating their aid policies toward the Pacific.

11. These were Egypt, Ghana, the Republic of Congo, Angola, South Africa, Tanzania, and Uganda.

12. Angola, the second largest oil producer in Africa, is said to have supplied 50 percent of China's imports of oil from Africa in 2006, when it became China's largest trading partner on the continent with bilateral trade valued at US$10 billion, surpassing that of South Africa.

13. The same logic underlies China's approach to resource-rich countries in the so-called North. Australia is a prime target of this Chinese strategy.

14. China entered the World Trade Organization (WTO) in 2001 as a non-market economy. Ever since then, one of the main thrusts of China's economic diplomacy has been to seek the recognition by other WTO members, mostly through bilateral agreements, of China's market economy status so as not to be subject to punitive actions initiated by WTO members, such as the anti-dumping measures imposed by the European Union. By the end of 2006, sixty-six WTO members recognized China's market economy status. But China's three largest markets, the United States, the European Union and Japan, have yet to do so.

15. The British diplomatic mission in Kiribati, which was locally staffed, was also closed during this period.

16. Lakhmi Puri, Director of the United Nations Conference on Trade and Development (UNCTAD) made this observation in May 2004. Since then the "silent revolution in South-South trade" has certainly been accelerated.

References

ABC Radio. 2006. "South Pacific and Australia-China Relations Analyzed." Correspondents Report, 9 April. Accessed 15 March 2007 at http://www.abc.net.au/correspondents/content/2006/s1610923.htm.

Aid Watch. 2005. "Australian Aid to PNG: The Boomerang Effect Continues: Part II." February. Accessed 15 February 2007 at http://www.aidwatch.org.au/assets/aw00681/PNG%20Feb%2028%20final.pdf.

AusAID. 2006. "Australia's Overseas Aid Program 2006–07." Statement by the Honourable Alexander Downer MP. Canberra: Commonwealth of Australia, 9 May. Accessed 20 May 2007 at http://www.budget.gov.au/2006-07/ministerial/download/ausaid.pdf.

Australian Senate Foreign Affairs, Defence and Trade References Committee. 2005. *Opportunities and Challenges: Australia's Relationship with China.* 10 November. Canberra: Commonwealth of Australia. Accessed 10 January 2007 at http://www.aph.gov.au/Senate/committee/fadt_ctte/china/report01/index.htm.

BBC News. 2006. "China to Double Aid to Africa." 4 November. Accessed 15 November 2006 at http://news.bbc.co.uk/2/hi/asia-pacific/6115870.stm.

Bezlova, Antoaneta. 2006. "China's Soft Power Diplomacy in Africa." *Asia Times Online,* 23 June. Accessed 10 January 2007 at http://www.atimes.com/atimes/China/HF23Ad01.html.

Biddick, Thomas V. 1989. "Diplomatic Rivalry in the South Pacific: The PRC and Taiwan." *Asian Survey* 29 (80): 800–815.

Broadman, Harry. 2007. *Africa's Silk Road: China and India's New Economic Frontier.* Washington, D.C.: World Bank.

Christensen, Thomas J. 2006. 'China's Role in the World: Is China a Responsible Stakeholder?" Remarks before the US-China Economic and Security Review Commission. Accessed 10 December 2006 at http://www.state.gov/p/eap/rls/rm/69899.htm.

Dobell, Graeme. 2007. "China and Taiwan in the South Pacific: Diplomatic Chess versus Pacific Political Rugby." *Policy Brief.* January. Sydney: Lowy Institute for International Policy.

Dumbaugh, Kerry, and Mark P. Sullivan. 2005. "China's Growing Interest in Latin America." *CRS Report for Congress.* 20 April. Washington, D.C.: Congressional Research Service.

Elliot, Michael. 2007. "China Takes on the World." *Time,* 11 January. Accessed 11 August 2009 at http://www.time.com/time/magazine/article/0,9171,1576831,00.html

Feizkhah, Elizabeth. 2001. "Making Friends." *Asia Week.* 15 June. Accessed 2 March 2007 at http://www.asiaweek.com/asiaweek/magazine/nations/0,8782,129537,00.html

Fonua, Pesi. 2006. "Japan Increases Aid to Pacific Islands." *Matangi Tonga,* 29 May: 1.

Goldstein, Avery. 2001. "The Diplomatic Face of China's Grand Strategy: A Rising Power's Emerging Choice." *The China Quarterly* 168 (December): 835–864.

Hakim, Peter. 2006. "Is Washington Losing Latin America?" *Foreign Affairs* 85 (1): 39–53.

Henderson, John. 2001. "China, Taiwan and the Changing Strategic Significance of Oceania." *Revue Juridique Polynesienne* 1 (1): 143–156.

Henderson, John, and Benjamin Reilly. 2003. "Dragon in Paradise: China's Rising Star in Oceania." *The National Interest* 72 (summer): 94–104.

Johnston, Alastair I. 2003. "Is China a Status Quo Power?" *International Security* 27 (4): 5–56.

Jubany, Florencia, and Daniel Poon. 2006. *Recent Chinese Engagement in Latin America and the Caribbean: A Canadian Perspective.* Research Report. Ottawa: Canadian Foundation for the Americas. Accessed 2 March 2007 at http://www.focal.ca/pdf/china_latam.pdf.

Kurlantzick, Joshua. 2007. *Charm Offensive: How China's Soft Power is Transforming the World.* New Haven: Yale University Press.

Malik, Rohan. 2006. "China's Growing Involvement in Latin America." *Power and Interest News Report,* 12 June 2006. Accessed 15 March 2007 at http://www.pinr.com/report.php?ac=view_report&report_id=508&language_id=1.

Marlaud, Jean-Michel. 2006. "France and EU in the Pacific." Seminar for the National Centre for Research on Europe, 12 October. Accessed 10 January 2007 at http://www.europe.canterbury.ac.nz/seminars/2006_presentations/marlaud_apr2006_ncre.pdf.

Norris, Graham. 2004. "Pawns in the Game: Pacific Becoming Key Battleground between Taiwan and China." *Pacific Magazine,* 1 May: 14–15.

Pan, Ether. 2006. "China's Soft Power Initiative." *Backgrounder.* Council on Foreign Relations. 18 May. Accessed 18 February 2007 at http://www.cfr.org/publication/10715.

———. 2007. "China, Africa and Oil." *Backgrounder.* Council on Foreign Relations. Updated 26 January. Accessed 15 March 2007 at http://www.cfr.org/publication/9557.

Pei Minxin. 2006. "The Dark Side of China's Rise." *Foreign Policy* (March/April): 32–41.

Perlez, Jane. 2006. "China Competes with West in Aid to Its Neighbors." *New York Times,* 18 September. Accessed 12 August 2009 at http://www.nytimes.com/2006/09/18/world/asia/18china.html?_r=1&scp=1&sq=china%20competes%20with%20the%20west%20in%20aid&st=cse

Ramo, Joshua Cooper. 2004. *The Beijing Consensus.* London: Foreign Policy Centre.

Rice, Condoleezza. 2007. "Address to Eighth Pacific Island Conference of Leaders, 7 May." Washington, D.C.: US Department of State.

Servant, Jean-Christophe. 2005. "China's Trade Safari in Africa." *Le Monde Diplomatique* (English edition), May. Accessed 5 March 2007 at http://mondediplo.com/2005/05/11chinaafrica.

Shie, Tamara Renee. 2006. "China Woos the South Pacific." *PacNet,* no. 10A, 17 March. Accessed 12 August 2009 at http://csis.org/files/media/csis/pubs/pac0610a.pdf

Shirk, Susan. 2007. *China: Fragile Superpower: How China's Internal Politics Could Derail Its Peaceful Rise.* Oxford: Oxford University Press.

Squires, Nick. 2006. "British Sun Sets on Pacific as China Waits in Shadows." *Daily Telegraph,* 1 April: 7

Taylor, Ian. 2002. "Taiwan's Foreign Policy and Africa: The Limitations of 'Dollar Diplomacy.'" *Journal of Contemporary China* 11 (30): 125–140.

Taylor, Nicholas. 2007. "China as a Status Quo or Revisionist Power? Implications for Australia." *Security Challenges* 3 (1): 29–45.

Thompson, Drew. 2005. "China's Soft Power in Africa: From the "Beijing Consensus" to Health Diplomacy." *China Brief.* Jamestown Foundation. 13 October. Accessed 12 August 2009 at http://www.jamestown.org/programs/chinabrief/archivescb/cb2005/

US State Department. 2007. "US Engagement in the Pacific Islands Region: 2007 Pacific Islands Conference of Leaders and Core Partners Meeting." Fact Sheet. 8 May. Office of Spokesman. Accessed 20 May 2007 at http://www.state.gov/r/pa/prs/ps/2007/may/84410.htm.

Wei Ruixing. 2006. Remarks by H.R. Ambassador Wei Ruixing at the dinner meeting in honor of China-Oceania Friendship Association. 7 June. Embassy of the People's Republic of China in Papua New Guinea. Accessed 1 March 2007 at http://pg.china-embassy.org/eng/dsjh/t265381.htm.

Wen Jiabao. 2006. "Win-win Cooperation for Common Development." Speech at the Opening of the First Ministerial Conference of the China-Pacific Island Countries Economic Development and Cooperation. 5 April. Accessed 10 December 2006 at http://news.xinhuanet.com/english/2006-04/05/content.4385969.htm.

Windybank, Susan. 2005. "The China Syndrome." *Policy* 21 (2): 28–33.

———. 2006. "China's Pacific Strategy: The Changing Geopolitics of Australia's 'Special Patch.'" *Executive Highlights*, no. 393. Accessed 15 January 2007 at http://www.cis.org.au/exechhigh/Eh2006/EH39306.htm.

CHAPTER 3

Challenges, Opportunities, and the Case for Engagement

Michael Powles

The Present Debate

Some in the Pacific region see increasing Chinese influence and welcome it, look-ing to the opportunities they believe it could bring. Others, perhaps a growing number, appear to fear the same trend and look for ways of shielding the region from the impact of China's rise. My argument is that China's rise to great power status is unlikely to be short-lived. Its impact on the Pacific Islands region will be substantial and will require significant adjustment. However, the worst fears of some commentators seem excessive. I believe that the countries of the region, act-ing with energy and skill and cooperating as they have when facing past challenges, can influence the course of events in several areas of vital importance to them.

In April 2006 China's Premier Wen Jiabao visited the region to meet with Pacific Island leaders and government ministers. He spoke of a new partnership and agreed to provide several hundred million dollars' worth of preferential loans, tariff reductions, development assistance, and investment (Wen 2006a; see Ap-pendix for his statement). This was no sudden discovery of the Pacific; Chinese navigators had traversed the region many centuries before. Indeed, earlier still, the ancestors of present-day Polynesians and Micronesians moved southward from southern China and Taiwan and then through parts of Southeast Asia before embarking on their epic voyages to new Pacific homelands. Subsequent migra-tions eastward followed and, more recently, there have been increasing people-to-people contacts and commerce. Today, total trade between China and Pacific Island countries has reached a value of US$1.1 billion annually.

The dynamism and energy of East Asia—its peoples and now its economies—are widely recognized as significant features of the global economy. For their part, Pacific peoples suffer serious economic handicaps because of the vast distances of the Pacific, and the small populations and meager resource bases of many island countries. Strengthening Pacific-Asia partnerships has the potential to bring new vitality to struggling Pacific economies.

But others see China's increasing influence more in terms of threats and strategic competition than opportunities. Some observers in the region emphasize the dangers of a "dragon in paradise," and the image is certainly not that of the benevolent dragon of Chinese mythology but rather the aggressive pyromaniacal creature that England's patron saint was brave enough to slay (Henderson and Reilly 2003). One respected regional academic described China as "the most expansionist power in the world today" (Crocombe 2005). Others more specifically expressed concern and suggested that:

> China is not just filling a political vacuum created by Western neglect. It is incorporating the Pacific Islands into its broader quest to become a major Asia-Pacific power. China's long-term goal is to replace the United States as the preeminent power in the Pacific Ocean. (Henderson and Reilly 2003: 94)

> [T]he Pacific will become the main arena for a second cold war between the United States and China that will last for decades. (Kaplan 2005: 1)

> Rising Chinese activity in the region has a broader twofold purpose: to sideline Taiwan and to undermine ties between Pacific Island nations and regional powers such as the United States, Australia and Japan. (Windybank 2005: 29)

> China's move into the South Pacific was clumsy, arrogant and dangerous; Pacific nations need to be careful when dealing with such cynical revolutionary carpetbaggers. (*Islands Business* 2006)

In my own discussions over the past eighteen months with Chinese academics, officials, analysts, and retired diplomats, the message has been clear. China has two principal goals in the South Pacific: access to minerals and raw materials and countering Taiwan's efforts to recruit Pacific countries into its ranks. My own view is that both these goals are pursued against a background of self-recognition that China is now a major Asia Pacific power.

These are some of the widely diverging views. Who is likely to be right in this debate about China's role in the region?

Some Factors Likely to Influence China's Policies in the Region

Foreign observers have a distinctly poor record of trying to predict accurately what will happen in China, or what China will do internationally. What I would like to do instead is examine some of the factors that are going to determine the way China will relate to the Pacific region in the future.

Fearful that this might lead to what one book reviewer called "more mush from a sinologist," I would emphasize that I have no claims to be an academic sinologist. But I have lived and worked in China for several years, including three as New Zealand ambassador in Beijing, and have followed developments in China with fascination for much longer. My roots, though, are in New Zealand and Samoa; moreover, from a base in Suva I represented New Zealand for three years in Fiji, Kiribati, Nauru, and Tuvalu. I am convinced from this professional and personal experience of both China and the Pacific that Pacific countries need to start preparing together for changes to the regional environment. However one reads China's intentions, its rise and increasing influence will require significant adjustments within the region in the years ahead.

China's Rise

Much of the enthusiasm on the one hand and concern on the other is occasioned by the startling speed of China's economic and political rise. Every day new headlines give meaning to the bald statistics about record economic growth, rising living standards, and balance of payments surpluses. For example, in 2005 more Buick cars were sold in China than in the United States (Kwong 2007: 6). In the same year, China sold more to one American company, Wal-Mart, than it did to the United Kingdom (Green 2007), and just recently it was announced that China's central bank had overtaken Japan's as the world's largest official holder of foreign reserves (China Central Bank 2007: 14).

Is such growth sustainable? Here, as on most significant issues relating to China, the observers are split into opposing camps. Some very well qualified observers answer emphatically that China's rise will be followed quite soon by its fall. Gordon Chang predicted in 2001 that China "has five years, perhaps ten, before it falls" (Chang 2001: xix). In an article entitled "Does China matter?" Gerald Segal wrote that "at best, China is a second-rate middle power that has mastered the art of diplomatic theatre" (Segal 1999: 24). Pei Minxin sees China as being on a "[l]ong march to nowhere," stagnating in a "trapped transition" (Pei 2006). Perhaps the most colorful argument against the likelihood of stable growth is expressed in a recent article by Gordon Chang: "Mao regimented the Chinese people, oppressed them, clothed them in totalitarian garb, and denied them their individuality. Today, they may not be free, but they are assertive, dynamic, and sassy. A mall-shopping, Internet-connected, trend-crazy people, they are remaking their country at breakneck speed. Deprived for decades, they do not only want more, they want everything. Change of this sort is inherently destabilizing, especially in a one-party state" (Chang 2006).

On the other hand, equally well qualified observers, and in fact many more of them, take the opposite view.[1] Western business agrees, and literally billions of dollars are being invested in China on the assumption that China's rise is indeed sustainable. There are certainly economic and social factors that have the potential to derail China's rise. There is heavy indebtedness in the banking system, the income gap between rich and poor is growing dramatically, the gap between the prosperous cities and the poor countryside is potentially destabilizing, corruption is serious, there are serious deficiencies in the legal system, and in a public survey of many thousand Chinese the state of the environment was ranked as the country's greatest future challenge. The list could go on. Any of these factors, especially if several should combine, could stop China's rise in its tracks. But there is no secrecy about these challenges, and some are discussed daily in the local press. The government has programs aimed at addressing most of them. That does not mean that they will necessarily be overcome, but over the last two decades there is much evidence of the ability of China's government to tackle awesome economic and social challenges.

More serious in the view of many is the lack of significant development in the country's political system. The country is still ruled by a monolithic Communist Party whose leaders are not selected in a way that Western observers would regard as democratic, and popular accountability is limited. Movement toward both democracy and accountability is occurring but slowly. Some observers believe that political development will follow economic development. One has written: "This writer is one of those who believe that economic development will bring about China's political liberalization. However, it is most unlikely that the Chinese government will collapse. In the wake of ... Tiananmen Square ... it was a rather common view in the West ... that the CCP regime would collapse before long. Many have since realized that the CCP and the Chinese people are unusually adaptable to their environment, internal and external" (Yang 2006: 12).

Some observers argue that government has lost legitimacy since it abandoned Marxism in favor of materialism. Certainly there is now no dominant ideology as there was under Mao. Legitimacy rests instead on the government's ability to continue to provide increasing prosperity. Meanwhile, as fast as it can, it is encouraging the study of Confucius, debunked by Mao, to seek to underpin society with appropriate moral values. One very senior Chinese official remarked to me twelve years ago over a beer that on bad mornings he awoke fearing Chinese society would simply spin out of control through rampant materialism. On better days he believed that Confucian moral values could eventually provide the moral glue necessary to hold society together.[2]

Finally on this point, former New York Times China correspondent Nicholas Kristof, who still visits China regularly, has written: "My hunch is that the period of smooth sailing [since Tiananmen] is now coming to an end. I sense more fragility in the system than at almost any time in the 23 years that I've been writing or living in China.... There is a growing boldness in the land which is significant because the times when Chinese have risen to demand change (including 1989) have been when they have been feeling most bold.... China will end this century as the world's most important country ... but after a wild ride. My premonition is that ferment in China will grow and that the long calm since Tiananmen may be coming to an end" (Kristof 2006). Dangerous though it may be to make firm predictions about where China will be, economically and politically, at any particular point in the future, the evidence today clearly points to China's rise continuing, not least because of the extraordinary adaptability, energy, and resilience of her people. But the odds could well favor at times the "wild ride" Kristof predicts.

A Peaceful Rise?

If China's emergence to world power status were to be accompanied by the conflagrations that accompanied the rise, for example, of Germany and Japan in relation to Britain and the United States, the consequences for the Pacific would be horrendous. On the other hand, if China's rise were to be more like the rise of the United States in relation to Britain, the repercussions in our region would be more manageable. Examination of the "manifest destiny" phenomenon, the American belief in "the old idea of an anointed nation doing God's work in the world" (Dabney 2005: 35), gives little cause for optimism that the United States will easily adjust to China's rise to global power status (Pfaff 2007: 15). In any event, at least for the next several decades, China is most unlikely to challenge the existing world order militarily, not least because of the vast gulf in military might between China and the United States. Strangely, the impression one gets from some utterances coming out of Washington is very different, and "China threat" theories abound.

The Chinese inevitably look at their international situation today through the filter of history, leading them "to feel that their rise now is very appropriate and they see it in the context of a past century of humiliation" (Platt 2006: 23). The pride they have in China's long history is combined with the painful memory of the "Century of Humiliation" to give contradictory feelings of being both confident and vulnerable (Yang 2006). Predicting China's likely behavior internationally in precise terms will always be difficult.

Another factor relevant to China's rise—one over which China itself has little influence—is what one historian calls the "Decline of the West" (Ferguson 2006). In 2006, a British journalist reviewed what he saw as the weakening of US power and influence both globally and regionally, even in the Americas, and concluded that the United States will become increasingly preoccupied with managing its own imperial decline (Jacques 2006).Whether this is overstated or not, the question of how the United States, Japan, and other powers react to China's growing power will strongly influence how China itself uses that power. The United States could make efforts to accommodate China's growing role regionally and globally, and give it respect as a global player (Yang 2006). Or it could refuse to accept or negotiate its relative loss of influence, particularly in East Asia. In the latter situation, tensions would be likely to rise as "China-bashers" fuse anti-communism with attempts to ignite racist fears of a "yellow peril." And if global terrorism proves to be too illusory a threat by which to justify US strategic policies, China may be an attractive alternative threat. In this scenario, open conflict could ultimately be a possibility.

A more likely, less clear-cut, scenario is that the United States' response will combine accommodation and resistance, leading to a continuing policy of what one observer has called "congagement"—a combination of containment and engagement (Feffer 2006). Doubt as to which part of the congagement policy will be applied from day to day would add another element of uncertainty to international relations. It is interesting that former Australian Minister for Foreign Affairs Alexander Downer publicly urged Americans to be more relaxed about China because, unlike the old Soviet Union, the Chinese "are much more pragmatic and engaging with the rest of the world. They are not trying to change the architecture of the world" (Barnes 2007: 15).

Japan, for its part, will not find it easy to accommodate the changing strategic situation in Northeast Asia. Already there is talk of possible changes to Japan's constitution to enable a more vigorous defense role. Given the troubled history of the relationship between China and Japan, as well as some continuing tensions, and despite the economic imperatives favoring a harmonious relationship, there could well be difficult times ahead. The extent of the adjustment expected of Japan should not be underestimated (see Chapter 4). I recall a conversation with a departing Japanese ambassador to China over a decade ago in Beijing. In response to my enquiry about his retirement he said, only half-jokingly, "Oh, it will be rather busy as I need to persuade Tokyo that its aim should be to work toward achieving the same position in relation to China that Switzerland enjoys today in relation to Germany." I am not sure how much progress he is making or whether any progress at all would be realistic.

While most observers agree that China's military will be no match for America's for several decades, there are two danger points.[3] The first, widely recognized, is the issue of Taiwan, where any move toward formal independence is likely to be opposed militarily by China. The second, less widely discussed, is the possibility that political disruption within China could lead to irrational foreign action (Baker 2007).

For their part, China's leaders repeatedly reassure the outside world that China's rise is not a threat to any country. For example, President Hu Jintao told students at Yale University in April 2006: "In future China will continue to firmly stay on a course of peaceful development. It will not compromise the interests of anyone. China's development will provide opportunities for other countries" (Wu 2006: 7).

As well as this statement of policy intention and the military imbalance between China and the United States, China has powerful reasons for concentrating its efforts and the major share of its resources on economic development. Jian

Yang has written: "Economic development is also the key to internal stability. Indeed, it has been widely accepted in China that to develop its economy remains China's ultimate solution to all external and internal problems. [Yang cites several Chinese academic sources for this.] Internally, to claim its legitimacy, the Chinese government has to raise living standards substantially" (Yang 2006: 15).

Finally on this point, the record of China's actual actions internationally is encouraging. A Japanese observer emphasizes the degree to which China is already enmeshed in the international system: "It is hard to imagine how an economically successful China so enmeshed in global capitalism will threaten the very system that made it rich and middle class. Bourgeois success tends to diminish military efficacy in international relations" (Tamamoto 2005: 12).

The Chinese leadership will be well aware that their continuing political legitimacy depends on China remaining within an international system in which it can prosper. While some observers expect China to challenge the US preeminence in the international system eventually, thus far Beijing has gone out of its way to work within the existing international rules of the game. It has emerged as a major power without significantly disrupting the international order (Kahn 2006).

But there is no doubt that China has grown more confident in recent years.[4] In 2006 it successfully hosted a summit for most of Africa. Massive preparations were orchestrated for the Olympics in Beijing in 2008 and are underway for the World Expo in Shanghai in 2010. China has adopted a more prominent and outspoken role in the UN Security Council, supporting sanctions against North Korea but, with Moscow, vetoing a resolution on Burma. It has demonstrated a new willingness to contribute substantially to UN peacekeeping activities, becoming the largest troop contributor among the Security Council's permanent members. More recently, of course, there was China's dramatic destruction of one of its own satellites, demonstrating by the use of sophisticated missile technology that it does not accept American dominance in space (Bowring 2007).

Inevitably, observers have begun to speculate about the likely shape of a "new Sino centric order." One writes of a possible eventual division of the world into American and Chinese spheres of influence, but that seems a far distant possibility (Feffer 2006). A less far-reaching observation from the 2006 Davos meeting in Switzerland is that there is now a global consensus on China taking its place at the top table in a new multipolar world (New Consensus 2007).

Implications for the Pacific Islands Region

We cannot know precisely how all these possible developments and trends will impact the Pacific Islands region. They do illustrate, however, that the Pacific region is not being singled out for any greater attention than its proximity to China would justify. That China's rise, regionally and globally, will have a major impact on our region is not disputed.[5] The areas of possible impact can be divided into two categories: first, those which the countries of the region will be unable to affect significantly, where largely we will be spectators of events occurring in our own front yard; and second, those that we, with skill and possibly some luck, could significantly influence in the course of events.

Several observers, quoted earlier, have forecast a serious competition for strategic influence between China and the United States occurring in the Pacific Islands region (Windybank 2005; Kaplan 2005; Henderson and Reilly 2003). We have seen that the intensity of that competition and the course it takes will depend on many factors, including how China exerts its power and how the United States reacts. The United States administration declared 2007 to be "the year of the Pacific" and stated it would "be seeking to expand our engagement and reverse any perception that the United States has withdrawn from the Pacific…. America's involvement in the Pacific remains crucial to our national security, as we are, and will remain, a Pacific power" (Davies 2007). This sudden declaration of United States determination may be due in part to recognition that China is now playing an increasing role in the Pacific. If it signals the likelihood of more intense competition in the region, many will urge caution on both parties. Our voices will be heard, of course, but larger issues will determine the actions of both sides.

Then there is the issue of Taiwan. Taiwan vigorously seeks to entice Pacific Island countries into its own diplomatic camp, while China actively opposes these endeavors. There is no doubt that the way in which the contest for diplomatic recognition has been conducted has been harmful to several countries in the region. I agree on this (if not on a great deal else) with Susan Windybank when she writes: "The competition between Taiwan and China for the diplomatic allegiance of Pacific states is *adding* to the region's problems, but it's not *causing* them. The two Chinas' engagement is counterproductive, to say the least" (Windybank 2006).

New Zealand Foreign Minister Winston Peters has referred to the recent practice of "checkbook diplomacy" and warned: "Those who seek to manage their relations with the region in this way not only do great harm but also run significant risks to their own international reputation" (Peters 2006a). In response to questions after his speech, Peters was prepared to name names, saying, "I think Taiwan's involvement in the recent blow-up in the Solomon Islands is irrefutable." Australia's former Foreign Minister Alexander Downer has similarly criticized the practice of checkbook diplomacy (Downer 2006). Requests not to engage in this kind of scurrilous bribery and corruption have failed to curb it, and it now has to be hoped that public shaming will have an effect. My hunch is that eventually it will, especially if it is combined with the kind of cooperative approach I propose a little later on in respect of crime and governance issues in the region. I do not believe that the more combative approach recommended by some commentators would be fruitful (see, for example, Dobell 2007).

Some observers suggest that the "Taiwan issue" heads both Beijing's and Taipei's policy priorities for the Pacific. No doubt this is true for Taipei, but it is almost certainly not for Beijing. As John Henderson has written, "China is looking beyond the Taiwan issue to gaining recognition as a major Pacific power" (Henderson 2006: 137).

I turn now to some of the areas in which I believe Pacific Island countries could have influence on the role China plays in the region. Some of these involve issues critical to the region's future prosperity and stability.

Marine and Seabed Resources

The Pacific comprises more than a quarter of the earth's surface, and the Exclusive Economic Zones (EEZs) of Pacific Island states cover an area of nearly 20 million square kilometers. In addition there are huge maritime areas and recognized rights over highly migratory species of fish such as tuna, which spend much time on the high seas. The Pacific tuna resource alone is the world's largest and, while at risk, the one with the best chance of being harvested in a sustainable fashion. From early on China has been a responsible participant in negotiations intended to ensure the sustainable exploitation of the Pacific tuna resource.[6]

The fisheries resource currently provides the biggest source of foreign exchange (from license fees) for several Pacific Island countries, and excitement is mounting regarding the mineral potential on, or below, the ocean floor. Vast quantities of manganese, cobalt, and other minerals lie on the Pacific seabed, much of which is within the EEZs of the Cook Islands, Kiribati, the Marshall Islands, and Tuvalu. Polymetallic sulphides have been identified near Papua New Guinea and Fiji, and diamonds near Pitcairn. Exploration to date has been only partial. Exploitation is another matter, of course, but as the world's industrial powerhouses, including China, work through readily accessible supplies they will certainly turn to the exploitation of seabed resources.

The right of island states to these seabed resources (and to the fish in the seas above) derives from the 1982 UN Convention on the Law of the Sea (or UNCLOS). These countries are proportionately the greatest beneficiaries of the convention (Crocombe 2001: 309).[7] The creation of EEZs under UNCLOS has been likened to giving most countries additional provinces to manage and exploit. In the Pacific Islands, these new resource-rich "provinces" are in most cases many times the size of existing land areas. At present many Pacific Island countries are regarded as being comparatively resource-poor. This will change dramatically when the mineral resources of the seabed come to be mined. Just as mineral wealth contributes to the notion of Australia as the "Lucky Country," the Pacific Island countries, today the subject of so much negative news, one day might become known as the "Lucky Islands." The region certainly has an enormous interest in seeking to ensure that the rights provided under UNCLOS remain intact and are honored.

At his first summit meeting with Pacific leaders at Nadi in Fiji in April 2006, China's Premier Wen Jiabao announced some millions of dollars' worth of aid, concessionary loans, and tariff reductions. However, almost certainly the most valuable thing he brought was China's unequivocal commitment to respect Island countries' rights to these resources: "As a permanent member of the United Nations Security Council, China supports the Pacific Island countries in pursuing their legitimate interests regarding maritime resources exploration and protection" (Wen 2006b; see Appendix for full draft of his address).

This commitment is doubly valuable at a time when international law generally is under strain. Sir Brian Urquhart, a distinguished British international civil servant, has written: "The United States has done more than any other country to develop and strengthen both the concept and the substance of international law. It is nothing less than disastrous that a United States administration should have chosen to show disrespect for the international legal system and weaken it at a time when the challenges facing the planet demand more urgently the discipline of a strong and respected worldwide system of law" (Urquhart 2006). It is ironic perhaps that at such a time, the US administration should be calling on China to be a more "responsible stakeholder" in the international system (Zoellick 2005).

Small island states by their nature depend more on the international rule of law for their survival and prosperity than do large and powerful ones. Tuiloma Nerone Slade, then Samoa's ambassador to the United Nations and now a Judge of the international Criminal Court, said in 1999: "The rule of law in the affairs and the conduct of nations is of paramount importance to small states.... Ultimately the law is their most effective protection, an indispensable antidote to their insecurity and sense of vulnerability" (Slade 1999). At a time when United States support for international law is diminished and Europe still seems preoccupied with enlargement and other issues, the role of the major powers of East Asia in maintaining the international legal system becomes more important. Smaller countries will therefore need to look to the major powers of East Asia for international leadership in this crucial area.

Some observers might question whether the Pacific Island countries could conceivably have the capacity to wield effective influence in this area with China and Japan. The historical record suggests otherwise. Samoa's prime minister, speaking as chairman of the Pacific Islands Forum (PIF) in 2005, said: "I think it is fair to claim that by cooperating at a regional level, Forum countries have achieved, in a number of areas, more than they might have been able to do on their own" (Tuilaepa 2005). Their success in the international negotiation over rights to ocean and seabed resources was clearly such an area. And on many other issues internationally, through their collective action or in cooperation with other like-minded states on particular issues, the member countries of the PIF have achieved considerable success.[8] It has come, however, only after extensive collaboration resulted in a common Forum Island Country position, often requiring individual countries to subordinate particular national positions to a regional one. The tension between national and regional positions has been a feature of negotiations by countries in the forum, often within the framework of the successful Forum Fisheries Agency, on the protection and sustainable management of the Pacific tuna resource. Where a regional position has been achieved, which has frequently been the case, success has often followed in negotiations with, for example, distant water fishing states.

Negotiating common positions for endorsement by all Pacific Island countries may become more difficult in the future as new political currents flow through the region. Fortunately, under the terms of the Pacific Plan, the governments of the region will take steps to promote closer cooperation and, where appropriate, integration. Indeed, Pacific governments held that this would provide improved collective strength in dealing with the outside world. I therefore disagree strongly with recent suggestions from an Australian commentator that regional integration is a "dead end" and pursuit of it is "futile" (Windybank 2006). The importance to all countries of the region of protecting rights under international law to marine and seabed resources and, ultimately, the exploitation of those resources, cannot be overstated.

Good Governance and Foreign Aid

The issue of promoting and encouraging good governance has been on the agenda in the Pacific for many years. Recent developments in several Pacific Island countries suggest that these efforts have not been universally successful, despite the support of PIF countries and the commitment of Australia and New Zealand to give it high priority in their development programs.[9] Hugh White has recently discussed what is involved in achieving good governance in the Pacific: "The hard part is root and branch reform of governmental institutions and political culture.... The harsh fact is Australia does not know how to do this. There is no model anywhere in the world for a country like Australia to follow in playing an intimate role in trying to help a vulnerable state rebuild its government structure and political system. It goes well beyond the traditional conception of development aid, involving much more intrusive engagement in a nation's internal affairs. But there seems no alternative; normal aid does little to help these countries, and without some new form of help failure is very real" (White 2007: 36–37). I do not believe White exaggerates the enormity of the task. Indeed, it may be an open question whether it is in fact possible or appropriate to change a country's "culture." Terence Wesley-Smith has written recently of the real difficulty of transforming culture to enable Western-style institutions to operate. He goes further: "The idea of somehow engineering the wholesale transformation of the central values and practices of Oceanic societies to fit the mould of Western-style administration is deeply troubling" (Wesley-Smith 2007).

In any event, Australia and New Zealand, acting separately or together, are unlikely to be able to change the culture of any PIF country. To be successful the whole region would need to be involved, presumably through the PIF, so that it is demonstrably not a case of the rich neighbors, the former colonial powers, being the proponents and instigators of change in such a sensitive area. The region may not yet be willing to act jointly on such a project, in which case it would be sensible to wait until a consensus can be formed. (In many countries of the region a popular rethinking from *within* needs to be encouraged, and civil society will play a crucial role in that process.) When it is possible to act regionally, it will be important to have the full backing of major outside powers involved in the region. Here there could be a role for China. Its backing and part-financing of such a project could have enormous advantages for perceptions of the project itself (improved governance being seen not to mean simply the imposition of Western standards), and for *regional* governance in bringing China into a closer cooperative relationship with all members of the PIF.

I suggest this is not just naïve and unrealistic thinking. Only the most extreme adherent of the darkest "China threat" scenarios would believe that China could see any benefit in the instability that bad governance can bring. To the contrary, Beijing could well be sympathetic toward such a project. There are clear indications that it could be willing to cooperate in this field in the Pacific, where it is already supporting the regional cooperation programs of the Pacific Island Forum Secretariat. Late in 2006 New Zealand journalist Dan Eaton (2006), under the headline *China Extends Hand to New Zealand in the Pacific,* quoted positive statements on aid cooperation in the Pacific from both China's ambassador to New Zealand and New Zealand's foreign minister. The ambassador was specific: "In other words we want to work together with New Zealand, with Australia, consistent with the Pacific Plan. We are only good in a certain number of areas, like infrastructure, office buildings. Even in those areas we want to work with New Zealand. For example, in the Cook Islands people are criticizing us. They say that the court building did not have the right architectural style. Okay, in that area, perhaps we can work with you and your architects can come up with a better design and we can work on the brick and masonry, or sometimes our money is not enough and we can pool our money."

Asked about these comments, Foreign Minister Winston Peters is reported to have said that diplomats and aid officials were examining a range of joint projects that will be closely monitored: "We have in the past been concerned about the nature of China's engagement and the nature of Taiwan's engagement, which was a situation that leads to corruption. The Associate Foreign Minister [of China] and the Ambassador gave us a commitment to work together and to work along-side each other on projects to make the effort more effective and to ensure our money went further" (Eaton 2006). A New Zealand academic expert on the Pacific, asked about all this by the same journalist, is reported as saying: "I'll believe it when I see it" (Eaton 2006). Indeed, these reported statements from both the Chinese side and the New Zealand side may not yet reflect settled policy. But they do indicate a possible way forward.

Asian Criminal Influences in the Pacific

Closer engagement with China by the Pacific Island states could also be productive in countering increasing Asian crime in the Pacific. The problem is serious and is becoming more so. The drug trade has blossomed in the region over the past decade. In 2000 357 kilograms of heroin valued at US$500 million were seized in Suva, Fiji. In 2004, also in Suva, a large methamphetamine factory was discovered; evidence linked its equipment back to China and Hong Kong (Powles and Taylor 2005). Chinese mafia groups are said to have infiltrated and corrupted the highest levels of Papua New Guinea's police force, involving it in people-smuggling, money-laundering, prostitution, illegal gambling, fraud, and theft (Forbes 2005). According to Andrew Hughes, an Australian police officer who worked until mid 2007 on secondment as Fiji's police commissioner, organized crime is now the greatest security threat in the region (Skehan 2005).

Some observers go so far as to suggest that this criminal activity is sanctioned by Beijing, implying a dark and malevolent plot: "The crime is being perpetrated by organized syndicates, triads or snakeheads, on an unprecedented scale and it is operating within the context of a growing official Chinese presence.... Questions are increasingly being asked as to what the connection is between official Chinese policy in the region and the growth of these transnational criminal networks" (Powles and Taylor 2005: 33). I agree absolutely that the Chinese government has a responsibility to work to combat this Asian crime wave in the Pacific. However, I question that there is any likelihood of some kind of policy support or encouragement of these activities on the part of Beijing. (Thirty minutes reading local Chinese newspapers reveals a strange conundrum: while China's major cities are among the safest in the world, at times, particularly in the countryside, the authorities have real difficulty enforcing their own criminal law.)

Both Australia and New Zealand have police officers attached to their embassies in Beijing. I would find it hard to believe that the Chinese would decline to extend the liaison role of these police attaches beyond the strictly bilateral to encompass criminal activities in the Pacific, if that was the wish of regional countries. Liaising about a problem can fall a long way short of solving it. But if the necessary police resources are put into the job by Australia and New Zealand, and if the Forum Island Secretariat is involved, and if the effort is given appropriate high-level political backing by Australian and New Zealand and other Pacific leaders, improvement in the situation must be possible. I would reiterate the importance of a clear Pacific Islands role through the political support of their leaders and the involvement of the Forum Islands Secretariat.

Conclusion

The term "There goes the neighborhood" has been used by a number of academics lately about the Pacific.[10] I am distressed that this should be said of our home region and prefer to look ahead to a time when we will envy the resource-rich "Lucky Islands" that I mentioned earlier. Achieving that goal, however, is likely to require some new thinking, perhaps along the lines I have suggested.

I suggest that now is the time to develop common positions among the countries of the region and then engage with China on them. I have highlighted three priority areas—marine and seabed resources, governance and development, and crime prevention. Other subjects could follow. The process may not be easy. But perhaps guidance can be found in the words of ancestors on both sides.

The mystic Chinese philosopher Lao Zi of the sixth century B.C. gave thought to how large kingdoms should relate to small kingdoms and vice versa, and particularly how great kingdoms should conduct themselves:

> Therefore if a great kingdom humbles itself before a small kingdom, it shall make that kingdom its prize. And if a small kingdom humbles itself before a great kingdom, it shall win over that kingdom.... But in order that they both may have their desire, the great one must learn humility. (Lao Zi 1905, translation)

New Zealand Foreign Minister Winston Peters has looked back to his Maori ancestors and their mythology for wisdom on the challenges facing Pacific peoples today:

> Maori have an old saying: He rangi ta matawhaiti, he rangi ta matawhanui – the person with a narrow vision sees a narrow horizon, the person with a wide vision sees a wide horizon. There is no question that the Pacific occupies a wide horizon. Indeed it matters so much strategically because it accounts for one quarter of the globe. Yet for a region of such daunting size, the countries of the Pacific often have limited and narrow horizons. Rather than the grand aspirational vision that such a vast and commanding presence should afford, the vision much of the Pacific embraces is often restricted to survival and trying to keep up. The rest of the world is not standing still and waiting for the Pacific; it is growing faster and more dynamic by the day. (Peters 2006b)

It is clear that China can play a positive or a negative role in assisting the Pacific's future growth. I am optimistic that it will choose to be helpful.

Notes

1. See, for example, Gosset (2006a, 2006b), Fallows (2006), Yang (2006), Feffer (2006), Zhang (2003), and Spence (2005).
2. The writer was the New Zealand ambassador in Beijing from 1990 to 1993.
3. See for example Yang (2006), Feffer (2006), and Kahn (2007).
4. Kahn (2006) writes of the Communist Party encouraging people to discuss what it means to be a major world power and financing a twelve-part television documentary that studies other major powers.
5. Interestingly, but perhaps predictably, New Zealand commentators seem to be a little more sanguine about China's increasing role and influence in the Pacific than their Australian counterparts: see, for example, James (2006), O'Brien (2006), and Plimmer (2006), on the one hand, and on the other, Windybank (2005 and 2006), Powles and Taylor (2005), and Dobell (2007). But extreme predictions have appeared on both sides of the Tasman, see for example Simpson (2007).
6. From 2001 to 2004 the writer was Chairman of the Preparatory Conference of the Western and Central Pacific Fisheries Commission.
7. And see also Mansfield (2006: 150) where he refers to the enormous gains for New Zealand (achieving the fourth largest EEZ in the world) and the Pacific Islands. Mansfield comments: "It is very improbable that the balancing of interests that enabled the adoption of the Law of the Sea Convention could ever be reconstructed in the future and in any event it is highly unlikely that any attempted renegotiation would produce a result as favorable for New Zealand." This comment could equally be made in respect of the Pacific Island states.
8. For an account of their success at the United Nations, see Powles (2002).
9. For a full discussion of the commitment to improved governance on the part of Pacific Islands Forum countries, see Hassell (2005).
10. For example, Windybank (2006) and Wesley-Smith (2006).

References

Baker, Rodger. 2007. "Fears of a Perfect Storm." *Stratfor Forecasting*, 31 January.

Barnes, Greg. 2007. "Mining Australia's Goodwill." *South China Morning Post*, 30 January, 13–14.

Bowring, Philip. 2007. "Beijing's Satellite Blast Reverberates in Washington." *International Herald Tribune*, 21 January.

Chang, Gordon. 2001. *The Coming Collapse of China*. New York: Random House.

———. 2006. "China in Revolt." *Commentary Magazine*, December. Accessed 5 March 2007 at http://www.commentarymagazine.com/viewarticle.cfm/china-in-revolt-10798

China Central Bank. 2007. "Report." *Shanghai Daily*, 17 January.

Crocombe, Ron. 2001. *The South Pacific*. Suva: University of South Pacific Press.

————. 2005. "The Growing Chinese Presence in the Region." *Islands Business,* January. Accessed 4 March 2007 at http://www.islandsbusiness.com/archives/islands_business/index_dynamic/containerNameToReplace=MiddleMiddle/focusModuleID=3869/overideSkinName=issueArticle-full.tpl

Dabney, Lewis M. 2005. *Edmund Wilson: A Life in Literature.* New York: Farrar, Straus, and Giroux.

Davies, Glyn. 2007. *Statement before the Subcommittee on Asia, the Pacific, and the Global Environment.* 15 March. Washington, D.C.: House Committee on Foreign Affairs.

Dobell, Graeme. 2007. "China and Taiwan in the South Pacific: Diplomatic Chess and Pacific Political Rugby." *Policy Briefing,* January. Sydney: Lowy Institute.

Downer, Hon. Alexander. 2006. Speech to National Press Club. Canberra, 26 April.

Eaton, Dan. 2006. "China Extends Hand to New Zealand in the Pacific." *The Press,* 8 November 12-13.

Fallows, James. 2006. "Postcards from Tomorrow Square." *The Atlantic Monthly (December)*: 100–113

Feffer, John. 2006. "China and the Uses of Uncertainty." Foreign Policy In Focus, 12 December, Accessed 23 February 2007 at http://www.fpif.org/fpiftxt/3781

Ferguson, Niall. 2006. *The War of the World: Twentieth Century Conflict and the Decline of the West.* New York: Penguin Press.

Forbes, Mark. 2005. "Mafia Corrupt Police in PNG." *The Age,* 19 February.

Gosset, David. 2006a. "The Dragon's Metamorphosis." *Asia Times,* 18 December.

————. 2006b. "A New World with Chinese Characteristics." *Asia Times,* 7 April.

Green, Stephen. 2007. *China Radio International,* 18 January.

Hassell, Graham. 2005. "Good Governance, Human Rights and Conflict Resolution." In *Securing a Peaceful Pacific,* ed. John Henderson and Greg Watson, 239–244. Christchurch: University of Canterbury Press.

Henderson, John. 2006. "Pacific Issues for New Zealand." In *New Zealand and the World: The Major Foreign Policy Issues, 2005–2010,* ed. Brian Lynch, 131–140. Wellington: New Zealand Institute of International Affairs.

Henderson, John, and Benjamin Reilly. 2003. "Dragon in Paradise: China's Rising Star in Oceania." *The National Interest* (summer): 94–104

Islands Business. 2006. Editorial, May. Accessed 14 February 2007 at http://www.islands business.com/archives/islands_business/index_dynamic/containerNameToReplace=MiddleMiddle/focusModuleID=15723/overideSkinName=issueArticle-full.tpl

Jacques, Martin. 2006. "America's Decline and Fall." *Guardian Weekly,* 24 November.

James, Colin. 2006. "Foreign and Family: The Australian Connection – Sensible Sovereignty or Niggling Nationalism." In *New Zealand and the World: The Major Foreign Policy Issues, 2005–2010,* ed. Brian Lynch, 29–37. Wellington: New Zealand Institute of International Affairs.

Kahn, Joseph. 2006. "China Opens Public Discussion on Its Rising Power." *International Herald Tribune,* 8 December.

Kaplan, Robert. 2005. "How We Would Fight China." *The Atlantic Monthly,* June.

Kristof, Nicholas D. 2006. "Rumblings from China." *New York Times,* 2 July. Accessed 23 February 2007 at http://select.nytimes.com/2006/07/02/opinion/02kristof.html?_r=1&scp=1&sq=Rumblings+from+China&st=nyt

Kwong, Peter. 2007. "Rush to Modernize Revives Past Sins." *International Herald Tribune*, 10 January.

Lao Zi. 1905. (Also known as Lao-Tzu). Giles Translation. Verse 61, 34–35.

Mansfield, Bill. 2006. "Resource Diplomacy: New Zealand's Exclusive Economic Zone and the UNCLOS Treaty Regime." In *New Zealand and the World: The Major Foreign Policy Issues, 2005–2010*, ed. Brian Lynch, 149–154. Wellington: New Zealand Institute of International Affairs.

New Consensus. 2007. "New Consensus: A Multipolar World, Viewpoints." *International Herald Tribune*, 27 January.

O'Brien, Terence. 2006. "New Zealand and Asia: Discussion." In *New Zealand and the World: The Major Foreign Policy Issues, 2005–2010*, ed. Brian Lynch, 55–59. Wellington: New Zealand Institute of International Affairs.

Pei Minxin. 2006. "China is Stagnating in its 'Trapped Transition." *Financial Times*, 24 February. Accessed 3 March 2007 at http://www.ft.com/cms/s/0/aa1448d8-a4db-11da-897c-0000779e2340.html?nclick_check=1

Peters, Rt. Hon. Winston. 2006a. *Influences in the Pacific*. Address to the Commonwealth Parliamentary Association, Wellington, 16 August.

———. 2006b. Address to the New Zealand Pacific Business Council, 18 August.

Pfaff, William. 2007. "Manifest Destiny: A New Direction for America." *New York Review of Books* 54 (2): 15.

Platt, Nicholas. 2006. Reported in *Shanghai that's*. 9 November., 23.

Plimmer, Neil. 2006. "New Zealand and the Pacific." In *New Zealand and the World: The Major Foreign Policy Issues, 2005–2010*, ed. Brian Lynch, 141–146. Wellington: New Zealand Institute of International Affairs.

Powles, Anna, and Brendan Taylor. 2005. "The Double-Headed Dragon." *The Diplomat* (July): 32–33.

Powles, Michael. 2002. "Making Waves in the Big Lagoon: The Influence of Pacific Island Forum Countries in the United Nations." In *Contemporary Challenges in the Pacific: Toward a New Consensus*, vol. 1, special issue of *Revue Juridique Polynesienne*, ed. Stephen Levine and Tyves-Louis Sage, 59-76.

Segal, Gerald. 1999. "Does China Matter?" *Foreign Affairs* 78 (5), (September–October): 24–36.

Simpson, Alan. 2007. "China Looms as Key Player in Fiji." *National Business Review*, 19 January.

Skehan, Craig. 2005. "Chinese Gangs in Pacific Now Real Regional Threat." *Sydney Morning Herald*, 19 February.

Slade, Tuiloma Nerone. 1999. *Pacific Perspectives on International Law*. Address to International Law Association, Wellington, 8 July.

Spence, Jonathan. 2005. "The Once and Future China." *Foreign Policy, issue 146* (January/February): 44–45.

Tamamoto, Masaru. 2005. "After the Tsunami: How Japan Can Lead." *Far Eastern Economic Review* 168 (2): 10–18.

Tuilaepa, Hon. Tuilaepa Aiono Sailele Malielegaoi. 2005. *The Future of Regionalism in the Pacific*. Annual Pacific Lecture of the Pacific Cooperation Foundation, Auckland (22 March) and Wellington (23 March).

Urquhart, Sir Brian. 2006. "The Outlaw World." *New York Review of Books* 53 (8). Accessed 19 February 2007 at http://www.nybooks.com/articles/article-preview?article_id=18973

Wen Jiabao. 2006a. "Wen Pledges to Lift Island Ties." *Shanghai Daily,* 6 April.

———. 2006b. Address to First Ministerial Conference of the China-Pacific Island Countries Economic Development and Cooperation Forum, Nadi, Fiji, 5 April.

Wesley-Smith, Terence. 2006. "There Goes the Neighbourhood: The Politics of Failed States and Regional Intervention in the Pacific." In *Redefining the Pacific: Regionalism Past, Present and Future,* ed. Jenny Bryant-Tokalau and Ian Frazer, 121–126. Aldershot: Ashgate Publishing.

———. 2007. "Self-Determination in Oceania: New Roles for United States, Japan and Asian Power?" *Japan Focus,* 7 February. Accessed 12 July 2008 at http://www.japanfocus.org/-Terence-Wesley_Smith/2347

White, Hugh. 2007. "Muscular Dystrophy." *The Diplomat* (December/January): 36–37.

Windybank, Susan. 2005. "The China Syndrome." *Policy* (winter): 28–33. Accessed on 3 March 2007 at http://www.cis.org.au/POLICY/winter05/polwin05-5.htm

———. 2006. *The Changing Geopolitics of China's Special Patch.* Lecture to Victoria Branch of Australian Institute of International Affairs, 12 October.

Wu, Elaine. 2006. "A Rising China Threatens No-One, Hu Tells Yale Students." *South China Morning Post,* 22 April, 7.

Yang, Jian. 2006. "China's Rise: The Security Implications." *New Zealand International Review* 31 (5): 12–16.

Zhang, Yongjin. 2003. "Relationship Dynamics and Strategic Calculus: A China Perspective." In *China and New Zealand,* ed. James Kember and Paul Clark, 87–88. Auckland: New Zealand Asia Institute.

Zoellick, Robert. 2005. *Whither China: From Membership to Responsibility?* Remarks to the National Committee on US/China Relations. New York, 21 September. Accessed 12 February 2007 at www.ncuser.org/articlesandspeeches/Zoellick.htm.

CHAPTER 4

China's Advances in Oceania and Japan's Response

Kobayashi Izumi

Introduction

The recent and vigorous growth of the Chinese economy and the associated development of its global resource diplomacy have made Japan feel threatened and uncertain about its future. In addition, China's and Taiwan's competition to provide aid to Oceania's independent island states affects Japanese diplomacy in several ways. In this chapter I will discuss how Japan is reacting to China's and Taiwan's activities in Oceania, and examine Japan's foreign aid policy toward these island nations.

Increase in Japanese ODA to Counter China

At the Fourth Japan–Pacific Islands Forum Summit, held in Nago City, Okinawa, in May 2006, Prime Minister Jun'ichiro Koizumi declared that Japan would distribute a total of 45 billion yen in Overseas Development Aid (ODA) to member nations of the Pacific Islands Forum (PIF) over the next three years. This signaled a massive increase of more than 50 percent in ODA: until then, annual Japanese aid had only reached a total of 10 billion yen.

In the early 1990s Japan had proudly contributed the world's largest amount of ODA. However, greatly affected by its struggling economy, Japan's ODA has fallen by approximately 10 percent each year since 1998, and in 2001 the United States took over as the world's largest aid donor. Likewise, Japan's aid to PIF member countries has also been on the decline (Ministry of Foreign Affairs 2006). This decline was further exacerbated by the fact that the main focus of aid funding by the Japanese government and the Japan International Cooperation Agency was on Africa, not Oceania. So just what were the prime minister's political intentions when he suddenly announced a 50 percent increase in ODA to Pacific Island nations, especially under such adverse conditions?

The reason for the increase in aid from Japan is relatively simple. The boost was not only a kind gesture toward Oceania but also a reaction to an announcement by Premier Wen Jiabao of the People's Republic of China at the China–Pacific Island Countries Economic Development and Cooperation Forum held in Suva, Fiji, just one month prior to the Japan–Pacific Islands Forum Summit of May 2006. Premier Wen Jiabao promised that in the next three years China would loan the seven countries that participated in the summit 40 billion yen in order to further encourage economic development. China's high profile declaration of aid at a conference held immediately before Japan's similar summit not only indicated a clear restraint on Japan's actions in the Pacific, but also showed the extent of China's presence in that region. The Japanese government could not disregard this kind of action by China. All the achievements accumulated over the twelve years of Japan–Pacific Islands Forum Summits would be cut in half by China's aggressive aid actions.

Japan's decision to increase aid to PIF member countries was hurriedly made during the one-month time frame immediately following China's announcement and before the Japan–Pacific Islands Forum Summit. One might guess that this decision was derived not from well-thought-out foreign policy or with reference to a program of aid reform, but rather as a simple numerical retaliation against China. Two points add weight to this conclusion. The funds for a 50 percent increase in ODA were not part of a special budget. Instead, the government simply reallocated money from the general ODA budget. Some portions of Japan's aid exceed that proposed by China, yet the amount of aid actually needed was not even investigated. These points indicate that the increase in aid, while a shift in quantity, did not necessarily reflect a change in policy toward Oceania. In fact, the aid initiative announced at the Fourth Pacific Islands Forum Summit was simply based on concepts taken from the Okinawa Initiative proposed at the Third Summit held in 2003. It was merely a continuation of a previous aid policy that until this point had not been influenced by China's actions in the region.

Japanese ODA is intended to focus on economic growth, sustainable development, good governance, security, and people-to-people communication and exchange. This means an emphasis on supporting programs and technical cooperation to enhance these five elements from the ground up (Ministry of Foreign Affairs 2000).

As mentioned earlier, Japanese aid has recently been geared toward Africa and South Asia, whereas aid for Oceania has been gradually decreasing. It is most likely, then, that the decision to increase aid for PIF member countries owed more to the efforts of the Oceania Division of the Ministry of Foreign Affairs than to Prime Minister Koizumi himself. This can be ascertained by taking a closer look at the Japanese policy making process. Many decisions on serious issues that have a heavy influence on the nation are ultimately dependent on the prime minister's own judgment. However, most other matters are dealt with using a policy making process that draws on the work of think tanks in the various government ministries before receiving the approval of the prime minister and other cabinet ministers. It is safe to say that in this case certain bureaus within the Ministry of Foreign Affairs played the "China card" to push the prime minister to grant more aid to Oceania. This was a smart move because Japan has been particularly sensitive to all aspects of China's actions, especially recently.

A Strong Interest in China

Japan's concern with China's recent moves in the Pacific must be seen in the context of the greater Asia Pacific region. In April 2007, the Japanese National Diet established the Basic Marine Law. The fact that no law like this had previously been passed seems to reflect the complacency of Japanese political strategy. However, each ministry of the Japanese government did in fact have its own marine policy, and the prime minister's action merely unified what was already there.

The reason why incoming Prime Minister Abe rushed to create this law had to do with China's actions in the East China Sea. In recent years China has been repeatedly test drilling and developing new gas fields along the boundary of Japan's Exclusive Economic Zone. Chinese submarines have also been frequently spotted in the vicinity of Japanese territorial waters. Furthermore, according to US Department of Defense reports, China has also deployed several intermediate and short-range missiles within range of both Japan and Taiwan (*Sankei Shimbun*, 26 May 2007, 2). For these reasons, Japan has paid special attention to the Straits of Taiwan and the East China Sea in order to avoid any sort of armed crises in these areas. In addition, there is tension with neighboring South Korea over competing claims to Takeshima Island, a small island in the Sea of Japan, and with North Korea over nuclear and abduction issues. With these issues piling up, Japan feels the need for constant preparedness in its coastal waters.

Japan is also actively discussing cooperation among East Asian nations. As well as the issues already mentioned, economic trends associated with the ever-expanding Chinese economy increasingly demand attention. In July of 2006, China established a Free Trade Agreement (FTA) with ASEAN (Association of Southeast Asian Nations), thus increasing its profile in this region. China's economic ties with ASEAN continue to grow, and in fact its trade with Thailand has surpassed that with the US and is now second only to Japan. Until recently, Japan had powerful economic ties with other ASEAN nations, but with China's increasing presence in the region, Japan is now sensing the impending crisis of China eventually taking over leadership of the East Asian community. Japan fears not only China's activities in East Asia, but also its relations with Russia, handled under the framework of regional organizations like the Shanghai Cooperation Organization. In fact, China's regional presence today is much more significant than in the past, and Beijing is involved in many of the international problems that concern Japan—a situation that was quite unimaginable during the US-Soviet cold war. Furthermore, China and Japan have had a deep and long-running relationship due to geographical proximity and historical entanglements, and Chinese trends and activities have always been of interest to Japan. Chinese initiatives in the Pacific are no exception.

Cuts in Aid to China

Compared to other parts of the Asia Pacific region, events in Oceania are not of urgent concern in Japan. For example, Japanese scholars and journalists have not paid much attention to the aggressive aid policies toward island countries pursued by China and Taiwan, being instead almost totally consumed by Chinese activities that have a more direct influence on Japan. Nevertheless, Japanese bureaucrats and diplomats continue to pay close attention to Chinese aid to the island nations, both because it gives China more influence in the region and because Beijing uses that influence to expand its negative campaign against Japan.

Japan's 2005 bid to reform the United Nations by seeking a permanent seat on the Security Council was backed by PIF nations. However, a closer look at individual nations' positions on this matter reveals that neither the Kingdom of Tonga nor the Federated States of Micronesia—both of which recognize China—explicitly supported Japan's induction into the council. China has pursued an aggressive anti-Japan campaign in nations that receive its aid, not only among Pacific Island nations but also in Africa (Kobayashi 2007). Although China was not entirely responsible for the outcome, the lack of support for the Security Council bid came as quite a big shock for Japan, and it has recently begun rethinking its aid policies in Africa.

China's activities in Africa are widely reported in the Japanese media. Over the years Japan has sent large amounts of aid to help China's development, and many felt that China should show more appreciation for those efforts. Instead, Beijing has used its own ODA to target resource-rich African countries—and to foster anti-Japanese sentiments. According to Japanese officials, China's actions were "downright inexcusable," which quickly became a big issue for the Japanese public.

Japan began its Chinese aid program in 1979, sending a grand total of more than 3.436 trillion yen by 2005. Of this, 3.1 trillion yen took the form of an international loan, which China did not consider aid, but rather "economic cooperation." This may be because China, as big and prominent as it is, had too much pride to accept assistance from its tiny neighbor. It is this kind of attitude that the Japanese public strongly opposes, and there has been much talk within the National Diet that perhaps China should graduate from the Japanese aid system.

In April 2005 the Japanese government announced its decision to stop giving loans to China after the 2008 Summer Olympics in Beijing (Ministry of Foreign Affairs 2006). China did not want to give up Japanese aid too easily, but after hearing the word "graduate" Premier Wen Jiabao said he was offended to think that the relationship between China and Japan was "like that of a teacher and pupil" (*Asahi Shimbun*, 31 March 2005, 15).

Although still receiving assistance from Japan, China continued its anti-Japan campaign by sending ODA to other developing nations. This kind of pattern has become common in Oceania, and the Japanese government has no valid means of opposing it. However, if present trends continue, all the trust and influence Japan has built up among island nations since the 1970s will become buried under China's aggressive aid campaign. This is why the Japanese government, feeling the impending threat of China, quickly resolved to provide PIF nations with 45 billion yen in aid as a short-term solution.

Japan's Assistance to PIF Members

China's reasons for getting actively involved in Oceania are to terminate Taiwan's diplomatic relations with island nations, to counter the US and Australian presence in the region, and to secure marine resources, including fish, and ensure a supply route to these resources. The Chinese ambassador to Papua New Guinea once stated: "instead of relationships like those with the old colonial powers such as the United States, Australia, and Japan, we should collaborate with our fellow developing nations, and deepen our relationship with island nations through our country's will to provide aid" (personal interview, February 2007). Taiwan, on the other hand, wishes to maintain its relationships with the few countries that recognize its sovereignty and to protect its place in the international community as an independent state. It also seeks to maintain its access to fishing grounds and fishing resources. It can be said that Taiwan is approaching island nations and competing with China to provide them with aid. Both Taiwan and China have distinctive relationships with the Pacific Islands—and clear diplomatic strategies for handling one another's moves in the region.

What about Japan? The country is located quite close to several Pacific Island nations, and its ODA is sometimes larger than that provided by other former colonial powers. What exactly is the country's motivation to provide ODA? A growing number of observers in the world of academia are quite interested in this subject. My research laboratory is often visited by researchers and graduate students from places like the United States and Australia who ask questions like "What is Japan's political policy toward island nations?" and "What national interests motivate these government policies?" Most of them seem to believe that Japan sends assistance to Pacific Island nations in order to protect its fishing grounds for bonito and tuna, and some in the islands also share this belief. In fact, even the policy papers produced by the Ministry of Foreign Affairs list this as the first of three reasons why Pacific Islands are so important to Japan. The second stated reason is to protect important shipping routes. The third is to have reliable partners in the international arena (Ministry of Foreign Affairs 2005). These reasons have been formally and publicly announced by the Japanese government, so no matter which section of a government office is asked, the exact same answer is given.

However, whenever I am asked these questions I answer that it is not because Japan wants to maintain its fishing grounds. In 2005 Japan's GDP was calculated at 503 trillion, 316.5 billion yen, and of that only 200 billion yen came from the bonito and tuna fishing industries—a mere 0.04 percent of total GDP (Ministry of Agriculture, Forestry and Fisheries 2006). In other words, the Japanese bonito and tuna fishing industries do not really have enough influence to sway foreign policy. In fact, for economic reasons all major Japanese fishing corporations have moved away from catching bonito and tuna and into the business of importing fish. The idea that fish need not necessarily be caught because they can simply be imported, is now prevalent in the industry.

So why is such a great deal of Japanese aid spent on marine-related projects? There are two possible answers. First, marine-related industries are often almost the only means of developing the resources of island nations. Secondly, when starting aid programs for island nations, it is easy to draw on the personal connections and information already established and employed by Japanese fisheries specialists. With both the fishermen's jobs and food safety in mind, the Japanese Fisheries Agency long ago began running programs under its own budget to maintain Pacific fishing grounds. Because of these programs, fisheries specialists have been better able to collect important information and conduct substantial exchange with island nations than the Ministry of Foreign Affairs. This suggests that Japan has been running numerous fisheries projects, not because of the importance of the fishing industry but because no other executable or high-priority projects have been discovered. Since the very beginning of its assistance to island nations, the majority of Japan's projects have been marine-related. However, today's projects span a wide variety of fields including education, sanitation, environment, and communications. In general, fewer projects have anything to do with the fishing industry.

In his insightful book *Essence of Decision: Explaining the Cuban Missile Crisis,* Graham Allison (1971) argued that policy making can be classified into one of three models: rational actor, organized process, or bureaucratic politics. He analyzed the decision-making processes within the large organization of national government and came to the conclusion that policies are not always made by rational means, but are rather the result of the power relationship between several departments (the second model) and the diplomacy of bureaucratic politics (the third model). So in trying to understand the true rationale of certain policies and decisions, using only the first model can be misleading. In contrast to many in academia, those with political or administrative experience can easily understand this sort of analysis. It is easy to misunderstand a situation because once a policy has been formulated, the bureaucrat in charge will compose an exceedingly rational explanation that may not reflect any of the behind-the-scenes interactions. The best bureaucrat is the one who is the most talented at this type of task.

In my view the true basis for Japan's assistance to these islands is not primarily that Japan wishes to preserve its fishing grounds. A better answer can be found by taking Allison's second and third models into consideration.

Future Directions for Japanese ODA Policy

The growth in Japanese ODA began with reparations following World War II. With the aim of satisfying domestic needs, Japan utilized a scheme to encourage export-oriented development. However, following the economic boom of the 1980s, the focus of ODA shifted outward in order to contribute to the stability and development of the international community and to an international society grounded in humanitarianism. Perhaps one reason why Japan is still viewed favorably by the recipient countries is that Japanese aid is not accompanied by any overt political pressure or regulations.

Of course, Japan's decision to distribute ODA was not grounded in a desire to be a dominating political force. Japan distributed ODA so it could reduce the surpluses on its books and fend off criticism for being a lone economic power in the international community. Under the abstract concept of a "contribution to the global community," Japan used ODA for practical purposes, not even thinking ahead about coherent strategies or the support it could get in return, and things grew from there. Unfortunately, due to the recession in the Japanese economy the country has had to cut its ODA budget since 1988. Recently, however, there has been vigorous discussion about the need for more ODA as a strategic instrument of diplomacy. The increasing frequency of this argument indicates that ODA was not used very strategically in the past. So if Japan creates friendly relations with neighboring islands, the motivation for its ODA donations to Pacific Island nations will be construed as nothing more than an abstract notion of being for the Japanese national interest.

Even if Japan now wants to use ODA in strategic ways, the system is designed in such a way that this is extremely difficult to do. Specifically, ODA budgets are not only handled by the Ministry of Foreign Affairs, but are also used by all other ministries except for the Ministry of Defense. Aid distributions from each ministry are decided upon separately. Because total Japanese ODA is made up from the combination of ODA from various ministry budgets, when the need for an urgent and strategic large sum of aid arises, funds cannot be disbursed without preparing a special budget. For this reason, one cannot see the true political intentions behind aid to the Oceania region without using Allison's second and third models. Likewise it is evidence of the political intentions behind why, in response to China's actions, Japan decided to quickly donate 45 billion yen in aid.

Surprisingly, until recently the Japanese ODA distribution system was able to operate despite these discrepancies. Although the system lacked concrete goals, recipient nations have often given Japan high marks for basing its ODA on humanitarian rather than political motives. Nevertheless, ODA budgets have been shrinking, and changes in Japanese internal affairs are bringing about a need for more effective and strategic use of aid. This is especially true in places like Oceania, where another donor country like China has come into the picture. Many are now voicing the opinion that the Japanese aid system needs to be reconfigured. Given the growing awareness of this issue, the Japanese government is currently considering political reforms that would unify Japanese ODA policy. In this sense, China's recent proactive aid programs have encouraged Japan to reform the way it administers its aid.

References

Allison, Graham T. 1971. *Essence of Decision: Explaining the Cuban Missile Crisis.* Boston: Little, Brown and Company.

Asahi Shimbun. 2005. National daily newspaper, morning edition.

Kobayashi, Izumi. 2007. *China and Taiwanese Influence Among Pacific Islands and Outlooks for the Future II.* Tokyo: Japan Institute for Pacific Studies.

Ministry of Agriculture, Forestry and Fisheries. 2006. *Annual Report on Fishing and Cultivation Industry Manufacturing Statistics.* Tokyo: Ministry of Agriculture, Forestry and Fisheries.

Ministry of Foreign Affairs. 2000. *Our Common Future.* Tokyo: Ministry of Foreign Affairs.

———. 2005. *Policy Paper.* Tokyo: Ministry of Foreign Affairs.

———. 2006. *Official Development Assistance: A Report.* Tokyo: Ministry of Foreign Affairs.

Sankei Shimbun. 2007. National daily newspaper, morning edition.

CHAPTER 5

The Overseas Chinese Experience in the Pacific

Bill Willmott

Much of the recent literature on "Chinese in the Pacific" has been concerned with the Beijing/Taipei competition and/or the growing role of China in aid and trade in the region. As a social anthropologist, my interest in Chinese communities has been sociocultural rather than political, so the policies and activities of successive Chinese governments have not received attention from me except to the extent that they affected the structure and activities of each Chinese community. Indeed, the activities of the Chinese government (whichever is active in a specific country) often has very little to do with the local Chinese community in that country.[1]

In 1990, when I began research on the Chinese communities in the South Pacific, there were few academic publications on the subject.[2] In terms of books, there were only David Wu's valuable study on Papua New Guinea (Wu 1982), Stuart Greif's less than satisfactory book on Fiji (Greif 1977), Gérald Coppenrath's outdated book on Tahiti (Coppenrath 1967), and Nancy Tom's fictionalized account of Western Samoa (Tom 1986). Bessie Ng Kumlin Ali's recent book on the Chinese in Fiji is an excellent addition to the Pacific literature (Ali 2002).

At the turn of the century, the total population of Chinese in the Pacific Islands was fewer than twenty thousand people living in sixteen countries and territories. Nevertheless, looking at the different communities in such a broad and diverse region, one cannot but speculate on what it means to be "Chinese" on the little islands of the vast Pacific Ocean.[3] The main purpose of this chapter is to demonstrate the wide range of differences that become apparent in studying these disparate communities. They are socially as well as spatially disparate, as there is little contact among the Chinese communities in the islands; each is isolated from the others.

Far too often academics appear to lump together Chinese of very different origins, classes, communities, and even historical periods. But the disparity between Chinese communities—and within some communities—belies such simple categorization. Professor Wang Gungwu has outlined four different types of Chinese identity based on ethnic, cultural, political, and economic norms (Wang 1988: 11–16). He suggests that differing identities based on one or other of these four criteria may emerge in different situations. While his model is problematic in various ways (see Hirschman 1988), it does warn us against assuming that all "Chinese" are culturally or politically identical. Antagonisms between resident Chinese and newcomers to the Pacific in recent years certainly demonstrate that point clearly.

The Chinese who came into the South Pacific in the nineteenth and early twentieth centuries were very different from the most recent wave, which began in the 1980s. Indeed, earlier migration patterns follow the global history of overseas Chinese migration summarized by Professor Wang, who has categorized Chinese migration over the last two centuries as falling into four patterns (Wang 1989). These four patterns are manifest in the South Pacific as separate waves of migration. The first and most persistent pattern is *huashang,* Chinese traders, those who went abroad to seek commercial opportunities. Later in the nineteenth century another type emerged, *huagong,* overseas workers, most of them contracted to non-Chinese companies. The *huaqiao,* sojourners, appeared in the first half of the twentieth century and established communities with continuing connections to the motherland, often including both *huashang* and *huagong.* Now a new phenomenon has emerged in the past three decades, that of the *huayi.* This fourth pattern comprises those of Chinese ancestry who are no longer tied to their motherland but move rather freely in the global economy, re-migrating to take advantage of new opportunities.

Such peripatetic migration does characterize some of the earlier Chinese in the Pacific Islands, who went first to California, on to the Victoria gold fields in Australia, and then elsewhere in the Pacific to follow perceived opportunities. It seems likely at that time, however, that they were strongly linked, socially and sentimentally, to their villages in China, so they differed greatly from the modern *huayi,* who are detached from those origins.

Even before the first wave of *huashang,* Chinese entered the South Pacific at the end of the eighteenth century as cooks and carpenters on ships seeking sandalwood and *bêche-de-mer* (trepang), although no Chinese settled in the islands until the 1840s.[4] They arrived in the New Hebrides (now Vanuatu) in 1844 and in New Caledonia in 1846 (Willmott 2005: 33, 53), but there are no descendants of these first-comers among the current Chinese populations of these islands. It was the resolute traders, the *huashang* who followed them after the middle of the nineteenth century, who became the first Chinese settlers in the South Pacific.[5]

These first settlers formed the nuclei of small Chinese trading populations that have continued until today in all but two of these countries, their children mixing with more recent arrivals to sustain Chinese communities. The exceptions are the Cook Islands and Kiribati, where the handful of Chinese traders in each archipelago married local women and their children did not invoke their Chinese identity to the extent of maintaining a Chinese presence on the islands, although one or two speak Chinese today. In Kiribati, the fact that both President Anote Tong and opposition leader Harry Tong (two brothers) have a Chinese father indicates the extent to which the descendants of I-Kiribati mothers have become indigenized.

Following the advent of Chinese traders in various islands, a second wave of migration comprised Chinese indentured laborers (*huagong*), who were imported in fairly large numbers to French Polynesia (Tahiti and the Marquesas) from 1865, German New Guinea from 1891, German Samoa from 1903, and Nauru and Banaba (Ocean Island) from 1906 (Willmott 2004: 166–170). Those going to Tahiti were Hakka, recruited first in Swatow and later in Hong Kong, while those who went to New Guinea were from Singapore, Macao, and Swatow, probably including both Hakka and Cantonese. The Chinese laborers in Nauru, Banaba, and Samoa were Cantonese from Macao and Hong Kong. One contingent of Chinese indentured labor was also recruited in Macao in 1884 for the nickel mines of New Caledonia, but the experiment was not repeated because other sources of labor proved more economical (Willmott 2005: 54). As with the traders in the Cook Islands and Gilbert Islands, descendants of the few Chinese laborers who settled in New Caledonia with their indigenous wives have disappeared into the Kanak population.

The third wave of Chinese migration to the Pacific began during the period between the wars, when all these countries except Tonga were French, British, Australian, or New Zealand territories. In six of them (French Polynesia, Western Samoa, Fiji, the New Hebrides, the Solomon Islands, and Papua New Guinea), *huaqiao* communities developed that included the Chinese wives and children of traders. The presence of these organized communities provided the opportunity for part-Chinese children of mixed marriages to participate as Chinese. The major Chinese association in the Pacific at this time was the Guomindang (China's National Party, also written as Kuomintang), absent only in the New Hebrides, where a Chinese community organization was founded instead (Willmott 2005: 37). The most elaborate community was in Tahiti, where the size of the Chinese population allowed the growth of several Chinese associations, including several schools and three Guomindang associations (Coppenrath 1967: 59–63).[6] A Chinese school was established in Fiji in 1936 (Ali 2002: 153).

The Pacific War seriously disrupted the Chinese communities in Nauru, Banaba, New Guinea, and the Solomon Islands, many of whom were evacuated when the region was occupied by the Japanese. In the other countries, however, the war economy strengthened the position of the Chinese, even though migration was interrupted for two decades (1940–1960). In the following years, some Chinese left Pacific Island countries as they approached independence, but strong communities remained in most. Now, during the fourth wave of global Chinese migration (*huayi*), they are experiencing economic and demographic growth while, paradoxically, the Chinese associations that structured the communities are in decline. New immigrants are entering from Hong Kong, Taiwan, China, and Southeast Asia to diversify these communities even further and fragment their identities along new dimensions.

From this brief historical review, it can already be seen that diversity characterized these communities, one significant demographic difference being historical sex ratios. In Nauru the Chinese workers were strictly segregated from the indigenous people, but in both Western Samoa and Tahiti some of the male Chinese laborers lived with island women before the Pacific War. Their offspring were therefore raised in two cultures while the men maintained a Chinese community, which allowed their children to develop a salient Chinese identity. In contrast, the lack of Chinese community in New Caledonia, Kiribati, and the Cook Islands denied the laborers' children any opportunity of maintaining the salience of a Chinese identity.[7] Hence, the Chinese communities in Apia and Papeete today include many who also claim Polynesian as well as their Chinese heritage.[8] The dearth of intermarriage elsewhere makes this complication far less relevant in most other South Pacific countries.

Another demographic variable with cultural implications is the provenance of the Chinese residents in these countries. Many of the nineteenth-century Chinese traders were Hokkien, from the port of Xiamen in Fujian Province. By the turn of the century, however, Cantonese migrants far outnumbered the Hokkien, and most of the veterans of the first and second waves are Cantonese. The Cantonese language therefore predominates in the South Pacific, except in Tahiti and New Caledonia, where Hakka is spoken because the large number of Hakka laborers linguistically dominated the community in Tahiti, which later provided migrants to New Caledonia.[9]

Unlike the Southeast Asian Chinese communities, then, and more akin to those in North America, Australia, and New Zealand, individual Pacific Island Chinese communities did not manifest much linguistic (sometimes called "subethnic": see Wang 1988: 17, n. 5) diversity to complicate their Chinese identity before about 1975. To be Chinese in Papeete or Nouméa was to speak Hakka, while to be Chinese elsewhere in the Pacific was to speak Cantonese, and the Chinese schools originally taught in these languages until about 1960.

Today, the situation is far more complicated. In Nuku'alofa, for example, where all the Chinese are recent immigrants, they come from Guangzhou and Hong Kong (Cantonese), Xiamen and Taiwan (Hokkien), Singapore, Shanghai, and other parts of China (Mandarin), even Inner Mongolia. For some time there was also a team of construction workers from Tianjin. Honiara also has some recent immigrants from the People's Republic of China (PRC) and Taiwan, and several Malaysian Chinese companies have staff resident there as well. A few Chinese from the PRC, Taiwan, and Malaysia live in Vanuatu along with the Cantonese majority and one or two Hakka families.

Somewhat less ethnically complicated are the Chinese communities in Tahiti and Nouméa, where the French authorities have permitted very little immigration other than a few temporary kitchen staff—all of whom are, however, Cantonese rather than Hakka. Western Samoa remains the most homogeneous, since all the new immigrants, including restaurant workers, are Cantonese, and there is as yet no immigration from Taiwan or Malaysia. In 1992 several dozen Chinese workers were building the new government office block in Apia, but their separation from the resident Chinese community was almost complete, symbolized and reinforced by the high wire fences surrounding the construction site where they lived.

Incidentally, Dr. Tan Chee-Beng once suggested that the one cultural characteristic common to all Chinese communities in the diaspora was the celebration of Chinese New Year (Tan 1988: 139). Alas, my research has discovered that even that diacritic can no longer be applied, as the Chinese in the Solomon Islands celebrate the New Year on 1 January and do not mark the lunar festival in any public manner.

Economically, too, the Chinese in the Pacific have become more diversified in recent years. Historically, the Chinese in the South Pacific were either indentured laborers or businessmen in the restaurant, retail, or import-export trade, extending to inter-island transport in the New Hebrides (Vanuatu) and the Cook, Gilbert, and Solomon Islands. In the last ten years, however, economic roles have become far more diverse with the reemergence of Chinese contract labor and the arrival of Chinese multinational corporations from Malaysia, Taiwan, and the PRC. In addition, some of the children of resident Chinese businessmen have returned from professional training overseas as doctors, dentists, accountants, and lawyers. It is therefore no longer possible to fit all Chinese into a narrow economic niche.

Chinese contract labor has been present recently in five of the Pacific Island countries: Fiji, Vanuatu, Solomon Islands, Tonga, and Samoa. The construction team for the government building in Apia, an aid project from the PRC, was brought on contract from China (*Islands Business Pacific,* March 1994, 50). Similarly, a new hotel complex near the Nuku'alofa airport was built by a team of about sixty workers contracted from Tianjin.[10] A Chinese construction company has the contract to build a dam on Malekula Island in Vanuatu, and several of the logging companies operating there are also from China, although I am unable to determine numbers. Similarly, of the ten foreign logging companies operating in the Solomon Islands, four are from the PRC and the others are Malaysian and Taiwanese; about a hundred workers from mainland China are involved. In Fiji, several hundred Chinese are working on contract in garment factories (Ali 2002: 96).

None of these workers represents economic competition for the local Chinese residents, who comprise primarily merchants, restaurateurs, and professionals.

In Tonga, the contract workers are an integral part of the Chinese community, participating in the Chinese association and enjoying daily contact with Chinese in their various businesses. In the other countries, however, they are isolated from the local Chinese, living in fenced compounds or outside the urban centers. They present some embarrassment for the local Chinese communities, since their behavior, often very different from that of the local Chinese, is identified as "Chinese" by the indigenous population.

Perhaps even more difficult for the local Chinese communities is the advent of Southeast Asian and Taiwanese businessmen, often representing large multinational companies. These men (I found no women among them) are identified as Chinese by the resident Chinese, and some have sought connections with the local Chinese community, invoking their common ethnicity as a reason for collaboration. Nevertheless, there is some animosity toward them for various reasons. In Fiji and French Polynesia, the antagonism is easily explained by the fact that local Chinese businesses have already grown and diversified to the extent that the prospecting companies represent direct economic competition. In other countries, however, international loggers and builders are not competing against local companies, as no local Chinese are engaged in these trades. Nevertheless, this foreign presence raises issues for them because it complicates inter-ethnic relations even more seriously than does the presence of Chinese workers.

One extreme example may suffice to make this point, even though the details must remain anonymous. The example is a Taiwanese businessman who arrived to do business in a country whose prime minister he managed to charm with proposals for major industrial investment. Many of the resident Chinese believe he is a charlatan, perhaps even corrupt, lacking capital of his own and without the business connections to gain large investment funds. The businessman then accused the local Chinese of "ripping off" the country by exporting their profits to Australia rather than investing them locally, an accusation all my informants took pains to demonstrate was false. The local Chinese have therefore been forced to activate their own political connections to defend themselves, and many are concerned that this man's business reputation will rub off on all Chinese.

Similarly, Tonga has suffered a series of Chinese con men from Hong Kong, Taiwan, and China, two of whom presented grandiose schemes to the late king and all of whom embarrassed the resident Chinese and annoyed Tongans. One Tongan family described their experience with a PRC businessman who entered into a joint venture with them to export sandalwood to China, then reneged on payment and left them with gross debts to friends and relatives. In Vanuatu and the Solomon Islands, many local Chinese believe the large logging companies will severely exploit the local population and environment for quick profits and then withdraw, leaving the resident Chinese to face the odium of this "Chinese" behavior. While some of this economic behavior is criminal, most of it is simply shrewd business practice that ignores the social relationships, developed over time, that characterize the "Pacific Way" of doing business. My research found no evidence of Chinese criminal gangs operating in the Pacific.

Current tensions have not developed along political lines, as they might have done forty years ago between pro-communist and pro-Guomindang factions—or, indeed, a hundred years ago between pro-imperial and pro-republican factions. Such political differences have negligible effects within Chinese communities today.[11] Rather, they relate to different experiences and outlooks. The Chinese settlers have adapted to their Pacific societies over decades and have developed a localized identity, adopting many aspects of Polynesian or Melanesian culture. They have found economic niches that in most cases have been of benefit to the indigenous population, although often in competition with European traders.[12] Most of them began modestly and were compelled to work hard and develop good relations with their customers. In contrast, many of the more recent immigrants come with a get-rich-quick mentality, whether as representatives of large Asian companies or as single men who start working in restaurants and then establish their own small enterprises—without the long apprenticeship in Pacific cultures that the previous settlers endured. Consequently, some of their business practices have offended both indigenous and Chinese residents.

Several of the factors I have mentioned were involved in the burning of Chinatown in Honiara in April 2005 and the destruction of Nuku'alofa's business center in November 2006. In both cases, an anti-government political demonstration turned into a destructive riot that burned a major part of the commercial center of town, although the differences are striking. Unlike the events in Nuku'alofa, where I had discovered considerable resentment of the Chinese ten years before, the incident in Honiara took me completely by surprise. There, I had found that relations between Solomon Islanders and Chinese had been cordial for decades despite the almost complete absence of intermarriage.[13] Resentment had been aroused, however, by rumors that some of the more wealthy Chinese businessmen were closely involved in supporting the current parliamentary leaders, for instance by giving them free lodging at the Honiara Hotel, owned by Sir Tommy Chan. There was also widespread suspicion that some of the aid from Taipei provided the prime minister with a personal slush fund.

While political issues may have provided some motivation for the riot's leaders, these men were able to gain crowd support to loot and torch Chinatown because of growing resentment over new economic roles assumed by some Chinese. Most established Chinese businessmen had maintained good relations with their customers, for some of whom they were wholesale suppliers as well as retailers of imported goods. At the same time they left to Solomon Islanders such enterprises as taxi services and fresh produce and small-goods retail, including stalls selling betel nut and single cigarettes (Chinese stores generally sell cigarettes by the pack or carton). Newly arrived Chinese, however, began to move into these lines in direct competition with indigenous enterprises. Also, one cannot ignore the fact that Honiara had a growing squatter population that was envious of anyone with property, and the Chinese shops held all the "goods" they coveted.

It is interesting that several of the well-established Chinese businessmen received timely warning of the impending invasion of Chinatown and were able to arrange protection to save their properties from looting and arson. The fact that the riot was foreseen in time to give warning indicates that it was not entirely spontaneous but was organized by anti-Chinese elements of the political elite. It also demonstrates that some Chinese had established good relations with some members of that elite.

The situation in Tonga was quite different from that in the Solomons. As in Honiara, the recent movement of Chinese into trades traditionally in the hands of Tongans, such as taxis, food stalls, and small dry-goods shops, caused resentment, as did their evident wealth compared to most indigenous Tongans. A major difference, however, was the fact that the Tongan Chinese community had originated very recently, while the Solomon Islands community had been in existence for nearly ninety years. Although none of the Chinese community was therefore involved in Tongan politics, their very presence in Tonga was resented by Tongan democrats because it relied on the king's unpopular policy of selling Tongan residency permits ("passports"), which began in 1982. Because all of the Chinese were recent immigrants, the protection that some of Honiara's Chinese experienced from their indigenous friends was not evident in Nuku'alofa. It is not possible, in my opinion, to gauge the extent to which the riot in Nuku'alofa can be attributed to anti-Chinese feeling. Demonstrations that started as attacks on the property of unpopular royalty and aristocrats soon enveloped Chinese establishments as well, since, unlike Honiara, Nuku'alofa had no Chinatown and many of the larger shops that fell victim to looters and arsonists along the main street were managed by Chinese.

These two tragic events manifest a new phenomenon in the Pacific Islands. While there was a small amount of violence against Chinese property in Vanuatu during the struggle for independence (Willmott 2005: 44), most countries had no experience of anti-Chinese incidents.[14] Now, with much more varied immigration and a more commercialized economy, ethnic conflict can emerge when some part of the Chinese community steps outside the traditional patterns of economic and ethnic relations. Clearly, there are significant differences among the Chinese communities in the Pacific Islands that we must not ignore if we are adequately to comprehend current events in the region. Even where things appear similar, historical and demographic differences can effect diverse outcomes both for the Chinese themselves and for the societies affected. We need to recognize that there are many varieties of Chinese experience in the Pacific today.

Notes

1. For example, in 1993 I asked a Shanghai businessman in Tonga if having a Taiwanese embassy caused problems. "None at all [*meiyou wenti*]," he replied. "We are all Chinese [*du Zhongguo ren*]." Tonga's switch to recognizing Beijing in 1998 did not affect this sense of unity.

2. For practical reasons, I limited my research area to Polynesia and Melanesia with the addition of Kiribati and Nauru from Micronesia, leaving out Papua New Guinea because David Wu (1982) and Christine Inglis (1978) had already provided adequate studies of that country. The rest of Micronesia had experienced completely different Chinese migration patterns, as had Hawai'i, of course, so my logistic decision was not entirely arbitrary historically or sociologically.

3. A paper I wrote in 1997 on this subject entitled "When is Chinese? Ethnicity and Identity Among the Chinese in the Pacific Islands" was never published because I lost my nerve. Some of it is repeated in this chapter, but I am happy to forward the original to anyone interested.

4. For a fuller statement of the early history of Chinese in the Pacific, see Willmott 1995. Chinese were living in the Sandwich Islands (Hawai'i) as early as 1802, when the first Chinese sugar maker set up his boilers (Willmott 2004: 163), but Hawai'i lies beyond the limits of this essay.

5. Traders were established in Tahiti in 1852 (Coppenrath 1967: 26,n.3), in Tevuka (Fiji) in 1855 and in Apia (Samoa) possibly in 1859 (Willmott 1995: 138. n.2). A few settled in Rabaul (German New Guinea) in the late 1870s (Wu 1973), in the Gilbert Islands about 1880 (Willmott 1995: 133), and in the Cook Islands in 1882 (Gilson 1980: 51). The first Chinese came to the Solomon Islands in 1912 (Willmott 2005: 10). The present Chinese community in Vanuatu traces its history to the arrival in 1912 of Ah Pow (*Zhang Yabao*), who served as a cook on the government ship *Euphrosyne* (Willmott 2005: 34). From Tahiti, the first Chinese restaurateur settled in New Caledonia in 1953 to inaugurate the contemporary community, the few Chinese traders who had lived there in the late nineteenth century having disappeared by 1926. Subsequent Chinese settlers in New Caledonia also came from Tahiti (Willmott 2005: 54–56). Except for two Anglican priests in the 1920s, both of whom left before the Pacific War, Tonga had no Chinese resident until a Taiwanese businessman arrived in 1974 (Willmott 1995: 136).

6. The original Guomindang in Papeete split in 1942 because of personality conflicts, and a third one was established at Uturoa a little later (Willmott 2006: 300).

7. The 1988 census in French Polynesia (the last that distinguished ethnicity) revealed that 14 percent of the Chinese had mixed parentage, almost all of them with Polynesian mothers. The total number of people claiming some Chinese ancestry was over twenty thousand, but most of these did not consider themselves Chinese. Among Chinese, there were 110 males for every 100 females, and the population was aging as families became smaller and more youth opted for Tahitian identity. Intermarriage has become quite common in Tahiti today.

8. In Apia, the Chinese community association was organized into two wings, one for Chinese and one for part-Chinese, using different languages in their meetings and

coming together in a governing committee of four Chinese and four part-Chinese (Willmott 2006: 303). This arrangement is not evident in the Chinese associations in Papeete, where divisions occurred along personal and political lines rather than ethnic (see note 6).

9. Some Chinese in Tahiti are at pains to demonstrate that their community is not descended from the indentured laborers but from independent traders who were also in Papeete throughout (see, for example, Vognin 1994). Their arguments are persuasive, which accounts for the careful formulation of my statement, since the first traders spoke Hokkien and the next came from the Australian gold fields (Willmott 1995: 134) and thus would have spoken Cantonese.

10. It is interesting that the Taiwanese company building the hotel contracted its labor from the PRC in 1992, a combination that would not have been possible even three years before.

11. For example, the Kingdom of Tonga Chinese Association (*Tongjia Wangguo Zhong-hua Huiguan*) unites Chinese from Taiwan and the mainland without apparent conflict.

12. Vociferous denunciations of Chinese traders throughout the twentieth century can be found in such magazines as *Pacific Islands Monthly*, complaining that their frugal habits and small profit margins were "unfair" to British and Australian traders and accusing them of unhygienic and corrupt practices. One sometimes hears similarly racist statements today from expats living in the islands or Islanders in New Zealand and Australia. Complaints to colonial authorities in the past usually fell on deaf ears, however, because most administrators recognized that the presence of Chinese traders was beneficial for the indigenous population.

13. Solomon Islanders call local Chinese "Waku", a Pidgin corruption of the Cantonese Wahkiu (*Huaqiao*); I was repeatedly assured that it is not a derogatory term. The only two Chinese that anyone could remember marrying Melanesians had moved out of the Chinese community into their wives' village culture.

14. In the artificial situation of both Nauru and Banaba, where Chinese contract labor worked in the mines, there were several incidents of industrial unrest, some of which became violent (see, e.g., Williams and Macdonald 1985: 188, 201–203), but they represented conflict between labor and management rather than between ethnic groups. On both islands, Chinese relations with locals was described as "cordial" though minimal.

References

Ali, Bessie Ng Kumlin. 2002. *Chinese in Fiji*. Suva: Institute of Pacific Studies, University of the South Pacific.

Coppenrath, Gérald. 1967. *Les Chinois de Tahiti: de l'Aversion à l'Assimilation 1865–1966*. Publications de la Société des Océanistes no. 21. Paris: Musée de l'Homme.

Gilson, Richard. 1980. *The Cook Islands 1820–1950*. Ed. Ron Crocombe. Wellington: Victoria University Press.

Greif, Stuart William. 1977. *The Overseas Chinese in Fiji*. Taipei: College of Chinese Culture.

Hirschman, Charles. 1988. "Chinese Identities in Southeast Asia: Alternative Perspectives." In *Changing Identities of the Southeast Asian Chinese since World War II*, ed. Jennifer W. Cushman and Wang Gungwu, 23–31. Hong Kong: Hong Kong University Press.

Inglis, Christine. 1978. "Social Structure and Patterns of Economic Action: The Chinese in Papua New Guinea." PhD dissertation, University of London.

Tan Chee-Beng. 1988. "Nation-Building and Being Chinese in a Southeast Asian State: Malaysia." In *Changing Identities of the Southeast Asian Chinese Since World War II*, ed. Jennifer W. Cushman and Wang Gungwu, 139–164. Hong Kong: Hong Kong University Press.

Tom, Nancy Y. W. 1986. *The Chinese in Western Samoa, 1875–1985*. Apia: Western Samoa Historical and Cultural Trust.

Vognin, Sophie. 1994. "La population chinoise de Tahiti au XIXe siècle." In *Le Peuplement du Pacifique et de la Nouvelle-Calédonie au XIXe Siècle (1788–1914), Condamnés, Colons, Convicts, Coolies, Chân Dang*, ed. Paul de Deckker, 236–237. Paris: Éditions l'Harmattan (for l'Université Française du Pacifique).

Wang Gungwu. 1988. "The Study of Chinese Identities in Southeast Asia." In *Changing Identities of the Southeast Asian Chinese since World War II*, ed. Jennifer W. Cushman and Wang Gungwu, 1–21. Honk Kong: Hong Kong University Press.

———. 1989. "Patterns of Chinese Migration in Historical Perspective." In *Observing Change in Asia: Essays in Honour of J.A.C. Mackie*, ed. R. J. May and W. J. O'Malley, 33–48. Bathurst: Crawford House Press.

Williams, Maslyn, and Barrie MacDonald. 1985. *The Phosphateers: A History of the British Phosphate Commissioners and the Christmas Islands Phosphate Commission*. Melbourne: Melbourne University Press.

Willmott, W. E. 1995. "Origins of the Chinese in the South Pacific Islands." In *Histories of the Chinese in Australasia and the South Pacific*, ed. Paul Macgregor, 129–140. Melbourne: Museum of Chinese Australian History.

———. 2004. "Chinese Contract Labor in the Pacific Islands during the Nineteenth Century." *Journal of Pacific Studies* 27 (2): 161–176.

———. 2005. *A History of the Chinese Communities in Eastern Melanesia: Solomon Islands, Vanuatu, New Caledonia*. Working Paper No.12. Christchurch: Macmillan Brown Centre for Pacific Studies, University of Canterbury.

———. 2006. "The South Pacific: Fiji, Nauru, New Caledonia, The Solomon Islands, Tahiti, Tonga, Vanuatu, Western Samoa." In *The Encyclopedia of the Chinese Overseas*, 2nd ed., ed. Lynn Pan, 292–296, 299–303. Singapore: Archipelago Press and Landmark Books for the Chinese Heritage Centre.

Wu, David Yen-ho. 1973. "The Chinese in New Guinea: The Adaptation of an Immigrant Population." Paper presented at the 45th Congress of the Australian and New Zealand Association for the Advancement of Science (typescript), 34 pp.

———. 1982. *The Chinese in Papua New Guinea: 1880–1980*. Hong Kong: Chinese University Press.

CHAPTER 6

Chinese in Papua New Guinea

Hank Nelson

Introduction

The topic of the Chinese in Papua New Guinea (PNG) and, more broadly, in the Pacific Islands, has received much recent attention in the press in Australia and Papua New Guinea, on a Radio National program, and at a seminar at the Australian National University.[1] All recognize the increasing importance of the Chinese in the region—in numbers, wealth, and political power—and of immediate and long-term change.[2] Papua New Guinea is clearly different from the other Pacific states in its size and resources, as well as its shared and porous borders. Its relationship with China is therefore different, and the extent of that relationship is difficult to measure because some transactions and movements of people are illegal and Papua New Guinea's statistics are often unreliable.

Elsewhere, there has been rapidly growing unease about China's interest in South America and Africa. Joshua Kurlantzick observed that in 2004 he found no concern among American policy makers about China's activities in Africa, but by 2006 "it seemed as if I was being invited to a conference on China's interest in Africa nearly every week" (Kurlantzick 2007: 11). However, except among a few specialists, there has been relatively limited and late Australian interest in China's actions and policies in Papua New Guinea—in spite of proximity, a close economic relationship between China and Australia, and a long history in Australia of fearing Asian enemies seeping or rushing south.

New Guinea: *Taim Bipo*

Early Chinese traders entered New Guinea in the early 1880s. One of the most prominent, Ah Tam (also known as Lee Tam Tuck), a shipbuilder and merchant, may have arrived before Germany claimed the area in 1884. The first large group of Chinese came in 1889 as indentured laborers for the Germans. Wanting men experienced in plantation work, the Germans had contracted them in Singapore and the Dutch East Indies. Indentured laborers direct from China were recruited in 1898. Work on the plantations was hard, pay was low, and the death rate high; nearly all the survivors were repatriated at the end of their contracts. Most long-term Chinese residents were men who paid their own fares or arranged loans to have them paid, and took up employment as carpenters, cooks, plantation overseers, and merchants. By 1913 there were over 1,000 Chinese in German New Guinea, Chinatown in Rabaul was an established center, and many Chinese thought of themselves as being in New Guinea briefly while they made money to take home. Men outnumbered women by more than ten to one in the Chinese population.[3]

In its first commitment of troops overseas in World War I, Australia occupied German New Guinea in 1914 and acquired New Guinea as a Mandated Territory in 1921. When the Australians surveyed the foreign population of their new territory in 1921, they found there were 1,195 Chinese men and 229 Chinese women. Nearly all were Cantonese speakers from See Yap. They were engaged primarily in commerce, but significant numbers worked as artisans and in primary industry. The Australian Immigration Act was immediately applied, limiting further Chinese immigration, forcing those given temporary entry to gain exemption from the dictation test, and imposing other restrictions. Chinese men with wives and children in China could not bring their families to New Guinea, Chinese men whose wives died could not bring another woman to New Guinea to look after their children, and Chinese people faced restrictions on buying land and obtaining licenses to operate businesses. Restrictions on the immigration of Chinese women made it more likely that Chinese men would marry mixed-race or New Guinean women, but most of the children from such marriages were brought up within the Chinese community.

By the end of the 1930s, many Rabaul Chinese families had converted to Christianity, or at least identified with the Methodist or Catholic missions and sent their children to mission schools. The wealthiest of the Chinese were sending sons overseas for education, some to Australia and some back to Hong Kong or China. In 1941 Bernard Chan came back to Rabaul after attending a superior private school, Wesley College, and studying law at Sydney University. He was better educated than nearly all Australians in New Guinea, and it was obvious he would not be contained within the three-tier hierarchy of races—Europeans, Asians and Melanesians—that was recognized in written and unwritten law in Rabaul. But war swept aside the old order and it was only partially rebuilt in the postwar period.

With Japan at war in China as of 1937, the Chinese in New Guinea were well aware of the threat from Japan. Official visitors from China spoke at the Kuo Ming Tang (National Party) club in Rabaul, and many New Guinea Chinese had family at risk in China. The Chinese in Rabaul offered to form a unit to fight alongside the Australians, and initially the Australians agreed that they could form an ambulance unit of about thirty members. Although the Chinese provided uniforms and equipment for their young men, the Australians were cautious about non-Australian citizens joining the defense force, and Australian regulations required recruits to be "substantially of European origin or descent." The Australians decided that they would rather have the help of the Chinese as Red Cross volunteers. Some forty years later, the few survivors of the Chinese who turned up for duty in the confusion of the Japanese assault on 23 January 1942 were admitted to the Australian veterans' organization, the Returned Servicemen's League.

In late December 1941, Australia evacuated white women and children but rejected pleas to allow Chinese women and children to take refuge in Australia. That decision was reversed a few months later when Chinese from Wau on mainland New Guinea were flown to Australia, and eventually over 300 Chinese were evacuated. However, the decision not to allow the majority of the Chinese women to leave was resented. In spite of this, several Chinese in Japanese-occupied New Guinea took great personal risks to help Allied airmen and coast-watchers and provide information about the Japanese. Chin Hoi Meen, who had worked for the administration in the prewar period and became a successful merchant after the war, was presented with an MBE and the King's Medal for his services. More than thirty-five Chinese were killed by the Japanese, another seven died as a result of Allied bombing, and all suffered deprivation and loss of capital assets. However, most survived the war (Cahill 1972).[4]

The Postwar Period

The war damage compensation scheme introduced by the Australian government was indifferent to agency or race. It paid whether the damage was caused by the Allies or the Japanese, and Melanesians, Chinese, and Europeans alike could apply for the loss of objects large or small, personal injury, and the death of relatives. The Chinese, already attempting to rebuild their businesses, were well placed to invest their compensation payments and to meet the needs of villagers who had their own payments to spend. Soon the Chinese were expanding their businesses, stocking high-priced cameras, electronic equipment, and clothing, and selling to Europeans. This change from running small trade stores catering to villagers had begun before the war, and it accelerated in the late 1950s. The strict policy against any further immigration of Chinese was maintained, but petty discriminatory laws were repealed. Minister for Territories Paul Hasluck moved to have the population of Papua and New Guinea divided into two: an indigenous majority and a foreign minority (Hasluck 1976: 333). Mixed-race people were to join one group or the other, and Asians with necessary residential qualifications could apply for Australian citizenship. As most Chinese then living in New Guinea had been born there, many were able to apply. A few Chinese shifted to Australia, and more moved into the neighboring Territory of Papua and changed the nature of merchandising in Port Moresby. Before the war, there had been almost no Asians in Papua, with the eighty-eight Filipinos being the dominant group. There were just five Chinese recorded in the 1933 census of Papua (Commonwealth of Australia n.d.: 574). In Port Moresby, Luk Poi Wai (popularly known to the Australians as "Luke Warm Pie") ran a tailor's shop above Koki. His was then the only Chinese family in Port Moresby.

The decision to allow the New Guinean Chinese to take Australian citizenship was an early and significant change in the White Australia policy. The turmoil in postwar China and the victory of the Communists had effectively prevented the New Guinean Chinese from visiting mainland China, which had increased the community's tendency to look south. By the 1970s and 1980s young Chinese were losing their fluency in Cantonese.

In the 1966 census, the first comprehensive census of the two Australian Territories of Papua and New Guinea, 64 men and 17 women (81 total) in Papua and 297 men and 188 women (485) in New Guinea claimed to have been born in China, a total of 566. When asked their nationality, 206 men and 76 women (282) in the two territories said they were Chinese. But when asked their "race," 1,391 men and 1,064 women (2,455) said they were Chinese. Of these, 273 were living in Papua. Being Chinese was by then about physical and cultural identity. For most, it was unrelated to nationality or place of birth. The 3,303 Chinese lived among an indigenous population of 2,150,317, and were part of a non-indigenous population of 34,669, of whom 17,847 had been born in Australia (Territory of Papua and New Guinea n.d.).[5]

By independence in 1975, many of the Chinese in Papua New Guinea had Australian citizenship and investments in Australia, and had educated their children in Australia. In Papua New Guinea they were still often socially separate from Australians, living unostentatiously and keeping clear of politics, although both Sir Julius Chan and Perry Kwan (who had a Chinese father and Filipino mother) were elected to the House of Assembly in 1972, and Robert Seeto served a long time as premier of New Ireland Province. Chan, by background, office, and longevity, is an exceptional figure in Papua New Guinea politics. Prime minister from 1980 to 1982 and again from 1994 to 1997, Chan was born in 1939 on Tanga Island, off New Ireland, the son of Chin Pak from China and Tin Koris of Nokon village south of Namatanai, New Ireland. Chin Pak, who arrived in New Guinea in 1921, was a plantation owner and trader. During the war the family was confined with other Chinese near Namatanai. After primary schooling at Rabaul, Julius went to Marist Brothers, Brisbane, and began a degree in agricultural science at the University of Queensland. Returning to New Guinea after a motorcycle accident, he worked in public service, took Australian citizenship, and went into the successful family shipping and trading business. He was first elected to Parliament as member for Namatanai in 1968, when he claimed to speak and read Cantonese, English, and Pidgin. After independence he became a citizen of Papua New Guinea. He was the founding minister for finance in the first Somare government. Defeated in the 1997 election, Sir Julius stood for the New Ireland provincial seat in 2002 and again lost, but his son, Byron Chan, won his old seat of Namatanai. Both father and son regained their seats in the 2007 general election.

In the last years of Australian administration, Papua New Guineans infrequently and in minor incidents expressed resentment against Chinese storekeepers. On the eve of self-government more Chinese shifted to Australia, but the transition to independence was accompanied by little overt racial antagonism. Through the first two decades of independence the Chinese continued their obvious role in the economy and inconspicuous role in the political, social, and cultural life of the nation. When Chinese stores were looted, the attacks were opportunistic and the initial cause was not resentment of the Chinese. For example, in 1997 when the Papua New Guinea Defense Force seized the Sandline International mercenaries employed by the national government to quell the separatist movement in Bougainville, the public demonstration in Port Moresby spilled into a retail area and Chinese shopkeepers suffered along with other merchants: "Men, boys and even girls poured into shops helping themselves" (Dorney 1998: 295). Papua New Guinea's national elections became festivals of democracy and small parties formed and reformed in alliances, but except for politicians negotiating in Chinese restaurants, the Chinese community remained outside politics. In her survey of the impact of Papua New Guinea–born Chinese on the 1987 elections, Margaret Wilson wrote that their "direct effect on the 1987 elections was probably negligible"; they "prefer to remain unobtrusive both politically and socially" (Wilson 1989: 102, 8).

By the 1980s the foreign population of Papua New Guinea was undergoing significant change. In 1971 the foreign population had been over 50,000, and the most numerous group by nationality was Australian. Around 3,500 were Asians, and nearly all of these (about 3,000) were Chinese by ethnicity, though not by place of birth or nationality. The total number of foreigners in Papua New Guinea declined after independence as Papua New Guineans took their places in the workforce and foreigners, uncertain of their future, chose to leave. According to the official censuses, non-citizens have continued to leave. At the same time, the composition of the non-citizen population has been changing. It is now more male, includes fewer children, and is therefore probably more transient. But most marked has been the change in nationality. In 1980 over half of the non-citizens were Australians—as they had been in 1966. In fact, in 1980 there were more Australians and New Zealanders in Papua New Guinea than the total of number of foreigners recorded in the year 2000. The fall in the real and relative number of Australians was marked: between the 1990 and 2000 censuses the "numbers of migrants from Australia and Europe halved" (Papua New Guinea 2003: 39).

In 2000 only 19 percent of all non-citizens had been born in Australia. In round figures, the number of Australians had fallen from more than 20,000 on the eve of self-government to under 5,000 thirty years later. Those few Australians are in a much greater Papua New Guinea population, estimated at over six million in 2007.

Sometime in the 1980s, the numbers of Australians in Papua New Guinea were surpassed by Asians. But initially those figures were misleading, as the 1990 census (and the subsequent count) said that while "Indonesians" were the largest group of non-citizens, most of them were living in the Western Province and were Melanesian refugees from Irian Jaya (Papua). The greatest number crossed the border in 1984, when over 10,000 people sought refuge east of the Fly River. Many are still in Western Province (May 1986: 120).[6] But even excluding the border-crossers, Asians now outnumber Australians among non-citizens. The most numerous of the foreigners in the 2000 census by place of birth were: Indonesians 23 percent, Australians 19 percent, and Malaysians 13 percent.

In the census figures, the Chinese appear to be missing. One explanation is that the old Chinese, the descendants of those migrants who were living in Mandated New Guinea, had left Papua New Guinea, were born in Papua New Guinea, and/or had Australian or Papua New Guinean citizenship. In any case they do not show in the statistics as Chinese and are now few in number. Most have become part of two-step migration: having shed part of a culture, picked up part of another, and added new genes in Papua New Guinea, they have moved to Australia.

The New Chinese: From Southeast Asia

The old Chinese have been overtaken by three other groups. The first are Chinese from Southeast Asia. They have come from Indonesia and Singapore, but predominantly from Malaysia. Publicly, they have been most associated with the Rimbunan Hijau (PNG) Group.[7] Beginning operations in Sarawak as a timber company in 1975, Rimbunan Hijau is now said to generate over a billion dollars (US) annually through its involvement in resource exploitation and other businesses in Southeast Asia, Africa, Oceania, Russia, and China. Since its initial involvement in logging in Papua New Guinea in 1989, Rimbunan Hijau has built a substantial headquarters and broadened its operations, most obviously by publishing a daily newspaper, the *National*, since 1993. In the range and extent of its investments in logging permits, sawmills, a veneer mill, oil palm, trading, travel, shipping, retailing, superannuation, and property development, and in the number of Papua New Guineans employed (over 4,000), Rimbunan Hijau is a significant force in the economy.[8] It has been different from most other companies in its direct engagement with politicians and its aggressive public relations.

Its public promotion and profile are in direct contrast to those of the old Chinese companies.

Tan Sri Datuk Tiong Hiew King, the founder of the Rimbunan Hijau Group, has played a key role in Sarawak politics and served as a Malaysian senator. Some commentators have seen him coming out of a system in which businessmen, bureaucrats, and politicians combine to pursue an agreed common good. But critics have seen a system corrupted, so that all arms of the lawmaking, administering, and enforcing institutions serve the interests of elite businessmen. In Papua New Guinea there have been many claims of corruption, ranging from the involvement of senior politicians and officials (the prime minister and the Minister for Forests have had interests in logging concessions), to the provision of prostitutes for workers, to the use of police to intimidate landowners. The harshness of the criticism is apparent in press headings such as "corporate criminals," "global bully on the loose," "profiting from plunder," and "the rape of PNG." The Rimbunan Hijau Group has publicly and vigorously defended itself, pointing out that much criticism has come from environmental groups like Greenpeace that might be expected to oppose logging irrespective of policy and practice. Local communities have claimed that while the company has made high profits, they have been left without the agreed infrastructure. The parliament on Manus was told that there had been no reforestation and "the west coast airstrip, schools, aid-posts, roads, and other infrastructure have not been built as promised" (*Post-Courier*, 28 February 2007, 7). In its own publications, Rimbunan Hijau has, not surprisingly, countered by listing the benefits that have flowed to those who sold logs: "At the opening of the new SDA church in the Edevu Elogogo area where Rimbunan Hijau has a sawmill, a local councilor said: 'Apart from the church, the company has also assisted in building our school, a bridge, 24 hours free electricity and a road further inland toward Mount Koiari'" (*RH Group Newsletter*, October–December 2005).

To manage companies and provide special skills along with the sweat of the unskilled, Rimbunan Hijau and other companies have brought in many foreign workers. Just how many is uncertain, and some may be in Papua New Guinea only briefly while a particular logging operation is underway. Some estimates of people brought into the country at any one time by Malaysian Chinese have been as high as 5,000. Sometimes associated with them are Chinese from Indonesia, and when their workers are included another 1,000 may be added to the total number of Malaysian Chinese.

The New Chinese: From the People's Republic of China

A second group of Chinese are those coming from the People's Republic of China in accord with Chinese government policy. Since agreement was reached in 2005 with the Chinese company Metallurgical Group Corporation (MCC) to develop the Ramu nickel and cobalt mine, that movement has increased and been under greater scrutiny. MCC, one of the biggest construction companies in the world, is state-owned, and China will take the entire output of the Ramu mine. The biggest project undertaken by the Chinese anywhere in the Australia-Islands region, the open-cut mine will require extensive infrastructure, including a long slurry-carrying pipeline and the development of a port on the Madang coast. The subsidiary of MCC that has started preliminary work has brought in workers, some of whom are said to be unskilled and low-paid by Papua New Guinean standards.

Apart from the imported workers, the development of the mine has raised a number of issues. The Chinese government has been willing to provide funds for the infrastructure required by the mine. Because MCC is government-owned, it is difficult to distinguish between foreign aid and a commercial venture that might wish to offset infrastructure development costs against tax concessions. This has particular relevance as MCC has negotiated a generous ten-year tax holiday. Questions have also been raised about the extent to which MCC will make disclosures as required by public companies listed on Western stock exchanges. Perhaps inevitably, some landowners are dissatisfied, either because they are not included in the 2.5 percent stake allocated to them, or because they believe that the share is not high enough. Again inevitably, there are questions about the environmental impact of the mine, particularly of the discharge of tailings into the sea near Madang (*Post-Courier,* 7 February 2007). There have also been angry complaints from Papua New Guinea workers at the construction sites because of the poor housing, pay rates below the legal minimum, crude toilets, and separate compounds for Papua New Guinean and Chinese workers.[9]

Revelations about the conditions at work sites after a visit by Labour Secretary David Tibu brought an angry public response. The press printed uninhibited letters, such as that by "Disgusted, Waigani":

> How can we allow such a company [MCC] to enter our country, rip off our resources and treat us like pigs. This is totally inhuman. This is another classic "under the table" deal without proper documents, procedures and contract agreement to govern the mining company…. I recommend a termination and deportation of these people and their company. (*Post-Courier,* 7 February 2007, 3)

There have also been guarded suggestions that some officials or politicians have been rewarded for decisions favoring the mining company. Governor of Enga and leader of the People's Party Peter Ipatas claimed that his demand for a renegotiation of the Ramu mine agreement was part of the fight against corruption (*Post-Courier,* 31 January 2007; *National,* 21 February 2007). He also suggested that the bringing in of Chinese workers may have violated Papua New Guinea's laws. The allegations of corruption were given increased substance when Ombudsman Peter Masi said he was investigating reports that Madang leaders had been awarded contracts "relating to the mine ... and in breach of the Leadership Code" and that the National Housing Corporation had been pressured to sell Madang properties to developers (*Post-Courier*, 21 February 2007).

The New Chinese: The Unsanctioned

A third group of Chinese entering Papua New Guinea has also arrived from the People's Republic of China. Evidence leading to convictions in Papua New Guinean courts or from Labour Department enquiries reveals that many hold forged work permits, have obtained visas by unknown means from the Papua New Guinea embassy in Beijing, or obtained visas for one reason but switched to other activities and overstayed (*Post-Courier*, 8 December 2006, 22 December 2006, 23 January 2007). Some have been engaged in illegal or marginal businesses such as gambling, selling cheap products counterfeiting prestige brands, or—in one report—selling fake toothpaste (*Post-Courier*, 10 November 2006). From observing who runs stores and food stalls and from newspaper reports, it appears that these Chinese migrants are numerous, and while most are in the main towns, they are working widely throughout the country—from the islands to the Highlands. Most are probably battling to make their way and exploiting whatever opportunities they can; while they may cut a few corners, they are not "criminals." A few seem to be tough, gun-carrying, and presumably connected to gangs or organized crime.

The recent migrants from China have provoked resentment. It is expressed in newspaper articles as well as letters to the editor:

> The influx of Asian businesses and their cheap products can wipe out the small economy of East New Britain. Government agencies revealed the new Asian businesses sell cheap products at mark-up prices and do not reinvest their money in the province. Instead, they send all their money out of the country through a particular commercial bank where they do not pay any fees or taxes. The agencies also revealed many of these new Asian businesses do not comply with PNG's tax laws—leaving the province deprived of the much-needed goods and services tax.... In Kokopo at least eight new shops, all owned by the same group, have sprung up around the town in less than two years. The agencies said that these Asians were all from the same area in China and came in as one group before they mushroomed throughout the town with different shops. (*Post-Courier*, 10 November 2006, 3)

The Department of Labour and Industry stated that in one year it had issued 450 work permits to foreigners to "work in the retail and wholesale businesses" in East

New Britain (*Post-Courier*, 23 August 2007). Papua New Guineans point to the tight security in the stores and say that if there are local people on cash registers, they are closely monitored. One letter writer spoke nostalgically of "our old time Chinese friends" and contrasted them with the "discriminatory" new merchants (*Post-Courier*, 5 December 2006). Infrequent and opportunistic looting of Chinese stores has continued, such as during a day of "chaos" in Kainantu in October 2006 (*National*, 16 October 2006). In the wake of the 2007 general elections a letter circulated in the Western Highlands threatening to investigate all "Asian" businesses and evict all those found to be breaking Papua New Guinea laws. The police reacted quickly, threatening that the letter writer would be "really hammered" (*National*, 15 August 2007).

The apparent ease with which visas have been obtained at the Papua New Guinea embassy in Beijing has been cited as one reason why Ambassador Max Rai has been replaced by John Momis. Minister for Foreign Affairs and Trade Paul Tiensten acknowledged the need to halt the flow of illegal immigrants, which was giving the "department a bad name" (*Post-Courier*, 9, 13, 14 February 2007, 14 March 2007). Estimates—some impressionistic guesses—of the numbers of the recent Chinese migrants engaged in small businesses suggest that they can be measured in thousands, probably over 5,000. Adding a few Chinese from Singapore and including those who have come with resource companies, that means a Chinese population of over 10,000. They are by far the most numerous of all foreigners in Papua New Guinea. And they are almost invisible in the 2000 census.

There are few migrants from Taiwan in Papua New Guinea, and tension between the Republic of China and the People's Republic of China is less marked in Papua New Guinea than in some other Pacific islands, such as the Solomon Islands, where Taiwan provides support for particular politicians to ensure continued recognition.[10] But the division between the two Chinas still impinges on Papua New Guinean politics. It did so dramatically but without consequence in 1999 during the last days of Bill Skate's prime ministership, when he made a secret trip to Taiwan to secure funds for his failing administration (and allegedly for himself) in exchange for abandoning Papua New Guinea's One China policy and recognizing Taiwan. However, soon after his return he was defeated in the parliament and replaced by Prime Minister Mekere Morauta.

More recently, the Chinese embassy in Papua New Guinea has "strongly protested" against Taiwanese participation in the Pacific Islands News Association (*National*, 9 February 2007). The association was to hold a conference in the Solomon Islands, and the Solomon Islands Media Association accepted a donation from Taiwan of US$65,000. In return—or coincidentally—the Taiwanese were allowed to send a large delegation to the conference. The Chinese made it clear to the Papua New Guinea Media Council, the largest contributor to the association, that it did not want the Taiwanese getting seats among the Islands media. The

Chinese thought that if the Papua New Guinea government supported the One China policy, then its media should do the same. That was scarcely a declaration of support for an independent press, but it did illustrate the sensitivities of China to any issues involving Taiwan.

Conclusion

There is almost no similarity or continuity between the Chinese in Papua New Guinea now and the Chinese residents of the 1930s, who, even if born in New Guinea, held an alien certificate of registration that identified the bearer with a thumbprint. The Chinese were then a minority, largely unprotected by a home government, subject to petty discrimination, deliberately avoiding party politics, and only entering the public area to make a general show of being loyal citizens in such events as the Rabaul Empire Day parade.

The Chinese in Papua New Guinea now outnumber Australians by two to one. Some are backed by a powerful government in China that is extending its global political and economic reach, and some have connections to other governments in Southeast Asia. They are engaged in billion-dollar resource projects, have joined vigorously in public debate, and show expertise in public relations. One of the major resource firms owns a national daily newspaper that is partisan when the interests of the parent company are involved.

The Chinese have become involved in public decision-making from the highest to the lowest levels.[11] Some influence on decision-making results from the appropriate lobbying by those with a case to argue. Some of the payments made to political parties are within the range that individuals and companies normally contribute in democratic systems. However, a review of the public record in the courts and the ombudsman's reports indicate that a few Chinese change or subvert government decisions by corrupting elected and appointed officials. The very presence of so many illegal migrants working in jobs where they do not have the appropriate license is indicative of widespread low-level violation of government regulations. Judging from the evidence presented to the T. E. Barnett enquiry between 1987 and 1989, and from latter reports and practices in other countries, the timber industry has long been rife with malpractice. And it must seem disturbing to the companies that developed the Panguna and Ok Tedi mines that the Ramu nickel and cobalt mine appears to have violated established standards for international companies, such as providing fair wages and conditions for local workers, employing and training a maximum number of local workers, not importing unskilled workers, paying a reasonable return to local governments, ensuring just compensation for landowners, and conducting preproduction environmental impact studies.

Outside commentators must be cautious not to accuse the Chinese of illegal or undesirable actions as though they are the only national group involved. The Chinese stand out because they are new, numerous, and involved in the largest and most public ventures, not because they are the most venal. Commentators also have to accept the obvious, that the Chinese have every right to pursue national, company, and personal goals in Papua New Guinea. Scrutiny of legality, morality, and mutual benefit to Papua New Guineans must, of course, be applied equally to all foreigners.

I will conclude with four final observations. First, states such as Papua New Guinea are at increased risk. Where the bureaucracy has difficulty enforcing policy, and where government officials and politicians from the central offices to the most distant local level governments are vulnerable to large and small inducements, states have great difficulty getting a fair return on their resources or even controlling the composition of their own population. And once the bribes have been paid, the erosion of institutional strength and civil trust is rapid. Second, China will continue to play an increasingly important role in the region. The issue is not whether it will exercise greater influence, but how and in what direction. In Africa, where China has become a major donor and trade partner, it has operated outside the conditions that the previously dominant national and international aid agencies have tried to impose. In Papua New Guinea the issue is complicated: because there are at least four groups of Chinese (the fading presence of the old Chinese, the Chinese out of Southeast Asia, and the sanctioned and unsanctioned immigration from mainland China), there is not just one official China policy.

Third, Australia continues to speak—and issue reports—as though it is not just the dominant player in the region, but virtually the only big player. This is where the rest of the world expects Australia to have expertise, and where Australia provides most aid, guides development, and intervenes at times of natural and manmade disasters. When Papua New Guineans suggest that they do not want to be beholden to Australians and that there are alternatives, this is scarcely taken seriously in Australia. It should be, and in future it will have to be. While the Australian government has been closely monitoring the growth of the Chinese economy, so important to the Australian resources boom, and has expressed its concern about tensions between China and the United States, its recent formal statements have given slight recognition to the increasing importance of China in Papua New Guinea and the wider Southwest Pacific (Department of Defense 2007).

Fourth, Papua New Guineans resent what they see as migrants taking jobs and business opportunities, buying favors, and taking wealth out of the country. It is possible that Australia will one day have to intervene to protect Chinese migrants whose lives and property are under threat. Perhaps Australia will fly the Chinese to Manus or Nauru: that would indeed be a "Pacific solution"—the term given to the previous government's policy of processing and holding illegal migrants and refugees on islands like Nauru where they do not have recourse to Australian courts.

Notes

1. This chapter is a revised version of *The Chinese in Papua New Guinea,* Discussion Paper No. 3, 2007, Canberra: State Society and Governance in Melanesia project, Australian National University. The Australian Territory of Papua and the Australian Mandated Territory of New Guinea were administered separately until 1942, when they were combined under the army unit entitled the Australian New Guinea Administrative Unit. The combined administration continued in the postwar period as the Territory of Papua-New Guinea until 1949, when it became the Territory of Papua and New Guinea. "Territory of" and "and" were dropped in 1972, and as of 1975 the name Papua New Guinea was continued by the independent nation. To avoid excessive changes some names are here used anachronistically.
2. *Australian,* 9 and 12 February 2007. The Radio National Program was on 8 February, and the seminar at ANU was an all-day workshop on 9 February 2007.
3. The main sources on the history of the Chinese in Papua New Guinea are Peter Biskup (1970), Peter Cahill (1972, 1996), Christine Inglis (1972, 1978), and David Y. H. Wu (1982). See also Chin Hoi Meen, obituary, *The Times of Papua New Guinea,* 23 April 1982.
4. Casualty figures are only for those Chinese in camps near Rabaul.
5. The number of Australians is understated because some "Australians" had been born in Papua and New Guinea. "Citizenship" was not an effective measure of "Australian" as Australians were then classed as "British."
6. The 2000 census (Papua New Guinea 2003: 39) indicates that 23 percent of overseas-born non-citizen migrants were born in Indonesia and 19 percent in Australia.
7. The company's own website is at: www.rhpng.com.pg
8. The *RH Group Newsletter* is available on the company website.
9. See, for example, Rowan Callick (2007) in the *Australian,* 9 and 12 February; *Post-Courier,* 8 February 2007; *National,* 7 February 2007. See *Post-Courier,* 14 March 07 for an inspector's report on substandard conditions in a logging camps in East Sepik.
10. There were some Taiwanese in New Guinea between 1942 and 1945. They were then Formosans, residents of a Japanese colony and conscripted into the Japanese army, often in non-combatant auxiliary and labor units.
11. The *Post-Courier* and the *National* of 28 February 2007 contained similar reports on the failure of Rimbunan Hijau to meet its obligations to communities where logging has taken place on Manus. The difference in the reporting of the two papers is not always obvious.

References

Australian. Daily national newspaper, Sydney.
Biskup, Peter. 1970. "Foreign Coloured Labour in German New Guinea." *Journal of Pacific History* 5(1): 85–107;

Cahill, Peter. 1972. "The Chinese in Rabaul, 1914–1960." MA thesis, Department of History, University of Papua New Guinea.

———. 1996. "Chinese in Rabaul—1921–1942: Normal Practices or Containing the Yellow Peril?" *Journal of Pacific History* 31(1): 72–91

Commonwealth of Australia. No date. *Census of the Commonwealth of Australia 30ᵗʰ June, 1933*, vol. 1. Canberra: Government Printer.

Department of Defense. 2007. *A Defense Update 2007*. Canberra: Government of Australia, Department of Defense. Accessed 14 February 2007 at: http://www.defence.gov.au/ans/2007/chapter_1.htm

Dorney, Sean. 1998. *The Sandline Affair: Politics and Mercenaries and the Bougainville Crisis*. Sydney: ABC Books.

Hasluck, Paul. 1976. *A Time for Building: Australian Administration in Papua and New Guinea 1951–1963*. Melbourne: Melbourne University Press.

Inglis, Christine. 1972. "Chinese." *Encyclopaedia of Papua and New Guinea*, ed. Peter Ryan, 170–174. Melbourne: Melbourne University Press.

———. 1978. "Social Structure and Patterns of Economic Action: The Chinese in Papua New Guinea." PhD thesis, London School of Economics.

Kurlantzick, Joshua. 2007. "Beijing Envy." *London Review of Books,* 5 July, 11.

May, Ron. 1986. "East of the Border: Irian Jaya and the Border in Papua New Guinea's Domestic and Foreign Politics." In *Between Two Nations: The Indonesia–Papua New Guinea Border and West Papua Nationalism,* ed. Ron May. Bathurst: Robert Brown.

National. Daily newspaper, Port Moresby.

Papua New Guinea. 2003. *2000 Census National Report.* Port Moresby: National Statistical Office.

Post-Courier. Daily newspaper, Port Moresby.

Territory of Papua and New Guinea. No date. *Population Census 1966, Preliminary Bulletin No 20, Summary Population.* Konedobu: Bureau of Statistics.

Times of Papua New Guinea. Daily newspaper, Port Moresby.

Wilson, Margaret. 1989. "The Trader's Voice: PNG-Born Chinese Business and the 1987 Elections." In *Eleksin: The 1987 National Election in Papua New Guinea,* ed. M. Oliver. Port Moresby: University of Papua New Guinea.

Wu, David Y. H. 1982. *The Chinese in Papua New Guinea 1880–1980.* Hong Kong: The Chinese University Press.

CHAPTER 7

Fiji's "Look North" Strategy and the Role of China

Sandra Tarte

Introduction

China's potential to play a growing role in the South Pacific and to challenge the predominance of Western influence has long been noted (Godley 1983). However, China's recent activities in the region have attracted widespread interest, along with speculation about its long-term strategic objectives. While most assessments have highlighted the rivalry with Taiwan as a key factor in China's policies, commentators have also referred to the "campaign by China to become the heavyweight of the Asia Pacific region and curb the political and military reach of the United States," and concern has been raised about the region's potential "to contain a collection of states that owed their primary allegiance to a country outside the (Western) alliance" (Feizkhah 2001: 24). Other concerns raised about China's role in the region have included claims that it is a contributor to international criminal activities and that it would interfere in domestic politics as a way to protect Chinese citizens abroad (Field 2001; Henderson and Reilly 2003; Crocombe 2005; Windybank 2005).

Fiji is regarded as a pivotal state in the region—a regional hub and a relatively influential player in regional politics. It was the first Pacific Island state to establish diplomatic relations with China. It also has an active and influential local Chinese population. For these reasons it is considered a "natural focal point" for both China and Taiwan's involvement in the South Pacific (Biddick 1989: 803). Relations between Fiji and China have grown more prominent in the period since 2000. This was a result of two main factors: the post-coup Fiji governments' efforts to diversify diplomatic and economic relations away from traditional partners, and the Chinese government's push to enhance its position in the region, particularly in the context of escalating tensions with Taiwan.

This chapter explores these diplomatic efforts by China and Fiji and what they have yielded in political, economic, and security terms. It highlights the role of increased aid commitments in promoting closer political ties. However, China's contributions to Fiji's overall economic development so far appear limited. Chinese efforts to establish a presence in Fiji's tuna fishery provide an example of the problems that have hampered closer economic relations. There is also the continuing issue—for China—of Fiji's "unofficial" ties with Taiwan.

Background to Fiji-China relations

When Fiji attained independence in 1970, about 1 percent of its population (or about 5,000) was of Chinese origin. The Chinese had come to Fiji as free settlers in the early part of the twentieth century—all from southern China—and as a community they played a significant economic and commercial role in the country (Yee 1974).

Fiji joined the United Nations soon after independence, when the question of who should hold the seat for China—the People's Republic of China (PRC) or the Republic of China (Taiwan)—was being debated. Although Fiji supported the seating of the PRC, it did not accept that Taiwan should simultaneously be expelled from the UN; thus it refrained from voting on the issue when subsequently it was put to the General Assembly in 1971 (Low 1981: 85). This position of "neutralism" reflected Fiji's approach to the China issue, which was to seek to maintain relations with both China and Taiwan.

In 1971 Taiwan established an official trade mission in Fiji, the East Asia Trade Centre, which was a channel for technical cooperation, mainly in agriculture (Biddick 1989). Meanwhile, the admission of the People's Republic of China to the UN and the normalization of relations between the United States and the PRC led Fiji to establish diplomatic ties with China in 1975. A Chinese embassy was established in Suva in 1976 (Low 1981: 88). China and Taiwan remained relatively minor partners for the next ten years or so. In the mid 1980s China was providing just 1.75 percent of Fiji's foreign aid. In 1985 China's Communist Party General Secretary Hu Yaobang visited Fiji, where he announced that China's policy toward the region embodied three principles: respect for the domestic and foreign policies of the island states, respect for close relations between them, and respect for their treaty arrangements with other powers. A number of initiatives with Fiji followed, including a preferential sugar agreement and special business links with designated Chinese provinces (Biddick 1989).

Following the 1987 coups, the military-led government of Sitiveni Rabuka launched a new foreign policy initiative aimed at diversifying aid and trade partnerships.[1] This sought to break the dependence on trade and aid links with Australia and New Zealand, which had been disrupted by economic sanctions. Among the East Asian countries targeted by Fiji in this campaign were Japan, South Korea, the People's Republic of China, and Malaysia. Significantly, the PRC was the first country to extend an official invitation to visit China to Fiji's post-coup minister for foreign affairs. This visit took place in November 1987, and the minister "pledged that Fiji would work to strengthen and expand the existing good relationship into mutually beneficial dimensions" (Low-O'Sullivan 1989: 37).

Coincidently, however, Fiji's political crisis provided an opportunity for Taiwan to enhance its status in Fiji. The post-coup government courted closer ties with Taiwan in order to benefit from economic support, and the Taiwan office in Fiji was upgraded to the Republic of China Trade Mission in 1988, with consular privileges. High-level meetings also took place between the Fijian and Taiwanese leadership (including a visit to Taiwan by Fiji's interim prime minister). Although protesting these developments, the Beijing government refrained from any retaliation and instead focused on building its support amongst the local Chinese community (Biddick 1989). As of the late 1980s this community included an influx of new Chinese migrants (from mainland China), attracted by government incentives aimed at luring investors to the tax-free garment industry, among other things. These incentives included the prospect of acquiring Fijian citizenship, which also made Fiji a potential stepping stone to Australia and New Zealand. Meanwhile, many descendants of the original Chinese settlers in Fiji migrated in the early post-independence era to Australia, New Zealand, and North America (Yee 1974).

Fiji's first attempt at a "Look North" policy did not radically change its foreign policy orientation or foreign economic ties. According to an assessment by Fiji's interim foreign minister in 2001, this was because "not much aggressiveness was put into finding new markets and follow-ups" (Gurdayal 2001: 10). Not surprisingly perhaps, once relations were normalized with traditional partners (Australia, New Zealand, and the United Kingdom), long-standing economic ties were again restored. However in the 1990s, Fiji—like other Pacific Island countries—had to contend with a changed foreign-policy context. The overwhelming concern was the prospect of marginalization in the post–cold war era and in the new trading environment ushered in by globalization. Thus there was a perceived need to broaden foreign policy ties wherever possible—including foreign aid partnerships.

Relations with China developed gradually in the 1990s, based on modest flows of aid and trade. A bilateral trade agreement was signed with China in 1997 to provide a framework for expanding trade between the two countries. The Fiji-China Business Council was launched in 1997. Military links also began in 1995 with the first of a series of aid packages, comprising nonlethal military supplies, to the Fiji Military Forces. On a visit to Fiji in 1998, Chinese Minister for Defense General Chi Haotian declared: "The development of China-Fiji relations not only serves the fundamental interests and common aspirations but also benefits regional development and stability" (Maclellan 2000: 12). Meanwhile Fiji maintained fairly productive ties with Taiwan, and in 1996 a joint communiqué was signed between Taiwan and Fiji dealing with mutual recognition of each other's system of government and various areas of cooperation.

By 2000, both China's and Taiwan's aid and diplomatic efforts in the region had intensified and were beginning to attract widespread interest and comment. This coincided with growing tensions in Taiwan-China relations. These tensions were evident at the regional negotiations for the establishment of a tuna management and conservation regime for the Central and Western Pacific Ocean—a process in which both China and Taiwan participated more or less as equals.[2] This reflected Taiwan's status as a major "distant water fishing nation" in the region. In 1999, Taiwanese fishing vessels accounted for 164,107 tons of tuna taken from the Exclusive Economic Zones of Pacific Island states. China accounted for just 2,026 tons (Gillett et al. 2001: 9).

At this conference, China vigorously opposed any moves to allow Taiwan to be a member of the future commission, arguing that it should only be an observer. Taiwan maintained its right to full contracting party status. Both sides stepped up efforts to build political support for their respective positions among the Pacific Island states. Ultimately the issue was resolved when Taiwan accepted something less than contracting party status, but with membership rights. It also accepted the nomenclature of Chinese Taipei (Tarte 2002).

It was against this broader background that political events in Fiji led to renewed emphasis on relations with China. A military-installed interim government led by Prime Minister Laisenia Qarase took office in mid 2000 and, in the face of foreign criticism by traditional partners, adopted a new Look North policy for Fiji. The interim administration subsequently formed the first elected government in September 2001 and held office until 2006. Although it was reelected in May 2006, the Qarase government was deposed by the Fiji Military Forces in the coup of December 2006.[3]

Fiji-China Relations since 2000: "Visit Diplomacy"

Like the previous effort in 1987, Fiji's new Look North policy was an attempt to ward off the effects of the economic crisis that stemmed from Fiji's political turmoil in 2000. According to Fiji's interim foreign minister in 2001, Kaliopate Tavola, the aim of the Look North policy was to "look for new markets for our exports, to diversify the sources of our imports, and to look for new partners in terms of investment and development assistance" (Gurdayal 2001: 6). Fiji particularly hoped to tap into China's sugar market and secure a preferential price-based government-to-government trade agreement. Fiji had had such an agreement in the late 1980s, but it had long since lapsed.

While Fiji pursued the Look North policy fundamentally for economic and financial reasons, diversifying Fiji's foreign relations was also thought to make for "good politics." There were "security reasons" as well. As in 1987, Fiji's close ties with Australia and New Zealand suffered as a result of opposition to the political developments in Fiji in 2000. While Foreign Minister Tavola predicted that relations with Australia and New Zealand would remain strong ("like any good neighbors, we quarrel at times"), he also said that it was in Fiji's interests to diversify its foreign relations: "We are in the middle of the Pacific and we need to balance our relations, south, north, east and west. Our geography requires us to do that." He noted that "Asian countries" based their policies on "non-interference," which he described as a "good approach diplomatically and internationally" (Gurdayal 2001: 6).

To promote this Look North policy, Tavola then embarked on a visit to Tokyo, Seoul, and Beijing in mid 2001. During the China leg of the journey, he officiated at the opening of Fiji's new embassy in Beijing on 11 July 2001 (the cost of which was shared between Fiji and China). According to the Fiji government, the establishment of the mission was "in recognition of the need to engage a major emerging world power" (Government of Fiji n.d.). During this visit, China agreed to provide a grant of F$28 million (US$12.1 million) for the construction of a large sport facility (to be ready for the 2003 South Pacific Games in Fiji). It also made a "quick decision" to fund the re-servicing of the Fiji parliament's public sound system (Gurdayal 2001). This set a pattern of high-level visits during the next four years between Fiji and China—termed "visit diplomacy"—at which a number of economic cooperation deals were signed. This is similar to the *omiyage gaiko* or "souvenir diplomacy" of Japan that became common in the 1970s and 1980s (Tarte 1998).

In the following year, a number of high-level Chinese officials visited Fiji, including the Chinese minister for agriculture, the chairman of the Chinese Communist Party, the vice minister for lands, and the head of the Chinese Foreign Affairs Ministry section dealing with Oceania. Reciprocal visits from Fiji took place, the key one being the first visit by Prime Minister Qarase in May 2002. At the invitation of Premier Zhu Rongji, the prime minister led an official twenty-five–member mission, accompanied by a private-sector trade and business delegation.

The visit was promoted as part of the Fiji government's Look North policy, and the expectation was that bilateral economic and trade cooperation would be strengthened. The Chinese president hoped that Fiji would continue its observance of the "One China" policy "to ensure smooth development of Sino-Fijian friendly relations" (Xinhua 2002). This policy was reaffirmed by Prime Minister Qarase, who also thanked the Chinese government for its cooperation since the political crisis of 2000. Mr. Qarase expressed appreciation for China's "pragmatic view" that Fiji's political situation was best left for the country's people to resolve (Elbourne 2002).

On this visit, the Fiji government received an "unrestricted" grant of F$7.5 million (US$3.4 million) from China—to be used however the government chose. One report stated that it might be used to purchase two ships to service the outer islands (Radio Australia 2002). A number of Memoranda of Understanding (MOU) were signed between Fiji government ministries and the Chinese government. This included one MOU on fisheries, which established the Joint Venture Agreement between the China National Fisheries Corporation and the Fiji National Fishing Company. During this visit the prime minister witnessed the departure from the Chinese city of Dalian of four China National Fisheries Corporation fishing boats bound for fishing operations in Fiji. According to reports, the Chinese government also offered to establish mahogany processing plants in Fiji.

Fisheries ties featured prominently during a further visit to China by Prime Minister Qarase in mid 2004. Accompanied by the fisheries minister and other officials, Qarase met with Premier Wen Jiabao and with officials of the China National Fisheries Corporation. A request was reportedly made for a fishing boat to serve as a training and research vessel. During this visit China also agreed to provide another F$6 million (US$3.4 million) to Fiji in financial assistance. (Radio Fiji/PINA Nius, 9 July 2004).

Prime Minister Qarase again visited China in mid 2005 as guest of Premier Wen Jiabao to mark thirty years of diplomatic relations between the two countries. While no new aid package was announced on this visit, it was revealed that Fiji had been granted Approved Destination status for Chinese outbound tourists.[4] The visit provided an opportunity for China and Fiji to reaffirm the One China policy as the basis of the bilateral relationship. The Fijian prime minister stated: "As long as we are in government there will be no change in that policy" (Fijilive 2005). In the wake of this visit, the Chinese ambassador to Fiji predicted that China would "work to push the bilateral relationship to new heights in the years ahead" (Komai 2005: 11).

These "new heights" appeared to be in sight in April 2006 when the Fiji government hosted the first-ever visit of a Chinese premier to a Pacific Island country. Wen Jiabao visited Fiji to open the first China–Pacific Island Economic Development and Cooperation Forum in Nadi. In addressing this summit, Wen announced that China would provide about US$383 million in preferential loans to Pacific Island countries over the next three years. This would be used to "boost cooperation in resource development" and to "set up a special fund to encourage Chinese companies to invest in Pacific island countries" (Wen 2006; see Appendix for his statement). The Fiji and Chinese governments also signed five bilateral agreements covering technical and economic assistance, including one providing for the development of a hydro-power plant on the northern island of Taveuni. An agreement covering cooperation between the Fiji Office of the Director of Public Prosecutions and its Chinese counterpart was also concluded. In August 2006, there was a follow-up visit by the Chinese foreign minister when a further economic and technical cooperation agreement worth US$1 million was signed.[5]

The sharp deterioration in relations between Fiji and its traditional partners (especially Australia and New Zealand) following the military coup in December 2006 led to the Look North strategy again being invoked. According to military commander and coup leader Frank Bainimarama, "We have relied for too long on our metropolitan neighbors and they are taking us for granted" (Fijilive 2007a). But he also declared that the Look North move was not to replace Australia and New Zealand, but to compensate for what Fiji had lost. According to Bainimarama, "We have to talk to China about continuation of military courses which have been stopped by Australia and New Zealand" (Fijilive 2007b). He expressed confidence that China would always be there to support Fiji: "We have always had close ties with Beijing. I have already made one official visit there at the invitation of the People's Liberation Army and we've had two senior officers at China's defense college since 2000" (Davis 2006: 4). In mid 2007, the Bainimarama government announced the appointment of a new ambassador to China, Sir Jim Ah Koy, a prominent part-Chinese, part-Fijian businessman. This appointment was accepted by Beijing; a sign that relations between the two states remained unaffected by the political turn of events.[6]

Taiwan and the "One China" policy

Taiwan remains a fundamental issue in China's relations with Fiji and is the main source of friction between the two sides. According to Fiji's former Foreign Minister Kaliopate Tavola, this is because "China looks to Fiji to be a leader in the region in terms of the One China policy" (Interview, January 2007, Suva). When Fiji's new Look North policy was adopted in 2000, China became increasingly sensitive to any links with Taiwan and made repeated efforts to dilute Fiji's ties with Taiwan. Reports circulated in mid 2001 that the Chinese government was putting pressure on Fiji to "cut off its relations with Taiwan"—and China was urged to show a "more understanding attitude toward our [Fiji's] position" (*Fiji Times*, 20 June, 2001, 5).

China's protests and attempts to pressure Fiji have had little effect, and ties between Taiwan and Fiji have, if anything, grown closer in recent years. As stated by Prime Minister Qarase in 2004, the Fiji government's position is that, while it remains committed to One China and aims to strengthen official ties and cooperation with the People's Republic of China, "we are glad that this does not stop us maintaining trade, economic and cultural associations with Taiwan" (Qarase 2004: 3). To underscore this relationship, the Fiji Trade and Cultural Office was opened in Taipei in 2002, funded entirely by the Taiwanese government. Meanwhile Prime Minister Qarase met with Taiwanese President Chen during an unofficial "technical transit" at Nadi, Fiji, in May 2005. This visit was vigorously opposed by the Chinese government, which accused Taiwan of "sowing discord in our friendly relations with Fiji" (Komai 2005: 11).

China is also highly sensitive to Fiji's aid connections with Taiwan. According to Fiji's first ambassador to China, a "major hurdle" in building a working relationship with China was government ministries that did not respect the One China policy and continued to receive "gifts and donations" from Taiwan. He warned that such links with Taiwan "could totally destroy the relationship with China" (Rarabici 2001: 2). However, Fiji's Ministry of Foreign Affairs has had little control over these links, since individual ministries (including the Office of the Prime Minister) request and receive assistance directly from the Taiwan trade mission in Fiji.

Soon after the December 2006 coup the Taiwan issue arose again when the first military-appointed prime minister, Dr. Jona Senilagakali, suggested in an interview that if sanctions were imposed on Fiji by its neighbors "we'll have no choice but to go to Indonesia, Taiwan and China to enlist their support" (Fiji Broadcasting Corporation 2006). But the military regime very quickly issued a statement reaffirming its adherence to the One China policy. According to the military commander, "[t]he Chinese government came across and said: 'We heard you mention Taiwan.' So we just wanted to confirm to them that we still recognize the One China policy" (Davis 2006: 4).

Taiwan is likely to remain an aid and trade partner with Fiji. Its interests are to keep a presence in Fiji and to seek to influence the Fiji government. This influence is exercised both directly (such as through offers of aid and other gifts) and indirectly through the local Chinese community (numbering about 6,000). This community, which was once predominantly aligned with Taiwan, now includes many new migrants from the mainland and Hong Kong. Both the Chinese and Taiwanese governments attempt to woo the community: for example, both support the Yat Sen School in Suva, which is run by the Fiji Chinese Association. However, according to some community leaders, Taiwan "works the system better" and is more effective than China in building and maintaining relations with both the Chinese community and the Fiji government.[7]

Economic Relations: Problems and Perceptions

Fiji's new Look North policy has so far not yielded significant economic gains or benefits, aside from a number of large aid commitments. Even in respect to aid commitments, problems have become evident. These include the Chinese government's reluctance to accommodate Fiji's preference for multi-year program aid as opposed to ad hoc project aid. It has also been noted that aid announcements have at times been made without the groundwork in place to actually implement the aid. This was the case with the soft loan package announced in

April 2006 by Premier Wen. A year later no funds had been disbursed to Fiji, despite projects being identified, because the modalities for delivering this aid were yet to be agreed. According to Fiji's ambassador-designate to China, Fiji was aiming to secure 40 percent (F$240 million, or US$153 million) of the regional allocation (Matau 2007: 7). Reflecting another problem with aid, Fiji's former ambassador to China has commented that the Fiji government does not always follow through on aid offers. For example, he claimed that Fiji used up only 20 percent of China's scholarship allocations (*Fiji Times* 2006).

Two big economic issues for Fiji are tourism and trade. But despite high hopes and expectations, growth in these areas has so far been limited. Although Fiji has attained Approved Destination status and an Air Services Agreement with China, there are still no direct flights between China and Nadi. It remains to be seen whether Fiji really is an attractive tourist destination for Chinese. While the Chinese ambassador to Fiji has claimed that Chinese tourists "like the people, nice weather and beautiful scenery" (Komai 2005, 11), only 1 percent of Fiji's tourists are in fact from China. Nor are there any Chinese investments in the tourism sector, although a Chinese company has acquired majority shareholding in Fiji's main domestic air carrier (*Fiji Times,* 21 March 2007, 12).[8]

In July 2006 Prime Minister Laisenia Qarase hosted a visit by the Chinese ambassador to Qarase's home village of Mavana, on an island in the Lau group. During this visit the prime minister predicted that China would "surpass Australia and New Zealand as Fiji's main trade partner in the near future" (Bola 2006: 15). This seemed a far-fetched prediction, however, given existing low levels of trade between the two countries and notable obstacles (economic, cultural, and logistical) to developing this further.

According to Fiji's Bureau of Statistics, in 2004 and 2005 China did not feature as either a significant source of imports or as a major export market. In 2005 it accounted for just 0.3 percent of Fiji's exports and 3 percent of imports. (If Hong Kong is included, the figures rise to 1.4 percent and 4.2 percent respectively). In 2004 China accounted for 0.5 percent of Fiji's exports (1.7 percent with Hong Kong) and 3.3 percent of Fiji's imports (5.4 percent with Hong Kong). Meanwhile China enjoys a healthy surplus in its trade with Fiji. Putting Fiji's trade with China into another perspective, Fiji exported F$242,196,000 (US$139 million) worth of merchandise to Australia in 2005, compared with F$3,826,000 (US$2.2 million) to China. Despite it being a top priority on its agenda, Fiji has not succeeded in negotiating a preferential sugar agreement with China.[9]

Problems breaking into the China market were compounded by the lack of effort to cultivate appropriate connections during official visits. For example, business representatives who accompanied the prime minister on his 2002 visit to China expressed disappointment about the lack of opportunities to meet relevant counterparts, including those in the sugar industry. One group claimed that the government was more interested in pushing mahogany talks. In response the prime minister's permanent secretary stated: "Some of those in the business group should ask themselves why they went, when there was nothing useful for them to pursue" (Wise 2002).

According to the former Fiji ambassador to China, countries like Australia and New Zealand were still held in higher regard, and stakeholders needed to change their attitudes toward China: "Unfortunately it still remains a tendency for Pacific island nations to look at China as a country that produces criminals" (*Fiji Times* 2006). This view was echoed by Ambassador-Designate to Beijing Sir Jim Ah Koy: "The trouble is we continue to stereotype Chinese as Tongs, drug pushers and people who promote prostitution" (Matau 2007: 7).

These comments reflect yet another problem facing Fiji's economic relations with China, the association between recent Chinese arrivals in the country (many with Hong Kong connections) and organized crime. Spectacular examples of such Chinese-linked criminal activity in Fiji were the seizure of 357 kilograms of heroin in 2000 (valued at over US$145 million) and a methamphetamine factory discovered in 2004 (reportedly the largest such laboratory yet found in the Southern hemisphere). There have also been a number of murders of ethnic Chinese as a result of gang and business disputes. Criminal activity in turn is seen to be fostered by corruption within the Fiji government (especially in the immigration section) and weak monitoring, vetting, and policing capacity (Skehan 2005).

Corruption was also a major problem associated with Chinese involvement in Fiji's tuna fishery. The fishing sector provides a good example of how the China connection has been used to promote political interests in Fiji, in line with Chinese commercial and political interests. But the economic conflict this created with local established interests, and the widespread corruption that subsequently surfaced, meant that for many Chinese fishing operators their activity in Fiji was short-lived.

As part of its affirmative action program, the Qarase administration aimed to promote indigenous Fijian participation in the tuna industry (to achieve 50 percent participation by 2020). One strategy to achieve this was to encourage joint ventures with overseas partners who could provide the capital and experience. On his first visit to China, Prime Minister Qarase signed a MOU on fisheries with the Chinese government, designed in part to encourage Chinese fishing fleets to enter joint venture partnerships with indigenous Fijians. By the end of 2002, 44 Chinese flagged vessels had been issued with licenses to operate in Fiji's Exclusive Economic Zone (EEZ). However, this development met with strong opposition from local fishing operators, who claimed that the industry could not sustain an influx of more vessels. In 2000 there were 54 vessels licensed to fish in Fiji's EEZ. This number had risen to 131 in 2002. By the following year, fishing operators were declaring that the industry was on the point of collapse, with vessels catching 60 percent less tuna than in earlier years. While debate raged within the industry, and with government, about what was a sustainable number of licenses for the

Fiji EEZ, allegations began to surface that officials were receiving bribes from Chinese vessel operators in exchange for licenses. Evidence also began to emerge that many of the so-called joint ventures between indigenous Fijians and Chinese were in fact "$2 companies," in which the local partner had very little or no shareholding. Licenses were being issued to Chinese fishing companies that did not meet joint venture standards. Nor did the local "partner" receive any benefits (Foster-Hildebrand 2003a, 2003b; Lenati 2003; Lewa 2002).

By 2004, investigations into corruption allegations had led to the suspension and subsequent conviction of several senior fishing officials. A crackdown on the issuing of fishing licenses also led to the government's licensing committee rejecting 60 out of 84 applications (mainly by Chinese operators) because they did not meet the various joint venture and other criteria. The total number of licenses issued also fell to 75 in 2005 and 63 in 2006 (an estimated 24 were Chinese flagged in 2006). According to industry sources, "the Chinese threat has been contained."[10]

Conclusion

Over the past three decades the framework for closer relations between Fiji and China has been put in place. Since 2000 there has been noticeable progress in this regard, with the establishment of an embassy in Beijing accompanied by various aid and economic agreements. This trend may have gained further momentum since the military coup of December 2006. But while the framework and political sentiment supporting closer ties exist, the substance of this relationship has yet to materialize.

The above analysis points to a range of factors that continue to inhibit the development of closer relations between Fiji and China. These include the continuing "unofficial" ties between Fiji and Taiwan, and the lack of substantive progress in promoting economic ties, particularly in trade. Moreover, while the official view in Fiji toward China remains very positive, largely due to Beijing's policy of non-interference in Fiji's domestic affairs and willingness to give aid without strings attached, the public perception of China (and new Chinese migrants) tends to be more negative.[11]

Some commentators have predicted that the hostile reaction of Australia and New Zealand to the latest Fiji coup provides China with its "best chance yet of gaining a more substantial presence in Fiji and the surrounding region" (Davis 2007: 7). There is an alternative possibility, however. While not wishing to antagonize Fiji (or to push it into closer links with Taiwan), China will nevertheless be mindful of the wider regional audience and the need to balance its strategic and political interests in the Pacific. As a way to ensure its future influence in the region, China may not want to be too much out of step with the position on Fiji taken by the Pacific Islands Forum. Notwithstanding current tensions between Australia and several Pacific Island states, the Forum's position on Fiji appears to be fairly cohesive.[12] According to former Secretary-General of the Pacific Islands Forum Greg Urwin, China is considered an important partner in the region, and in particular in the implementation of the Pacific Plan (Pacific Islands Forum Secretariat 2006). This is a standing that China's leaders may well seek to preserve—albeit for their own interests rather than those of the forum.

It is also important to note that while China professes to be sympathetic to the "rights and interests of developing countries—including Pacific island countries" (Wen 2006), this is not at the expense of other pressing interests. Fiji officials have observed that at the World Trade Organization, China has not proved to be a friend of Pacific Island states—for example, by blocking proposals to assist small countries adversely affected by the liberalization of global trade. The path to creating a "new regional order with China as the natural leader" (Windybank 2005) is thus not as straightforward or as predictable as some have suggested.

Notes

1. Fiji experienced two military coups in 1987. The first, in May, deposed the newly elected Labor Coalition government. According to coup leader Colonel Sitiveni Rabuka, this government was not supported by the indigenous Fijian population. The second coup, in September, derailed an attempt by the then governor general to put together a caretaker government that included members of the deposed coalition. This coup was also led by Colonel Rabuka, who subsequently established an interim military government and declared Fiji a republic.

2. These negotiations, known as the Multilateral High Level Conference or MHLC, took place between 1997 and 2000, when the Convention for the Conservation and Management of Highly Migratory Fish Stocks in the Western and Central Pacific was concluded in Honolulu, Hawai`i.

3. In May 2000 a group of armed civilians stormed Parliament and took hostage members of the Labor Party–led coalition government that had been elected one year earlier. The "cause" was ostensibly the same as that of the 1987 coups: to return political power to indigenous Fijian control. The Fiji Military Forces subsequently seized power and, while negotiating the release of the hostages, installed an interim civilian government with former banker Laisenia Qarase as prime minister. Members of this government later formed a new Fijian political party and successfully contested the general elections of 2001. A government led by Qarase was formed; however, its relations with the military commander (Frank Bainimarama) soured over the next five years. This was mainly due to its pandering to nationalist Fijian interests and its links with Fijian leaders implicated in the civilian-led coup of May 2000 (and an army mutiny of November 2000). Following the election of May 2006, which saw the return to power of the Qarase government, relations deteriorated further, and the army executed a coup in December 2006. The stated aim of this coup was to "clean up" corruption and racism in the government.

4. Approved Destination status allows Chinese tourists to visit Fiji without having to apply for an exit visa from their government. In 2007 the (post-coup) interim government of Fiji announced an open visa plan for visitors from China that would allow entry into Fiji without first applying for an entry visa.

5. According to the Chinese embassy in Suva, 120 government officials and technical staff received training in China and attended workshops in 2006.

6. The Chinese government's response to the military coup in December 2006 was characteristically muted. A statement from the Chinese embassy in Suva simply declared that Beijing "would like to see Fiji maintain its stability" and hoped that "all parties involved could resolve their problems for the sake of economic development, political stability and people's harmonious life" (*Fiji Times*, 9 December 2006, 5).

7. This is the view of Chinese community leaders interviewed by the author in January and February 2007. The interviewees wished to remain anonymous.

8. Fiji's ambassador-designate to Beijing has made promotion of tourism his number one priority and has predicted that Fiji could attract 620,000 visitors annually from China. Fiji's current total number of tourist arrivals (from all destinations) is around 500,000 (Matau 2007: 7.).

9. Trade statistics vary depending on the source. The Chinese embassy in Suva cites the overall trade volume between Fiji and China in 2005 as $50 million and in 2006 as $70 million. According to a Chinese embassy official, Fiji's exports to China were constrained by the fact that most of the products that China would be interested in (such as marine products and bottled water) were already fully committed to markets elsewhere (Interview, Suva, September 2007).

10. This assessment was made by local fishing industry representatives interviewed by the author in Suva in January and February 2007. Details of corruption allegations were publicized in media reports in late 2003 and early 2004. For example, "Fishery Scam Expands," Radio Fiji One, 17 January 2004, and "Fiji License Scrutinized," Radio Fiji One, 26 January 2004.

11. One correspondent to a Fiji daily wrote of Chinese turning Fiji "into a huge Mafia zone … where black marketing, prostitution and gambling become things of the day" (*Fiji Times*, 29 May 2002, 6).

12. This position is laid out in the Forum Eminent Persons' Group (EPG) Report, Fiji, 29 January–1 February 2007. It called for, among other things, an early return to elected government. It also declared the military takeover of government "unconstitutional and unacceptable." An official at the Chinese embassy in Suva acknowledged that the Pacific Islands Forum has a role to play in helping Fiji resolve its problems. The EPG, he said, was respected by the Fiji government and respected by Pacific Island countries, "[s]o China respects the EPG." He said there was a need for "constructive dialogue" in dealing with Fiji's situation (Interview, Suva, September 2007).

References

Biddick, Thomas. 1989. "Diplomatic Rivalry in the South Pacific: The PRC and Taiwan." *Asian Survey* 29 (8): 800–815.

Bola, Jona. 2006. "Trade Weight Will Shift to China: PM." *Fiji Times,* 31 July, 15.

Crocombe, Ron. 2005. "The Growing Chinese Presence in the Region." *Islands Business,* January, 24–27.

Davis, Graham. 2006. "Regime Looks at China." *Sunday Times,* 31 December, 4.

———. 2007. "The New Power Game." *Fiji Times,* 9 February, 7.

Elbourne, Frederica. 2002. "Qarase Pays Tribute to Asia." *Fiji Times,* 29 May, 5.

Feizkhah, Elizabeth. 2001. "How to Win Friends." *Time,* 4 June, 24–26.

Field, Michael. 2001. "Chinese Presence in the Pacific Increases. *Fiji Times,* 2 June, 36.

Fiji Broadcasting Corporation. 2006. AM Report, 7 December. Accessed on 13 March 2007 at http://www.radiofiji.com.fj/

Fijilive. 2005. "Qarase Reaffirms Fiji Loyalty to China." 29 June. Accesses 23 January 2007 at *Pacific Islands Report* http://archives.pireport.org/archive/2005/june/06-30-12.htm

———. 2007a. News Report, 22 January. Accessed on 14 March 2007 at http://www.fijilive.com/

———. 2007b. "Bainimarama to Seek Trade, Military Ties with Asia." 29 January. Accessed on 21 March 2007 at Pacific Islands Report http://archives.pireport.org/archive/2007/january/01-30-f01.htm

Fiji Times. 2006. "Fiji Urged to Pursue Chinese Overtures." 6 April. Accessed 4 March 2007 at *Pacific Islands Report* http://archives.pireport.org/archive/2006/april/04-07-19.htm

Foster-Hildebrand, Sophie. 2003a. "Job Security Uncertain." *Fiji Times,* 5 November, 16.

———. 2003b. "Fishing Industry Takes Stock." *Fiji Times,* 6 November, 24.

Gillett, Robert, et al. 2001. *Tuna: A Key Economic Resource in the Pacific.* Manila: Asian Development Bank.

Godley, Michael. 1983. "China: The Waking Giant." In *Foreign Forces in Pacific Politics,* ed. Ron Crocombe and Ahmed Ali, 130–142. Suva: University of the South Pacific.

Government of Fiji. n.d. Website of Embassy of the Republic of Fiji Islands in Beijing, China. Accessed 18 August 2009 at http://www.fijiembassy.org.cn

Gurdayal, Mithleshni. 2001. "Adapt to Looking North Policy: Tavola." *Fiji's Daily Post,* 10 August, 6.

Henderson, John, and Benjamin Reilly. 2003. "Dragon in Paradise: China's Rising Star in Oceania." *The National Interest,* no. 72 (summer): 94–104.

Komai, Makareta. 2005. "We Need to Learn from Each Other." *Fiji Times,* 11 August, 11.

Lenati, Temo. 2003. "Low Catch Affects 200 Jobs." *Fiji Times,* 28 October, 3.

Lewa, Sainimili. 2002. "Tuna Boat Owners Protest on Licenses." *Fiji Times,* 11 June, 2.

Low, Mary. 1981. "The Foreign Policy of a South Pacific Microstate: Fiji 1970–1980." Unpublished MA subthesis, Australian National University.

Low-O'Sullivan. 1989. "Fiji's Foreign Policy: A Change in Direction?" *Review,* 10 (17): 32–40.

Maclellan, Nic. 2000. "Chinese Military Aid to the Pacific." *Pacific News Bulletin,* December, 12.

Matau, Robert. 2007. "Sir James Takes Fiji East." *Fiji Times,* 17 July, 7.

Pacific Islands Forum Secretariat. 2006. "China to Study Pacific Forum Proposals." News Release, 24 August. Accessed 4 March 2007 at *Pacific Islands Report* http://archives.pireport.org/archive/2006/august/08-30-rl.htm

Qarase, Laisenia. 2004. "Remarks at the Official Opening of the Heads of Missions Consultations." *Foreign Affairs Bulletin,* no. 1 (October): 3.

Radio Australia. 2002. "Fiji Receives Unrestricted Grant from China." 31 May. Accessed 14 January 2007 at Pacific Islands Report http://archives.pireport.org/archive/2002 /june/06-03-11.htm

Rarabici, Vasemaca. 2001. "Respect One China Policy, Says Fiji Envoy." *Fiji Times,* 9 September, 2.

Skehan, Craig. 2005. "Chinese Gangs in Pacific Real Regional Threat." *Pacific Islands Report,* 21 February. Accessed on 18 August 2009 at http://archives.pireport.org/ archive/2005/february/02-21-12.htm

Tarte, Sandra. 1998. *Japan's Aid Diplomacy and the Pacific Islands.* Suva and Canberra: Institute of Pacific Studies and National Centre for Development Studies.

———. 2002. "A Duty to Cooperate: Building a Regional Regime for the Conservation and Management of Highly Migratory Fish Stocks in the Western and Central Pacific." In *Ocean Yearbook 16,* ed. Elisabeth Mann Borgesse, Aldo Chircop, and Moira L. McConnell, 261–299. Chicago: University of Chicago Press.

Wen Jiabao. 2006. "Win-Win Cooperation for Common Development." Speech at the opening of the first Ministerial Conference of the China-Pacific Island Countries Economic Development and Cooperation Forum, Nadi, 5 April. Accessed 8 October 2006 at http://au.china-embassy.org/eng.

Windybank, Susan. 2005. "The China Syndrome." *Policy* (winter): 28–33.

Wise, Margaret. 2002. "Fallout Grows over Fiji's Trip: Some Business People Failed to Meet Contacts." *Pacific Islands Report,* 5 June. Accessed 18 August at http://archives .pireport.org/archive/2002/june/06-06-02.htm

Xinhua News Agency. 2002. "Fiji Prime Minister Qarase Confirms Support for One China." 28 May. Accessed 14 January 2007 at *Pacific Islands Report* http://archives .pireport.org/archive/2002/may/05-29-06.htm

Yee, Sin Joan. 1974. *The Chinese in the Pacific.* Suva: South Pacific Social Sciences Association.

CHAPTER 8

Milking the Dragon in Solomon Islands

Tarcisius Tara Kabutaulaka

Introduction

China's recent rapid economic growth and associated political power have enabled it to play a more pervasive and assertive role in global affairs. Even small and relatively isolated Pacific Island countries have felt the impact of China's rising power. This has provided opportunities as well as caused concerns for both island countries and the metropolitan powers that traditionally enjoyed influence in Oceania. In particular, there is concern that China's more assertive role will exacerbate its competition with Taiwan (Republic of China) for diplomatic recognition. This will, in turn, have economic, geopolitical, and geostrategic implications for the region. For Pacific Island countries, however, China's economic growth also provides new opportunities, a bigger market, and a source of investment free of the kinds of restrictions imposed by Western countries.

This chapter discusses the Chinese influence in the Pacific Islands, with a focus on the Solomon Islands. In particular, it examines the factors that influenced the Solomon Islands' decision to establish and maintain diplomatic relations with Taiwan, rather than China, and the implications of that decision. First, the chapter outlines the issues and debates associated with China's increasing presence in Oceania. Second, it provides a brief history of when and how the Solomon Islands established diplomatic relations with Taiwan, and the issues and debates surrounding that decision. Third, it discusses the nature of the Solomon Islands–Taiwan relationship and the interaction between the dynamics of domestic politics and diplomatic relations with Taiwan. Fourth, the chapter examines how the growing economic and political power of China and its more assertive presence in the region could affect Taiwan's ability to maintain its Pacific Island allies, particularly the Solomon Islands. This will have important geostrategic and geopolitical implications for the region, and for world politics more generally.

Although trade and investment were important in influencing the Solomon Islands' initial decision to establish diplomatic relations with Taiwan, these factors have become less significant over the years. Instead, the relationship is now influenced predominantly by the dynamics of the Solomon Islands' domestic politics. This demonstrates how the Solomon Islands' foreign policies, like those of most Pacific Islands countries, were determined by local concerns rather than by geostrategic issues. In the longer term, however, there is a possibility that the Solomon Islands might switch from Taiwan to China because of the growing importance of China as an economic partner.

China in Oceania

With its rapid economic growth and aggressive international diplomacy, China is asserting itself on the international stage and creating a new global order. The things that make China fascinating are its size and the speed of its economic growth: a population of 1.3 billion people and an annual economic growth of 10 to 12 percent. In the past decade, in response to Beijing's embrace of a neoliberal market economy, foreign businesses have flooded into China to take advantage of its cheap and readily available labor, as well as its rapid economic growth and industrialization, making China the world's factory. In recent years, however, Chinese businesses are also going out into the world to invest in all kinds of enterprises, including natural resource extraction, to feed the country's growing appetite for raw materials—much as Western countries did throughout the 1800s and most of the 1900s. Consequently, Chinese-owned companies are establishing themselves around the world as a force to reckon with in industries like mining, forestry, and fisheries. For example, a Chinese state-owned company owns 40 percent of the oil concessions in southern Sudan (Elliot 2007). In another case, in April 2006 the China National Offshore Oil Corporation completed a deal to buy a 45 percent stake in a Nigerian oil block for more than US$2 billion. These were part of a series of energy and minerals deals with African countries, including Sudan, Chad, Angola, and Zimbabwe. Chinese-made products are also flooding global consumer markets, including those in Africa. Trade between China and Africa is now worth more than US$30 billion and is growing rapidly (Griffiths 2006).

Beijing has been able to use this economic muscle to exert itself politically, posing as the next world power that could challenge—possibly even undermine—the global hegemony of the United States. This is accompanied by an aggressive international diplomacy that, in the past few years, has seen Chinese leaders tour the globe and host world leaders in Beijing. In 2004, for example, Chinese President Hu Jintao spent two weeks touring South America, and in 2006 he visited the United States, Russia, Saudi Arabia, Morocco, Nigeria, and Kenya. Also, toward the end of 2006 Hu hosted the leaders of forty-eight African countries in Beijing for three weeks. Premier Wen Jiabao was also busy visiting fifteen countries in 2006 (Griffiths 2006). In April of that year, Premier Wen met with leaders of the eight Pacific Island countries that have diplomatic relations with China. This international diplomacy comes with promises of Chinese assistance and investments.

For Pacific Island countries, China's economic growth and political assertion provide new opportunities as well as challenges. Hence, there are mixed reactions both in the region and outside. On the one hand, fresh opportunities arise as Chinese companies invest in the region, especially in natural resource extraction industries like fisheries, forestry, and mining. In Papua New Guinea, for instance, a Chinese-owned company has bought the Ramu nickel and cobalt mine in the country's Madang Province. In February 2007 Papua New Guinea Foreign Affairs and Trade Minister Paul Tiensten stated that Chinese investment was important because the Ramu mine project "had the potential to turn around the country's sagging economy" (Reuters 2007). Further, Chinese textile companies have set up shop in Pacific Island countries like Fiji in order to take advantage of their access to markets in Australia and New Zealand. China has also provided assistance in the form of aid and loans. In April 2006, for example, during the first Ministerial Conference of the China–Pacific Island Countries Economic Development and Cooperation Forum in Fiji, Chinese Premier Wen Jiabao (2006; see Appendix for full statement) expressed his country's commitment to its Pacific Island allies and promised that China will, among other things,

> provide RMB 3 billion *yuan* of preferential loans in the next three years to boost cooperation in resources development, agriculture, forestry, fishery, tourism, textiles and consumer products manufacturing, telecommunications and aviation and ocean shipping. The Chinese Government will also set up a special fund to encourage Chinese companies to invest in the Pacific island countries.

However, while these opportunities are welcomed, China's presence has also brought challenges. Chinese investors often have problems meeting the labor and environmental standards of the countries where they invest. The conditions in the garment sweat shops in Fiji, for example, have been a topic of concern and widespread discussion (Storey 2004). Poor labor and environmental conditions at the Ramu mine in Papua New Guinea have also been the center of much controversy, attracting the pointed criticism of Papua New Guinea Labour Secretary David Tibu, who stated: "The Chinese developer does not seem to have any standards and I will not allow my countrymen and women to be used as slaves" (Callick 2007: 5). Further, Chinese businesses often seem to attract Chinese citizens who engage in undesirable activities such as illegal resource extraction, drug and people smuggling, and murder, posing security challenges for Pacific Island countries (Radio New Zealand 2004; Field 2005). In 2000, for example, 357 kilograms of heroin were confiscated from Chinese citizens in Suva, Fiji. Further, in

2004 the biggest methamphetamine laboratory in the Southern hemisphere was found in Suva. These events have raised concerns about security threats associated with the entry of Chinese gangs into the region (Skehan 2005).

Much of the concern about China's growing presence in Oceania is expressed by academics and people in the media, most of whom are located outside the region. The debates surrounding China's assertive presence are often complicated by the struggle for diplomatic recognition between China and Taiwan, and by the fact that Pacific Island countries sometimes become entangled in that competition. The independent countries of the region are divided in their diplomatic ties, with seven having diplomatic relations with China while six recognize Taiwan.[1] Of the twenty-four countries around the world that recognize Taiwan, six (25 percent) are in the Pacific Islands, making them an important region for Taiwan. In reaction to the 2006 Chinese-organized forum in Fiji, Taiwan organized a forum with its six Pacific Islands diplomatic allies in Palau in September of the same year (see Appendix for the forum's communiqué). This was to ensure that Beijing did not win these countries to its side. Pacific Island countries often take advantage of this competition between Taipei and Beijing in soliciting aid and other forms of assistance.

In broader discussions, the reaction to China's assertive presence in the region has been mixed. Many island countries, including those that have diplomatic relation with Taiwan, have taken advantage of the trade opportunities that China provides. Palau and the Solomon Islands, for example, trade with China although they recognize Taiwan diplomatically. Similarly, Papua New Guinea and Fiji have trade relations with Taiwan but recognize China. For these countries, both China and Taiwan provide much-needed economic opportunities.

Concern that China's assertive role in the region could create problems dominates much of the academic, media, and policy discussions emanating from countries like Australia, New Zealand, and the United States. Much of this discussion is characterized by a "threat discourse" that portrays China's economic and political growth as well as the projection of that growth into the region as potentially dangerous, to be treated with care, especially by small Pacific Island countries that are perceived as having no capacity to deal with a giant like China. In the literature, China is portrayed as a threat to the dominance of the Western countries that have long enjoyed dominance in the region. There is, in other words, a tendency to represent China as a "big bad dragon" that must be denied access—especially strategic access—to the region. John Henderson and Benjamin Reilly (2003), for example, discuss China as a strategic threat to the region, while Susan Windybank talks about Beijing's role in Oceania's "arc of instability," contending that the competition for diplomatic recognition between China and Taiwan adds to existing regional problems. She argues further that the arrival of China as a major regional player, together with the diplomatic competition with Taiwan, "is counterproductive." However, in relation to Australia's role in the region, Windybank cautions against "what I'd call 'old' versus 'new' security thinking: China is not another Soviet Union and it's Chinese triads rather than Chinese military bases that we should worry about" (Windybank 2006).

These representations of China bear striking resemblance to the cold war discussions that informed the "strategic denial" policy adopted by the Western allies toward the Pacific Islands region. China and Taiwan are often portrayed as the "big bad dragons" because they are said to take advantage of the political and economic gullibility of Pacific Island countries and their leaders, creating political instability and conflicts within these countries. Australian journalist Graeme Dobell, for example, argues that the riots in Honiara (Solomon Islands) and Nuku'alofa (Tonga) in April and November 2006 respectively were caused, in part, by the diplomatic rivalry between Beijing and Taipei. He claims that in the Solomon Islands case, Taiwanese money helped prop up and bring back to power an unpopular government, hence attracting protests that led to the riot. Similar claims were made by fellow journalist Michael Field. Both, however, failed to provide evidence to show that China and Taiwan had a hand in the riots in Honiara and Nuku'alofa. Further, they discuss the events in Tonga and the Solomon Islands without providing any historical context, and without reference to the complex dynamics of local politics.

These discussions are often patronizing. They portray Pacific Islanders, and in particular their leaders, as passive victims of an external onslaught, unfit and unable to deal with China or Taiwan. They do not acknowledge that Pacific leaders are intelligent individuals actively making rational decisions that reflect national interests and complex domestic politics. In other words, Pacific Islanders—especially national leaders—are always trying to find ways to milk the dragons without being eaten by them. It is important to note, however, that this is not a bargain between equals. The small (Pacific Island countries) need to be realistic about understanding the goals (especially the long-term ones) of the larger powers. The late professor Ron Crocombe stated that Pacific Island leaders need to be aware that China and Taiwan are seeking the best outcomes for themselves, and that compared to Western or Pacific Island countries, China, Taiwan, and Japan tend to adopt a much longer-term perspective (personal communication, 11 December 2007).

China and Taiwan in the Solomons

At the time of its independence from Great Britain in 1978, the Solomon Islands' foreign policy slogan was "friend to all, and enemy to none," a phrase borrowed from neighboring Papua New Guinea's foreign affairs. While catchy, inclusive, and perhaps suitable for a new and small nation trying to establish itself in the international arena, this did not say much about the issues that informed the country's foreign policy. If anything, it demonstrated a naive perception of playing a neutral role in the international arena, one heavily influenced at the time by the bipolar ideological division between the East (communism) and West (democracy). Who Pacific Island countries interacted with was influenced (if not dictated) by their "traditional friends" and former or existing colonial masters—Great Britain, Australia, United States, New Zealand, and France. These metropolitan countries were determined to keep the Pacific a "Western lake" and developed a policy of "strategic denial" to exclude "communists" entirely from the region.[2] The newly independent island nations were not regarded as mature enough to be allowed to deal with Eastern bloc countries.

However, many of the Pacific Island countries were eager to express their independence, especially in foreign relations. Vanuatu, for example, joined the Non-Aligned Movement and established links with Libya, despite being chastised by Western countries for these actions. Similarly, Kiribati defied the advice of its traditional allies when it signed a fishing agreement with the Soviet Union in 1985. The Solomon Islands was also keen to forge an independent foreign policy while maintaining good relations with its traditional friends. In January 1983, for example, Prime Minister Solomon Mamaloni described the assistance of "traditional friends" as "boring" and said that the Solomon Islands should explore relations with countries with colonial backgrounds similar to its own, like Indonesia, Malaysia, Singapore, mainland China, Taiwan, India, and Bangladesh (*Solomon Star* 1983a).

In the early 1980s the Solomon Islands also debated whether to establish diplomatic relations with Taiwan or China. At that time the Solomon Islands had cordial relations with both countries, although there were indications that diplomatic relations would be established with Beijing. China had offices in Canberra and Port Moresby and was actively attempting to entice Honiara into a relationship. In April 1982, Minister for Foreign Affairs and International Trade Ezekiel Alebua visited China to initiate talks that would eventually lead to the establishment of diplomatic relations. Alebua met with Deputy Premier and Minister for Foreign Affairs Huan Hua, and the two signed an initial communiqué. On his return Alebua said that "a good foundation has been laid for future sound diplomatic and trade relations between both countries" (*Monthly Magazine* 1982a). On 10 April 1982 a Memorandum of Understanding (MOU) was signed in Honiara to pave the way for the development of trade between the two countries. The MOU involved the Solomon Islands Copra Board and a five-man trade team from the National Cereals, Oils and Foodstuffs Import and Export Corporation of the People's Republic of China (*Monthly Magazine* 1982a).

While this was going on, the Solomon Islands government was also warming up to Taipei. In June 1982 a Taiwanese trade exhibition was held in Honiara, the result of a visit by a group of Solomon Islands government officials to Taiwan in February and March of that year. Solomon Islands Deputy Prime Minister and

Minister for Home Affairs Kamilo Teke was impressed by the exhibit, which featured agricultural machinery, and later became an enthusiastic proponent of relations with Taiwan (*Monthly Magazine* 1982b).

By the beginning of 1983 interactions with Taipei were becoming more serious, and in March of that year a Taiwanese consular-level office was established in Honiara. Despite this development, Minister of Finance Bartholomew Ulufa'alu insisted that the Solomon Islands government "recognizes mainland China as the sole representative of the people of China," and that the relationship with Taiwan concentrated "mainly on promotion of investment, trade, and economic cooperation" (*Monthly Magazine* 1983). Despite Ulufa'alu's assurances, on 26 May 1983 the Taiwanese consular office was upgraded to embassy level and Suen His-tzung was appointed the first Taiwanese ambassador to the Solomon Islands. According to the official newsletter, *Government Monthly* (1983a: 9), "Mr. Suen said both governments also agreed to develop friendly relations and mutual cooperation for the purpose of raising mutual benefit from each other in the fields of trade and investment, technical and cultural exchanges."

The Solomon Islands government emphasized trade and investment as the major reasons for developing its relations with Taiwan. For example, Minister of Foreign Affairs and International Trade Dennis Lulei noted that "Taiwan could help Solomon Islands get a soft loan from the ADB since it is a member of the bank. It would also encourage Taiwanese investors." He said that Taiwan might also help to fund a new international airport and provide patrol boats (*Solomon Star* 1983b). The Taiwanese emphasis, however, was on securing diplomatic recognition that would give it legitimacy in the international arena.

Beijing was disappointed when the Solomon Islands established diplomatic relations with Taiwan. In April 1983 the Chinese embassy in Australia expressed surprise over the move to establish consular-level relations with Taiwan (*Solomon Star* 1983c, *Government Monthly* 1983a). On 18 August 1983, Chinese Ambassador to Papua New Guinea Hu Hongfan visited Honiara for a two-day round of talks with officials from the Ministry of Foreign Affairs and International Trade. In these he emphasized that his country would not establish diplomatic relations unless the Taiwanese Consulate-General in Honiara was downgraded to a commercial office. Government officials had told the Chinese that it was prepared to accommodate both countries based on its foreign policy of being a "friend to all and enemy to none" (*Government Monthly* 1983b).

China continued to encourage Solomon Islands to break relations with Taiwan. In September 1983, a six-man delegation led by Speaker of the National Parliament Maepeza Gina was invited to visit China. The *Government Monthly* (1983c) reported that the aim of the mission was "to observe their parliamentary system and how it works." It was also to visit industrial areas and observe social and economic developments. However, in Beijing the visiting delegation was told that "establishing diplomatic relation with Taiwan is an act of interference with [China's] internal affairs," and high-level officials refused to meet with them. Delegation leader Maepeza Gina reported that they were "unable to observe the Chinese Parliamentary system as much as expected because of major differences between the country's Parliamentary system and Solomon Islands parliamentary set up." However, he said that they were able to visit many agricultural development areas, educational institutions, and cultural centers before returning home. He also mentioned endorsing a document on possible assistance in the building of a new Solomon Islands National Parliament and a national sports stadium (*Government Monthly* 1983d). Although these projects had been discussed previously, the assistance never eventuated, and it was the United States government that ended up funding the construction of the national parliament building.

In response to Beijing's expression of disappointment, Prime Minister Mamaloni said that his government would establish diplomatic relations with Taiwan because it did not want communism:

> Leaders of the People's Republic of China (Communist China) must understand that Solomon Islands people do not accept communism because they wish to enjoy the freedom of democracy and the traditional values they have survived under for many years. It is for this reason that the Solomon Islands Government has established diplomatic relations with only countries who have shared the same democratic relations. (*Government Monthly* 1983e)

Mamaloni said that nothing had been achieved from the visits to China and emphasized that the Solomon Islands must benefit tangibly from diplomatic relationships (*Solomon Star* 1983d). Interestingly, the Solomon Islands had established diplomatic ties with Taiwan four months prior to the Maepeza Gina–led visit to China. Hence, the decision could not have been influenced by the fact that nothing tangible came out of that visit.

By the late 1980s, the Solomon Islands had become one of Taiwan's most trusted allies in the region. For the Taiwanese, this provided much-needed diplomatic recognition that enabled them to participate in the global arena. For the Solomon Islands, the expectation was that the relationship would lead to improved investment, trade, and budgetary assistance. There was also an expectation that the Solomon Islands could learn from Taiwan's development experience and benefit from its technology, especially in agriculture.

The Solomon Islands and Taiwan

The Solomon Islands' diplomatic relations with Taiwan have attracted a lot of attention, especially because of their alleged negative impact on domestic politics. To fully understand the situation, it is necessary to examine the nature of the relationship between the two countries. Taiwan's reason for establishing diplomatic ties with the Solomon Islands was clear: to gain international recognition of its independence and the legitimacy of its claim to a political identity separate from that of mainland China. For the Solomon Islands, on the other hand, the rationale for the relationship is less clear. Official rhetoric emphasizes economic development as the major factor influencing the relationship. From the beginning it was anticipated that Taiwan would provide trade opportunities and transfer technology, and that the Solomons would learn from and potentially emulate its development experiences (*Solomon Star* 1983b).

However, the reality has been quite different. The Solomon Islands has never had a strong trade link with Taiwan (see Illustrations 8.1 and 8.2). Nor has Taiwan ever been a major source of investments in the Solomon Islands. In fact, the value of Solomon Islands trade with China has been much greater than that with Taiwan (see Illustrations 8.1 and 8.2). This is partly due to the nature of the Taiwanese economy, which is highly mechanized and based on information technology, and therefore does not require the kinds of primary products that dominate Solomon Islands exports. China, on the other hand, has a massive demand for raw materials to sustain its rapid economic and industrial growth, including the timber and fish available in the Solomons. Although the Solomon Islands does not have diplomatic relation with Beijing, it trades more with China than with Taiwan.

Illustration 8.1 • Destination and Value of Solomon Islands Exports 2001–2006 (SI$ 000)

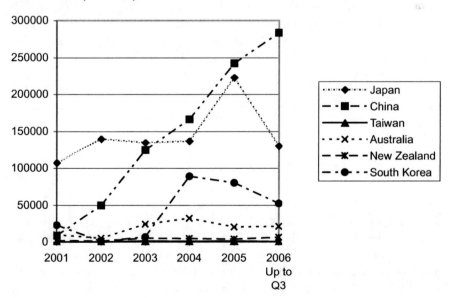

Illustration 8.2 ◆ Source and Value of Solomon Islands Imports
2001–2006 (SI$ 000)

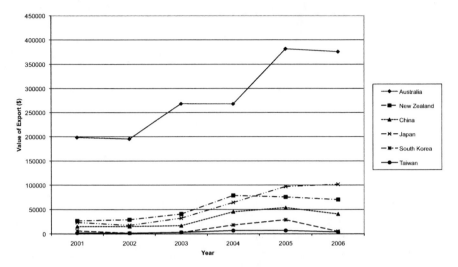

The fact that the Solomon Islands imports less from Taiwan than from China
(see Illustration 8.2) could be explained partly by the fact that many of the im-
porters in the Solomons are ethnic Chinese with connections to China rather
than Taiwan. Many of them came to the Solomons from China—especially from
Hong Kong after its transfer from British to Chinese rule—or have relatives
there. Further, Taiwanese businesses prefer to invest their money in China or
Southeast Asian countries, rather than in the Pacific Islands. As a member of the
Taiwanese General Chamber of Commerce said, "People in Taiwan and China
belong to the same ethnic group and we speak the same language. Although the
Pacific Islands enjoys abundant agricultural and marine resources, the political
instability, the less-than-ideal standard of living and the cultural discrepancy between that region and Taiwan would make Taiwanese think twice before going
there" (Chu 2000).

Political Dynamics

If trade has never featured significantly in the Solomon Islands–Taiwan relationship, then what factors have helped sustain it? The answer lies partly in the fact
that the Solomon Islands–Taiwan relationship is influenced by political and security imperatives rather than economic ones. Taiwan's interest is to gain and
maintain diplomatic recognition. Solomon Islands interests have been dictated
by the need for assistance—especially financial assistance—that could be readily

accessed to address immediate needs. For the politician that need is to gain and maintain political support. For the constituent, it is to have access to resources—especially goods and finance—to address immediate and often mundane requirements. Such assistance, therefore, often comes in the form of cash payments that are controlled (directly or indirectly) by politicians. The situation works well for both Taiwanese and Solomon Islands politicians. Continuing and readily available assistance from Taipei insures that Solomon Islands politicians will continue to give Taiwan diplomatic recognition.

Taiwan has been one of the country's major donors and has also provided assistance when and where other donors have been reluctant or unwilling to do so. From 1990 to 1998, for instance, Taiwan's grant assistance to the Solomon Islands amounted to SBD$103,695,380 (US$14.9 million). Between 1999 and 2004 Taipei contributed SBD$212,178,418 (US$30.5 million) to the Solomon Islands development budget. Taiwan also contributed enormously to the national budget from 2005 to 2007. For the 2007 development budget, Taiwan contributed 5 percent. Although this is small compared to contributions from Australia (64 percent) and the European Union (10 percent), it is not much less than the transfers from New Zealand (7 percent) and Japan (6 percent), and it exceeds those from the Asian Development Bank (3 percent) and the Solomon Islands government itself (4 percent).[3]

Taiwan provides assistance in a number of sectors, including agriculture, education, and health. In the education sector, for example, Taipei offers scholarships for Solomon Islands students to study in Taiwan; so far, they have been awarded to about thirty students. In July 2006 the Taiwanese government announced SI$16.7 million (US$2.4 million) in funding for local and overseas training for Solomon Islanders (People First Network 2006a). Further, in March 2007 the Taiwanese government donated SI$7.6 million (US$1 million) to give about 700 Solomon Islanders access to tertiary education (People First Network 2007). Taiwan was also responsible for the building of the National Referral Hospital.

Taiwan contributes to the government's development efforts more generally. In November 2006, for example, Taipei paid SI$20 million (US$2.9 million) to the Solomon Islands government's Millennium Development Fund, which was established to facilitate rural development policy (People First Network 2006b). Further, Taiwan gives SI$1 million (US$143,500) per member of parliament per year via the RCDF), and SI$10 million (US$1.4 million) a year for Micro Project Funds. It also supported the Poverty Alleviation Fund and other special funds administered by the Prime Minister's Office. In March 2007 the Solomon Islands Broadcasting Corporation reported that the Taiwanese government was providing roofing irons and water tanks for villagers in three constituencies on North and East Malaita (SIBC 2007).

Furthermore, in the years of civil unrest (1999–2003) when other donors were reluctant to give support because of concerns about corruption and the Solomon

Islands government's capacity to disperse aid, the Taiwanese government was the only one that came forward with assistance. In October 2002, while speaking at a function to mark Taiwan's National Day, Solomon Islands Prime Minister Sir Allan Kemakeza called on other countries and institutions to be like Taiwan, ready to provide assistance without being too judgmental about the governance situation in the country (*Pacific Islands Report* 2002b). In January 2005, during a visit by Taiwanese President Chen Shui-bian, Solomon Islands Governor General Sir Nathaniel Waena hailed Taiwan as "the only helper in Solomon Islands' dark days." In response, President Shui-Bian called Solomon Islands "Taiwan's most loyal ally in the Pacific" (*Solomon Star* 2005).

A common critique of Taiwan's support for the Solomon Islands is that the funds create dependency and have no positive impact on longer-term development. There is a certain element of truth in this. Taiwan often funds projects with high political returns for Taiwan, i.e. it sustains Solomon Islands diplomatic recognition of Taiwan. This is done by providing predominantly monetary assistance that benefits local politicians, perhaps not financially but in terms of rallying and maintaining political support from constituents. In the 2007 budget, for example, Taiwan contributed 21 percent in direct financial assistance to recurrent expenditure, as compared to only 6 percent in equipment (or capital expenditure), and no contributions in the form of technical assistance. It can be argued that this is basically a patron-client relationship, where Taiwan ensures that its politician clients in the Solomon Islands benefit directly and the politicians, in turn, use the money and goods to please their constituents and ensure that they continue to elect them to office. Indeed, this is a complex network of patron-client relationships that weaves all the way from the very local level to the international arena. The man or woman in a village in the Solomons receives Taiwanese money through politicians. He or she then renders support to the politician, and the politician, in turn, ensures that the Solomon Islands maintains its diplomatic recognition of Taiwan. One could argue that even if this situation does not necessarily contribute to long-term sustainable development, it does help to maintain political stability because those in power have access to the resources necessary to keep them in office.

It should also be noted, however, that Taiwan is not the only aid donor that attempts to influence local politics in Pacific Island countries. Others, including Australia, New Zealand, and the US, have done similar things. Australia, for instance, is at the time of writing attempting to use aid and trade to pressure the Frank Bainimarama–led military government in Fiji to hold national elections, and it played an important (although less visible) role in getting rid of the Manasseh Sogavare-led government in the Solomon Islands. It is therefore not unusual for aid donors to proactively attempt to influence the politics of recipient countries.

Controversy

The Solomon Islands–Taiwan relationship has not always been cordial. There have been controversies over allegations that Taiwanese support corrupts domestic politics and is not conducive to long-term economic development. In the lead up to the April 2006 election, for example, Taiwanese money was said to have been used to support favorite candidates. Member of Parliament for Rennell and Bellona Joses Tuhanuku accused Taiwan of funding the campaign of one of his opponents. In launching his Labour Party platform, Tuhanuku alleged that there was direct intervention from Taiwan:

> It is very shocking to observe that ROC or the Republic of China is now acting like a local political party, sponsoring candidates—including in my own electorate—involving itself directly in the business of Solomon Islands politics. It is very sad to witness even so-called senior members of our community, senior bureaucrats, chiefs and even church leaders who have already fallen victim to this insidious undermining of our nation. (*Solomon Star* 2006a)

Tuhanuku went further and alleged that there was also Taiwanese influence in the election of the prime minister:

> It's a sad fact that, come the declaration of election results on 6th and 7th of April, the same old game of temptation and corruption will begin to play out in the back rooms of Honiara's hotels, restaurants, casinos and taxis. Indeed, I believe those who distorted our political processes ... have already put in place a plan to repeat what they did in 2001, to keep their puppet in place, that is maintain the current Prime Minister following these general elections. The actions of this mission are so brazen and blatant. It is a sad fact that Solomon Islanders have in reality lost control of who heads our government and runs our country (*Solomon Star* 2006a).

Similar allegations were made by former MP for East Kwaio Alfred Sasako, who suggested that Taiwan had initiated a new practice of funding constituency projects through aspiring candidates for office, rather than through the sitting MP. He denounced this practice, saying that "[i]t is very frustrating to know that those who are supposedly helping us are now using such assistance to rope and strangle us" (*Solomon Star* 2006b). Both the Taiwanese embassy and the Solomon Islands government vigorously denied these allegations. They suggested that Tuhanuku and other MPs also benefited from the support Taiwan provided through the Rural Constituency Development Fund. However, in an open letter in the *Solomon Star* on 21 March 2006 (barely two weeks prior to the election),

Tuhanuku (2006) insisted that the real source of corruption was the Special Projects Fund. Here, Taiwanese money is put in a general pool controlled by Prime Minister Kemakeza, who selects those individuals who should apply for support from the fund. According to Tuhanuku, once a request has been made,

> Taiwan's dirty money comes flooding forward for the politician or candidate of the prime minister's choice.... Now in the past few months leading up to the election, these special projects are being used as the chief source of campaign funding for the Prime Minister's favorites who are expected, once elected, to back him and his Republic of China cronies. (Tuhanuku 2006)

Kemakeza quickly rebutted this charge, noting that Special Projects funding had existed for some time and that "[i]t has happened to all the Prime Ministers" (*Solomon Star* 2006c). Joses Sanga, MP for East Malaita and a former long-serving public servant, however, made an interesting comment with regards to these funds, originally introduced under the Bartholomew Ulufa'alu government:

> It is only when Kemakeza took office that the Prime Minister started using the fund for special projects outside of the normal procedures. [The] Prime Minister took on himself the administrative role which would have been normally done by the aid management and coordination ministry, or the Ministry of Planning and National Development. (*Solomon Star* 2006d)

The Solomon Islands–Taiwan relationship also attracted controversy when, in 2002, the Solomon Islands government offered to import industrial wastes from the Taiwan Power Company in exchange for financial remuneration. Under the proposal, the wastes were to be dumped on the island of Makira. This attracted widespread criticism from within the Solomons as well as from the international community (*Pacific Islands Report* 2002a). Although the proposal was later abandoned, it demonstrated that the Solomon Islands government was willing to please Taiwan in exchange for financial support.

Such criticisms about Taiwan and the way in which it disperses its assistance to the Solomon Islands are not unusual, and it could be that Taiwanese funding does influence domestic politics. Although I have no direct evidence to prove that Solomon Islands politicians were paid by Taiwan to make particular kinds of decisions, it is not far-fetched to assume that in the face of China's growing power, Taiwan will do as much as possible to ensure that the Solomon Islands stays on its side. There is, after all, a real possibility that the Solomon Islands could switch sides if Taiwanese assistance was not forthcoming. In October 2000, for example, Minister of Foreign Affairs Danny Philip, frustrated by Taiwan's reluctance to provide a financial aid package worth around US$60 million, canceled a scheduled trip to Taiwan for its National Day celebrations. He then traveled to Hong

Kong, where he met with Chinese officials to discuss a financial deal. China's Foreign Minister Tang Jiaxuan told Philip by phone that it was necessary for the country to accept the "One China" policy—and dump Taiwan—before the country was eligible to receive cash from China (Chu 2000). Although the Solomon Islands government later revealed that its ties with Taiwan were "intact," this incident shows that Honiara could easily break the connection if and when Taipei does not provide the appropriate assistance.

Conclusions

Taiwan is an important donor for the Solomon Islands, and is likely to continue to be so. On the other hand, the Solomon Islands is an important ally for Taiwan, all the more so because of the rise of China and its assertive presence in the region. Because of the perceived threat of China, Taiwan is likely to do all within its power to maintain and strengthen its relationship with Pacific Islands allies, including the Solomon Islands. It is also likely to become more strategic in its assistance, targeting areas that ensure the continuation of diplomatic recognition. This could mean patronizing particular politicians and providing cash donations, with little concern about the long-term consequences for national development goals. Despite the millions of dollars donated by Taiwan (and other donors, for that matter) there is little tangible impact in terms of improvement in the lives of the ordinary people of the Solomon Islands. This raises questions about whether Taiwanese assistance holds potential for long-term positive impacts.

Taiwanese assistance is likely to enhance the ability of sitting members of Parliament to strengthen their positions. This could be regarded as a positive outcome, although it might not necessarily mean better governance. If it enables corrupt and inefficient leaders to maintain their positions of power, then it might engender discontent in the society at large and even provoke violent social uprisings.

The Solomon Islands experience also shows that while trade and investment were identified as major factors in the initial decision to establish diplomatic ties with Taiwan rather than China, these have not been prominent features of the relationship over the years. Instead, China has become an important trade partner and is likely to become more important in the future because of its growing market and potential for investing in the Solomon Islands, especially in natural resource extraction. Although it would make more economic sense to have diplomatic relations with China, it is not necessarily economics that determines foreign policy, at least in the short term. The current situation is mutually beneficial politically for both Taiwan and the Solomon Islands.

However, economic interests do have the potential to change policies and political structures over the longer term. Pressure from the business sector in the

Solomon Islands could possibly lead to a change in allegiance from Taipei to Beijing, although trade links with China already exist and could develop further without formal recognition. If the Solomon Islands were to recognize the One China policy that Beijing espouses, then the Chinese authorities would need to learn to build and maintain the patron-client relations that have proved so important in the relationship with Taiwan.

For the Pacific Islands region as a whole, China's assertive presence does give rise to security concerns, especially for metropolitan countries like Australia and New Zealand. These concerns center on issues of drug and people smuggling, which have more to do with Chinese criminal organizations' ability to expand than with state polices in China. Further, strategic concerns have little to do with state-sponsored military security issues. It is unlikely that any Taiwan-China military standoff in the Taiwan Strait will play out in the Pacific Islands region. I do not think that China's assertive presence in the region poses as much of a military threat as we are sometimes led to believe. On the other hand, China's growing presence in the region could represent a positive development. It could provide more economic opportunities and give Pacific Island countries the opportunity to milk two dragons rather than just one—that is, provided they can avoid the danger of being milked by two dragons rather than one.

Notes

I am thankful to Donald Kiriau for his assistance in collecting data, and to Dr. Peter Larmour, Prof. Robert Kiste, and the late Prof. Ron Crocombe for reading and commenting on an earlier draft of the chapter. The chapter is, however, mine, and I take responsibility for the contents and any errors or misrepresentations.

1. The Pacific Island countries that have diplomatic relation with China are Fiji, Papua New Guinea, Tonga, Samoa, the Cook Islands, Vanuatu, and the Federated States of Micronesia. Those with diplomatic relation with Taiwan are the Solomon Islands, Palau, the Marshall Islands, Tuvalu, Nauru, and Kiribati.

2. Here, the term "communists" or "communism" was used loosely for any country that did not share the West's belief in neoliberal democracy or capitalism.

3. It is fair to note, however, that much of Australian aid is "boomerang aid" and probably goes back to Australia through Australian companies, consultants, advisors, etc. Taiwanese aid goes almost totally to Solomon Islanders through projects and the Rural Constituency Development Fund. It might not be distributed equally, but it does not go back to its country of origin in the same way that Australian aid does.

References

Callick, Rowan. 2007. "Chinese Mine Treating PNG Workers Like Slaves." *The Australian,* 9 February, 5.

Chu, Monique. 2000. "Islands' Investment Conference Draws Lukewarm Response." *Taipei Times,* 22 November, 3. Accessed 22 April 2007 at http://www.taipeitimes .com/News/local/archives/2000/11/22/62492.

Elliot, Michael. 2007. "China Takes on the World." *Time Magazine,* 11 January. Accessed 10 April 2007 at http://www.time.com/time/printout/0,8816,1576831,100.html.

Field, Michael. 2005. "Games of Chess: China's Intriguing Moves." *Islands Business,* May.

Government Monthly. 1983a. "Chinese Consul General in Solomons." *Government Monthly,* August, 9.

————. 1983b. "China Refuses Diplomatic Ties with Solomon Islands." *Government Monthly,* September, 10.

————. 1983c. "Solomon Islands Delegation Returns from China." *Government Monthly,* September, 5.

————. 1983d. "China Disturbed by Solomon Island Taiwan Diplomatic Relation." *Government Monthly,* October, 2.

————. 1983e. "SI Govt. Does Not Want Communism—PM." *Government Monthly,* October, 2.

Griffiths, Dan. 2006. "Big Business Brings Beijing to Africa." *BBC News,* 23 April. Accessed 28 April 2007 at http://news.bbc.co.uk/2/hi/africa/4931668.stm.

Henderson, John, and Benjamin Reilly. 2003. "Dragon in Paradise: China's Rising Star in Oceania." *The National Interest,* no. 72 (summer): 94–104.

Monthly Magazine. 1982a. "Relations with China Nearer." *Solomon Islands Government Monthly Magazine* 1 (4), 30 April, 1.

————. 1982b. "Minister Impressed with Taiwanese Trade Exhibition held in Honiara." *Solomon Islands Government Monthly Magazine* 1 (7), 31 July, 4.

————.1983. "SI Recognises Mainland China as Legitimate Gov't." *Solomon Islands Government Monthly Magazine* 1 (16), 30 April, 4.

Pacific Islands Report. 2002a. "Desperate Solomon Islands Under Pressure to Become a Waste Dump." *Pacific Islands Report,* 7 May. Accessed 21 April 2007 at http://archives .pireport.org/archive/2002/may/05-08-01.htm.

————. 2002b. "Solomon Islands Leader Appeals to Aid Community: Be Like Our Asian Friends." *Pacific Islands Report,* 11 October. Accessed 21 April 2007 at http:// archives.pireport.org/archive/2002/october/10-14-03.

People First Network. 2006a. "Taiwan Announces Multi-Million Dollar Education Finding for Solomons." *People First Network,* 19 July. Accessed 21 April 2007 at http:// www.peoplefirst.net.sb/news/News.asp?IDnews=6747.

————. 2006b. "Taiwan Paid Millennium Fund." *People First Network,* 30 November. Accessed 21 April 2007 at http://www.peoplefirst.net.sb/news/News.asp?IDnews=7302.

————. 2007. "Taiwan Releases Multi-Million Dollar Funding for Solomon Islands Education." *People First Network,* 6 March. Accessed 21 April 2007 at http://www .peoplefirst.net.sb/news/News.asp?IDnews=7581.

Radio New Zealand. 2004. "Fiji Police Charge Chinese National with Murder of Recent Immigrant." 28 June. Accessed 27 April 2007 at http://www.rnzi.com/pages/news .php?op=read&id=10718.

Reuters News Agency. 2007. "PNG Seeks Talks with China Firm over Nickel Mine. 14 February.

Skehan, Craig. 2005. "Chinese Gangs in Pacific Real Regional Threat." *Pacific Islands Report*, 21 February. Accessed on 18 August 2009 at http://archives.pireport.org/archive/2005/february/02-2-12.htm

Solomon Star. 1983a. "Solomon Islands Looks to Southeast Asia." 7 January.

———. 1983b. "Taiwan to Help S.I.—Lulei." 8 April, 5.

———. 1983c. "China Surprises at the SI-Taiwan Relations." 8 April, 5.

———. 1983d. "China Not in Favour of SI-Taiwan Ties." 23 October, 10.

———. 2005. "Taiwan's Most Loyal Ally in the Pacific." 1 February, 7.

———. 2006a. "Taiwan Denied Bribery Claims." 13 March.

———. 2006b. "Donors Accused of Interference." 15 March.

———. 2006c. "PM Refutes Tuhanuku's Claims." 25 March.

———. 2006d. "Sanga Replies to PM." 26 March.

SIBC. 2007. "Taiwan Provides Funds for Housing Project. *Solomon Islands Broadcasting Corporation*, 24 March. Accessed 22 April 2007 at http://www.sibconline.com.sb/story.asp?IDThread=149&IDNews=18481.

Storey, Donovan. 2004. *The Fiji Garment Industry.* Auckland: Oxfam New Zealand.

Tuhanuku, Joses. 2006. "Taiwan Funds Fill Solomons Ministers' Pockets." *Solomon Star,* 21 March.

Wen, Jiabao. 2006. "Win-Win Cooperation for Common Development." Keynote speech, China–Pacific Island Countries Economic Development and Cooperation Forum, Nadi, Fiji, 5 April. Accessed 30 March 2007 at http://news.xinhuanet.com/english/2006-04/05/content_4385969.htm.

Windybank, Sue. 2006. "China's Pacific Strategy: The Changing Geopolitics of Australia's 'Special Patch.'" Paper presented on 12 October. Accessed 24 March 2007 at http://www.cis.org.au/exechigh/EH2006/EH39306.htm.

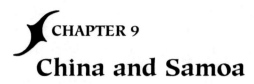

CHAPTER 9

China and Samoa

Iati Iati

Introduction

The only clue to the identity of the occupant of an unnamed grave in Samoa are four Chinese characters on the tombstone that literally translate as "dragon, came, thousand, miles." Alternatively, these may be read as "the dragon came from afar" (Tom 1986). The grave belongs to one of the many Chinese indentured laborers who came to Samoa during the early part of the twentieth century. The inscription was obviously intended to be descriptive, but it could also be seen as quite prophetic. Approximately eighty years after Chinese people first crossed the Pacific to Samoa, a new bridge was built when China and Samoa established diplomatic relations in 1975. The aim of this chapter is to try to understand the reasons for and the implications of this relationship for Samoa.

There can be no doubt that China's presence and influence are rapidly increasing in the Pacific Islands region. Although accurate statistics about China's economic activity in the region are difficult to find, the available information indicates dramatic increases in both trade and aid. More obvious signs are China-funded infrastructural developments, including the construction of sporting complexes and government buildings in a number of Pacific Island countries. The academic and media communities in Australia and New Zealand have responded very critically to this growing presence (Henderson and Reilly 2003; Windybank 2006; Feizkhah 2001). They express unease about the situation, asserting that the primary reason behind China's presence is self-interest, and that the interests of the region are secondary. It is often argued that Beijing is simply recruiting allies to support its One China policy or, as a corollary, countering Taiwan's attempts to gain recognition (Feizkhah 2001). Another popular argument is that China is seeking to usurp the place of the United States as the dominant power in the region, or that its regional pursuits are part of a larger challenge to Washington's global social, economic, and diplomatic hegemony.

These observers tend to describe China's increasing regional presence and influence in negative terms. Some argue, for example, that the China-Taiwan rivalry will exacerbate regional tensions and conflicts, while others worry because China is not part of the Western alliance of states promoting ideals of good governance and democracy. These responses are predicated on the assumption that Pacific Island states are weak and not in control of their foreign relations with powerful countries. In the context of a region seen to be unstable and riddled with corruption, weak democracies, struggling economies, and tendencies toward violence and conflict, Pacific nations are regarded as "vulnerable to manipulation" (Windybank 2006). China is assumed to be exploiting this vulnerability. Overall, China's involvement in the region, and particularly its rivalry with Taiwan, is regarded as compounding existing problems, tensions, and conflicts.

These perspectives are affirmed to some extent in the China-Samoa case, for example in the way that China has increased its presence in the post–cold war period and deployed its aid, as well as in the obvious importance of the One China policy. At the same time, a number of important aspects of the China-Samoa relationship, such as the pursuit of self-interest by Pacific Island countries and the impact of internal political dynamics on foreign relations, are neglected or obscured in conventional accounts.

China-Samoa Relations

China and Samoa established formal ties in 1975 with the signing of the Joint Communiqué on the Establishment of Diplomatic Relations, which came into effect on 6 November of that year.[1] Samoa was the second Pacific Island state to establish such an agreement, making its diplomatic relationship with China one of the longest-running in the region.[2]

One of the key factors affecting Samoa's decision to enter into this relationship was the attitude of the political leadership. When Samoa gained independence in 1962, the national government, and the prime minister in particular, took a very cautious approach to international relations. Malama Meleisea and Penelope Schoeffel (1979: 92) describe the government's overall approach as "to make haste slowly." In international affairs, this translated into a watered-down form of isolationism.[3] It was reflected in the fact that Samoa waited fourteen years after independence before seeking to join the United Nations. According to Meleisea and Schoeffel, at the time the Samoan government was uncertain about whether the benefits would outweigh the costs (Meleisea and Schoeffel 1979: 93). This cautious approach to international relations prevailed in Samoa until 1976.

A change in prime minister brought about a change in Samoa's foreign policy approach. In 1976, Tupuola Efi was elected prime minister and wasted little time in making his intentions clear. The government took the necessary steps to admit Samoa to the United Nations, which was accomplished in December 1976. Also in that year, Samoa hosted a group of officials from the Soviet Union at the independence celebrations. This new approach to international relations helped bring Samoa into a relationship with China. What motivated China is uncertain, although it is worth noting that there was some tension between China and the USSR during this period and China was attempting to limit Soviet influence. It is conceivable that Samoa's overtures toward the USSR might have been a factor in China's decision to establish a formal relationship with Apia. Given that China and Fiji established their diplomatic ties two days earlier, it might also have been part of China's larger Pacific policy.

The new international attitude of the political leadership was not the sole factor influencing Samoa's decision to enter into this relationship. Arguably, the government also wanted to attract the attention of other influential regional powers. According to Meleisea and Schoeffel (1979: 100), the hosting of the Russian delegation and the establishment of diplomatic ties with China can be interpreted as "a nudge in the ribs of the two leading metropolitan powers in the South Pacific, Australia and New Zealand. The message appeared to be that while Samoa was small and weak it was capable of finding large strong friends, if Western Samoa was overlooked by these two leading powers." If this was Samoa's strategy, it met with swift success. China opened an embassy in Apia, which at the time was the only diplomatic mission in Samoa besides that of New Zealand. Shortly after this Australia and the United States also established direct representation (Meleisea and Schoeffel 1979: 100).[4]

During the cold war period, the relationship between China and Samoa might be characterized as one of strengthening social and cultural ties. Much of the interaction during this period involved social, cultural, and educational exchanges, and the provision of medical assistance by China. In 1981, for example, the Chinese People's Association for Friendship with Foreign Countries visited Samoa. In 1982 China started awarding two scholarships per year for Samoan students to study in China, and the number has since risen. In 1983, a Chinese women's delegation visited, followed a year later by a Chinese cultural study group. In 1984, China sent two teachers to Samoa, and nine Chinese medical teams have worked in Samoa since 1986 (*Samoa Observer* 2002). In June 1987, China sent an acrobatic troupe to attend the celebrations of the twenty-fifth anniversary of Samoa's independence. These exchanges and forms of assistance continued into the post–cold war period.

The post–cold war period also witnessed an upsurge in diplomatic activity. In addition to the 1975 communiqué, Samoa and China have signed a number of agreements. They are not all strictly bilateral; some have been signed as part of multilateral agreements between China and members of the Pacific Island Forum. The bilateral agreements usually relate to matters of financial assistance from China, and it is interesting to note that all but one of these agreements, which are at least six in number, were signed after 1989.[5]

The year 1989 marked the end of the cold war, which in turn diminished the strategic value of the Pacific for the United States and other Western powers. China certainly increased its presence and influence in Samoa after 1989. However, if China was filling a gap left by the United States and its allies, it was doing so with some prompting from the Samoan government. Samoan Prime Minister Tofilau Eti was one of the first foreign leaders to visit China after the infamous Tiananmen Square protests in 1989. China quickly rewarded Samoa with a US$12 million grant for a new government building, and it has been suggested that this was something that Tofilau anticipated might happen (*New Internationalist* 1991).

Many diplomatic exchanges have taken place between China and Samoa since the end of the cold war. The website of the Ministry of Foreign Affairs of the People's Republic of China lists the people considered to be the "main Samoan personnel" to have visited China, including the Samoan head of state, prime minister, and various government ministers. According to this list, there have been twenty-three visits since 1976, twenty of them made during or after 1989 (MFAPRC 2003b). The same website also lists the number of "main Chinese personnel who have visited Samoa," which totals fourteen. The pattern is similar, with twelve of these personnel visiting after 1989.

Samoa's engagement with China has not been limited to the central government. In 1996, Samoa and the Hong Kong Special Administrative Region of China signed a mutual exemption of visas agreement, which allows Samoans who travel to Hong Kong to stay for thirty days without having to obtain a visa. The agreement provides similar privileges to those traveling from Hong Kong to Samoa. A similar agreement was signed in 2000 between Samoa and the Macao Special Administrative Region of the People's Republic of China.

Trade has grown quite dramatically since China and Samoa established a Trade Agreement in 1997. In 2002, the trade volume between the two countries was US$2.788 million, which represented a 20 percent increase from the trade volume in the previous year (MFAPRC 2003a). In 2006, the trade volume was US$13 million, a 117 percent increase from 2005 (Xinhua News Agency 2007). Although both countries have helped facilitate the increased trade, China has invested considerable money into encouraging trade with all of its Pacific allies, including Samoa.

The agreements signed by the two countries play an important role in establishing and affirming each country's expectations and responsibilities. They often serve as reference points during discussions between representatives of each country—reminders of both the foundations of the relationship and the base from which new directions can be charted. When Premier Wen Jiabao met with Prime Minister Tuilaepa Malielegaoi in 2005, for example, both reaffirmed their countries' strict adherence to the 1975 Joint Communiqué between China and Samoa and expressed their belief that it would serve as a foundation and driving force for further cooperation between the two governments (MFPRC 2005c). The meeting led to the adoption of a joint declaration between the two countries.

A year later, at a meeting with Tuilaepa, Chinese Foreign Minister Li Zhaoxing said that the "joint declaration issued by the two countries last year has charted the direction for long-term and stable development of Sino-Samoan relations in the new century" (China 2006).

The diplomatic exchanges help to strengthen the ties between the countries by reaffirming the terms of relationship and making adjustments to improve it. In a speech at the opening of the First Ministerial Conference of the China–Pacific Island Countries Economic Development and Cooperation Forum in April 2006, Premier Wen Jiabao said that the purpose of regular exchanges between governments, parliaments, political parties, and nongovernmental sectors was

> to enhance mutual trust and understanding; strengthen consultation and coordination on major international and regional issues; accommodate each other's interests and reinforce mutual support; and establish a new economic and trade relationship of mutual benefit that meets the needs of the island countries. (Wen 2006. See Appendix for full statement.)

During meetings between diplomatic officials from both countries, one subject is always discussed, or at least mentioned: the One China policy. Normally China reiterates its gratitude to Samoa for adhering to the One China policy, and Samoa responds by affirming its support of it. It is an indication of what is, ultimately, central to their relationship (MFAPRC 2005b). In a September 2007 interview, the secretary to the Chinese ambassador to Samoa, Mr. Wong, stressed that China was highly appreciative of the fact that Samoa had never wavered in its support of the One China policy (Interview, 20 September 2007).

Even exchanges involving nongovernment personnel have a positive effective on the relationship between the two countries. In 2003, Samoan journalist Terry Tavita visited China as part of a cultural exchange program. His editorial about his experiences, published in the *Samoan Observer*, the most widely disseminated privately owned newspaper in Samoa, was full of praise for China and its people. Tavita told of how he was greatly impressed by the achievements of the country, signified by its massive structures, none more so than the Great Wall of China. He associated these with the character of the Chinese people, which he noted was significantly different from how they are often stereotyped in Samoa: "Here in Samoa, the mention of 'Chinese' conjures up many stereotypes, some not very savory. They range from good business acumen to downright exploitive and sharkish money grabbing.... The average Chinese character, I found, is intelligent, laborious, peaceful and modest" (Tavita 2003, 4).

In addition to portraying a positive image of Chinese, Tavita highlighted the similarities between Samoans and Chinese. He noted in particular similarities regarding two fundamental characteristics of Samoan society: prioritizing the needs of the family over the individual, and being subservient and respectful to parents.[6] He stated: "Chinese remain loyal to their families and obey their parents. In fact, he said, they pay more attention to their parents than themselves" (Tavita 2003, 4). If Samoans held any inhibitions about Chinese migrating to their country, this article might have worked to allay them. While the editorial does not tell us how others have reacted to these exchanges, it certainly indicates the kind of outcomes that can be achieved.

This kind of response must also be understood in a historical context. Since arriving as indentured laborers during the late nineteenth and early twentieth centuries, the Chinese have woven themselves into the social, economic, and political fabric of Samoan life. Chinese cuisine has been incorporated into the Samoan diet, and a number of these dishes are now considered Samoan staple food items, particularly on special occasions. Many of the most prominent businesspeople in Samoa are descendants of early Chinese migrants, and many continue to carry the surname of these migrants. Similarly, a number of high-level government employees and even government ministers can trace their ancestry to these early migrants. Arguably, these ties have created a cultural milieu receptive to the idea of having more Chinese come to Samoa.

China–Taiwan Rivalry and Samoa

The rivalry between China and Taiwan is not a significant factor in Samoan politics. It is not unreasonable to think that the possibility of approaches from Taiwan provides an incentive for China to maintain a strong relationship with Samoa. Furthermore, in talking with government and nongovernment workers one senses that the Samoan government is firmly committed to its relationship with China. But while this may be the government position, it would be wrong to assume that people in general support this policy. An indication of how Taiwan might exert its influence emerged in the mid 1990s when traditional Samoan leaders led nationwide protests against the national government. The government accused Taiwan of providing funding to this movement. Nothing was ever proven, and Taiwan denied any involvement. However, it seems unlikely that the Samoan government would make such a bold accusation without reason.

Samoa seems to have responded to the China-Taiwan rivalry by putting all its eggs into the China basket, probably with very good reason. In a candid conversation, a former government employee expressed his belief that China would eventually emerge victorious from the China-Taiwan conflict. He also believed that this was the view of the Samoan government. Unlike many other Pacific Island countries, Samoa has never wavered in its support of China. Under these circumstances, it would be safe to say that the China-Taiwan rivalry is unlikely to have significant implications for Samoa.

China and Samoa's Traditional Benefactors

The rivalry between China and Samoa's traditional benefactors, on the other hand, may have significant implications for Samoan politics. Samoa's main aid and trade partners are Australia, Japan, New Zealand, and the United States, and it has also received considerable financial assistance from multilateral development organizations such as the Asian Development Bank, United Nations Development Program (UNDP), and the World Bank. All these donors share one characteristic: they are all part of or associated with the Western alliance of states that has traditionally been the dominant outside force in the Pacific region.

While the trend elsewhere in the Pacific in the post–cold war period might have been a general downgrading of the presence of these countries (Reilly 2001), this was not the case in Samoa. The level of financial assistance to Samoa from its traditional benefactors either stayed the same or increased. During the early to mid 1990s, Japan's financial assistance remained fairly constant (Japan 1999). In 1999, Australia increased its aid to Samoa by 6.8 percent, to US\$9.3 million (PACNEWS 1999). A 2006 report by the United Nations Conference on Trade and Development on Samoa states: "Over the last two decades, there has been little sign of a declining or erratic trend in aid flows, and the donor structure has been relatively stable" (UNCTAD 2006: 18). While the decline of donor attention may have given China more opportunity to increase its influence in the other parts of the region, this factor does not account for its growing presence in Samoa.

Like many developing countries, Samoa is dependent on aid. It is understandable, therefore, that Samoa welcomes aid from China. But there is another factor that makes Chinese aid appealing: it does not come with a set of impositions and conditions about governance in Samoa. This is different from the way that aid from Western donor countries is normally dispersed. Since the early 1990s, countries in the Western alliance have actively promoted a set of principles and policies that they consider necessary to improve governance. The good governance agenda has been promoted in conjunction with organizations like the UNDP, World Bank, Asian Development Bank, and Pacific Islands Forum. Countries like Australia and New Zealand channel much of their aid into programs designed to improve governance, and they also insist that recipient countries implement good governance policies (NZAID 2006: 9; *Pacific Beat* 2006). These conditions continue to be applied to Samoa.

Samoa has responded positively to these demands, and in 1996 the government embarked on a reform program based largely on the good governance agenda. Its policies were designed to create a sustainable economic base by strengthening the private sector and limiting the influence of the government in the economy. The policies were so well aligned with the good governance agenda that AUSAID identified Samoa as the standard for other developing countries (AUSAID 2001, 11). This is one of the reasons why the level of aid to Samoa from Western donors, particularly Australia, increased during the post–cold war period. According to the Australian High Commission in Samoa, "The much larger increase in funding for Samoa than other island countries reflects our belief that the government is committed to building a sustainable economic base in Samoa" (PACNEWS 1999). Currently, Australia is Samoa's largest aid donor, contributing approximately 30 percent of its total aid (Australia 2007). However, this does not mean that Samoa welcomes being told by donors what to do in its domestic affairs.

The government of Samoa has not openly criticized Western aid donors about aid conditionality. However, it is probably fair to say that it does not want its destiny determined by outside powers. It would be surprising if a country that spent most of the twentieth century fighting for independence, sovereignty, and the right to self-determination would suddenly decide to give these up (Davidson 1967; Meleisea 1987). Although China does not give as much aid as Samoa's traditional donors, the fact that these funds do not come attached to the conditions imposed by many Western aid donors must certainly be welcome.

This is not the only appeal of Chinese aid. Beijing's aid is also channeled into projects that are much more visible than those funded by other countries, except perhaps Japan. Chinese aid has gone toward the erection of the government building that stands in the center of the main urban area, the building of the new sports complex for the 2007 South Pacific games, upgrades to the national rugby stadium, and improvements in the road systems around urban areas. It is also being used to fund the construction of a new building for the Land and Titles Court, and will soon be channeled into the construction of another government building.

Recently, I held discussions with a number of people in Samoa about infrastructural improvements in the country. In each case, the improvements were credited to the Samoan government and China. In no case was Australia or New Zealand mentioned in the context of positive developments for Samoa. During one discussion with a high-profile lawyer in Apia, I was told that China's assistance to Samoa was highly valued, in contrast to assistance from Australia and New Zealand, which the lawyer argued was hardly visible. I asked his opinion of the critiques emanating from Australia and New Zealand regarding the absence of good governance conditions in China's aid. He was highly critical of these views, noting that although Australia and New Zealand had much longer affiliations with Samoa, China's assistance was felt to be much more significant. He went on to express considerable resentment of Australian and New Zealand assistance, contending that it has only been upgraded in response to the greater interest being shown by China (Interviews conducted between September 15 and 20, 2007 Apia, Samoa).

These comments, which are not dissimilar to those of other discussants, highlight at least one important point: the visibility of China's aid works quite effectively to promote its image as a benefactor to Samoa. The question is whether this is a strategic ploy or reflects other motives. In my interview with Mr. Wong from the Chinese embassy, I asked him this question. He answered that the projects China funds are undertaken in response to requests from the Samoan government. The construction of the new sports complex and government buildings, for example, were initiated by the Samoan government, not China. This presents a different perspective on the idea of Chinese aid being strategically deployed. The way it has been deployed certainly raises China's profile, but this could well be because China is responding to the needs of the recipient countries, rather than trying to impose its own development plans, as Australia and New Zealand are seen to be doing.

During the interviews, significant concern was expressed about what China might expect in return for its assistance. People often commented that nothing is free, and China's assistance may one day come at a cost that Samoa will not be able to meet. Particular reference was made to the possibility that land in Samoa might someday become involved. I asked Mr. Wong whether China might, in the future, seek to claim assets in a recipient country if loans could not be repaid. He pointed to the fact that in 2006 China forgave the debts of its Pacific allies. Samoa's debt had been approximately US$11.5 million (Xinhua News Agency 2006) and noted that if China intended to accrue assets from recipients for unpaid loans, it would not have canceled their debts. Mr. Wong's response seems credible, and the fear that Chinese might take over Samoan land may be unfounded.

Mr. Wong also stressed that China's intentions are simply to help a country that it considers an ally and a friend. He noted that China's overall aim is to create an international environment that is stable and secure, and establishing a strong network of allies and friends contributes to that goal. Moreover, he implied that China is not motivated simply by charity but also by self-interest, noting that China requires this kind of environment for its growing economy. The discussants' concerns reveal that Samoans are keenly aware of the potential threats that even a beneficent donor poses, and are not simply blinded by extravagant treatment. Moreover, it suggests that China's intentions are not as secretive as some appear to think.

Much of the apprehension about China's presence is based on the perceived internal weaknesses of Pacific Island countries, which would seem to leave them susceptible to exploitation. What is not often acknowledged is the fact that these countries have highly complex political systems that would make exploitation extremely difficult. Samoa, for example, has a dual political system where political power is divided between central and local governments (Va'a 2000: 165). The authority of both is guaranteed by the constitution, and other legislation ensures that local governments have all the authority associated with their traditions and customs. Whereas this division of authority and power makes political decision-making for the country as a whole extremely difficult (Sagapolutele 2000; Lesa

2000), it also erects considerable barriers to foreign powers seeking political influence. The idea that these islands are exceedingly vulnerable to outside manipulation needs to be rethought.

Conclusion

Much of the academic and media discourse about China's increasing Pacific presence is highly critical of recent developments. But is this justified? After all, much of the criticism appears to be mere speculation, and the only sure motive for China's presence concerns the One China policy. To be sure, China's growing presence and influence may reduce the influence of Western powers in the region, particularly Australia and the United States. But why should this be regarded as problematic, given that there is a feeling that the islands have been neglected by their traditional allies? Moreover, China's increasing presence in the region has provided considerable infrastructural development and boosted resources and skills within many Pacific Island countries. Of course, China's rising influence does mean that the hegemonic status of the region's former benefactors is being undermined. The critical assessments coming out of Australia and New Zealand are to be expected, but there is no reason to expect that these views will be shared in the islands themselves.

The usual reservations about China's presence do not seem to be reflected in Samoa's foreign policy relations with China, nor widely shared by the general population. Instead, China's claim of being a friend and ally seem to hold a much more integral place within the Samoan psyche. It is obvious why this is the case. In terms of infrastructure, Samoa has reaped considerable benefits from Chinese assistance, and China has also assisted in other very meaningful ways. Furthermore, any reservations about what China's intentions are—in particular about whether it is building up credit in support of future demands—can be allayed by its actions thus far. The cancellation of Samoa's hefty debt is a prominent sign that Beijing does not intend to hold Samoa to ransom for any of its assets. Still, the old saying that nothing is free is not without merit. Although at the moment it seems that all that Beijing wants is loyalty to its One China policy, foreign policy is susceptible to change. China has built up considerable goodwill, and perhaps even a moral debt, that it may seek to cash in sometime in the future.

Notes

1. The agreement was signed by Pei Tsien-chang, Representative of the Government of the People's Republic of China, and Tupua Tamasese Leaofi IV, Prime Minister and Minister of External Affairs of Western Samoa.
2. Fiji apparently established diplomatic relations with China two days before Samoa

(MFAPRC 2005b). However, there is some confusion on this matter. According to at least one scholarly article, and to the Chairman of the Standing Committee of the National People's Congress Wu Bangguo in 2005, Samoa was actually the first Pacific Island country to establish diplomatic relations with Beijing (MFAPRC 2005a).

3. Meleisea and Schoeffel refer to Samoa's international approach as "isolationism," but I would not go that far. After all, it still maintained close connections with New Zealand, with whom it signed the Treaty of Friendship in 1962, joined the Commonwealth of Nations in 1970, and encouraged the United Nations Development Program to establish its Pacific Regional headquarters in Apia in the early 1970s. Although Samoa did significantly restrict the extent to which it engaged the international community, it did not withdraw completely.

4. The United States closed its embassy in Samoa in 2001.

5. Agreements were signed in 1976, 1989, 1992, 1995, 1999, 2000, and 2007.

6. Within Samoan society, utmost respect is given to parents. It is a fundamental duty of children to obey and take care of their parents until they die. The family is also prioritized over the individual. The *aiga* (family) is the key group within Samoan social organization.

References

AUSAID. 2001. "Samoa Sets the Standard for Stability." *Focus,* June. Canberra: Australian Agency for International Aid and Development: 11–12.

Australia. 2007. *Samoa Country Brief.* Canberra: Australian Government, Department of Foreign Affairs and Trade. Accessed 14 December 2006 at http://www.dfat.gov.au/geo/samoa/samoa_brief.html.

China. 2006. "Chinese PM, Samoan PM Meet on Ties." Chinese Government's Official Web Portal, 1 August. Accessed 23 January 2007 at http://www.gov.cn/english//2006-08/01/content_351727.htm.

Davidson, J. W. 1967. *Samoa mo Samoa: The Emergence of the Independent State of Western Samoa.* Melbourne: Oxford University Press.

Feizkhiah, Elizabeth. 2001. "How to Win Friends: Beijing Is Courting Tiny Pacific Nations." *Time Pacific,* no. 22, 4 June: 34.

Henderson, John, and Benjamin Reilly. 2003. "Dragon in Paradise." *National Interest,* no. 72, (summer): 94-104.

Japan. 1999. *Japan's Official Development Assistance Annual Report.* Tokyo: Government of Japan, Ministry of Foreign Affairs of Japan. Accessed 18 August 2009 at http://www.mofa.go.jp/policy/oda/summary/1999/index.html.

Lesa, Keni Ramese. 2000. "Samoa Court Orders Bible Study Group to Leave Village." *Samoa Observer,* 14 September, 1.

Meleisea, Malama. 1987. *The Making of Modern Samoa: Traditional Authority and Colonial Administration in the Modern History of Western Samoa.* Suva: Institute of Pacific Studies, University of the South Pacific.

Meleisea, Malama, and Penelope Schoeffel. 1979. "Western Samoa: 'Like a slippery fish.'" In *Politics in Polynesia,* ed. Ron Crocombe et al., 81–115. Suva: Institute of Pacific Studies, University of the South Pacific.

MFAPRC (Ministry of Foreign Affairs of the People's Republic of China). 2003a. "Bilateral Relations between Samoa and China." 9 December. Accessed 5 April 2007 at http://www.fmprc.gov.cn/eng/wjb/zzjg/bmdyzs/gjlb/3422/default.htm.

———. 2003b. "Samoa: Bilateral Political Relations." 9 December. Accessed 6 April 2007 at http://www.fmprc.gov.cn/eng/wjb/zzjg/bmdyzs/gjlb/3422.

———. 2005a. "Chairman Wu Bangguo Meets with Samoan Prime Minister Tuilaepa." 10 May. Accessed 5 April 2007 at http://www.fmprc.gov.cn/eng/zxxx/t195428.htm.

———. 2005b. "Joint Communiqué of the Government of the People's Republic of China and the Government of Fiji on the Establishment of Diplomatic Relations between China and Fiji." Accessed 5 April 2007 at http://www.fmprc.gov.cn/eng/wjb/zzjg/bmdyzs/gjlb/3392/3393/t17053.htm.

———. 2005c. "Joint Statement between the Government of the People's Republic of China and the Government of the Independent State of Samoa." 9 May. Accessed 17 April 2007 at http://www.fmprc.gov.cn/eng/wjdt/2649/t194788.htm.

New Internationalist. 1991. "Western Samoa: Country Profile." no. 222, August. Accessed 18 August 2009 at http://www.newint.org/issue222/profile.htm.

NZAID. 2006. *NZAID Annual Review 2005/06—Pacific Regional Programme.* Wellington: New Zealand International Aid and Development Agency.

Pacific Beat. 2006. "Australia: Concern about Pacific Aid Conditions." Interview with Karen Iles of the Aid Watch Organization and Teresa Gambaro, Parliamentary Secretary to the Australian Minister for Foreign Affairs, 17 October.

PACNEWS. 1999. "Samoa Receives Increased Australian Aid." 17 May. Accessed 18 August 2009 at *Pacific Islands Report* http://archives.pireport.org/archive/1999/may/05%2D18%2D08.html.

Reilly, Benjamin. 2001. "Island of Neglect: Trouble in Paradise." *Asian Wall Street Journal,* 4 May. Accessed 18 August 2009 at *Pacific Islands Report* http://archives.pireport.org/archive/2001/may/05%2D07%2D01.htm.

Sagapolutele, Fili. 2000. "Samoa Prison Releases 54 Bible School Students." *Samoa News,* 2 August, 1.

Samoa Observer. 2002. "China Awards Scholarships to Samoans." 24 August, 3.

Tavita, Terry. 2003. "Samoans Could Learn from Chinese." *Samoa Observer,* 16 September.

Tom, Nancy Y. W. 1986. *The Chinese in Western Samoa 1875—1985: The Dragon Came from Afar.* Apia: Western Samoa Historical and Cultural Trust.

UNCTAD. 2006. Vulnerability Profile of Samoa. United Nations Conference on Trade and Development, CDP2006/PLEN/10, March 2006. Accessed 18 August 2009 at http://www.un.org/esa/policy/devplan/profile/vulnerability_profile_samoa.pdf

Va'a, Unasa L. F. 2000. "Local Government in Samoa and the Search for Balance." In *Governance in Samoa: Pulega I Samoa,* ed. Elise Huffer and Asofou So'o. Canberra and Suva: Asia Pacific Press, Australian National University, and Institute of Pacific Studies, University of the South Pacific.

Wen, Jiabao. 2006. Speech at the opening of the First Ministerial Conference of the China-Pacific Island Countries Economic Development and Cooperation Forum, 5 April. Accessed 4 May 2007 at http://english.gov.cn/2006-04/05/content_245681.htm.

Windybank, Susan. 2006. "China's Pacific Strategy: The Changing Geopolitics of Australia's 'Special Patch.'" Lecture to the Victorian branch of the Australian Institute of International Affairs, 12 October. Accessed 14 March 2007 at http://www.cis.org.au/exechigh/EH2006/EH39306.htm

Xinhua News Agency. 2006. "China to Fund New Court Building in Samoa." June 6. Accessed 27 March 2007 at http://www.china.org.cn/english/international/170551.htm.

———. 2007. "Senior Chinese Official Says to Enhance Cooperation with Samoa." 2 April. Accessed 15 September 2007 at *Chinaview.cn*, http://news.xinhuanet.com/english/2007-04/03/content_5930910.htm.

CHAPTER 10

China's Diplomatic Relations with the Kingdom of Tonga

Palenitina Langa`oi

Introduction

Western powers such as Australia, New Zealand, and the United States have warned the Pacific Island states about the corruption they see in the region. These practices include providing flags of convenience for shipping and the sale of passports. Such warnings have been regarded by many island states as an intrusion into their internal affairs (Herr 2007: 2). In trying to control corruption, the Western powers and other aid donors have imposed conditions for the aid that they provide to the Pacific Islands. These conditions include minimum standards of good governance and accountability, as well as more democratic political systems. Pacific Island leaders feel pressured by international expectations as well as by their limited resources, and are considering alternative means of reducing these pressures. As rising regional powers, China and Taiwan have used this situation to gain diplomatic recognition from island states by offering financial assistance with no preconditions attached. For their part, Pacific Island states, including Tonga, welcome these alternative sources of support. However, this situation brings social, political, and economic implications for the island states.

Chinese Migration to the Pacific and Tonga

To understand the current environment, it is important to outline the history of the migration of Chinese to the Pacific Islands and their eventual arrival in the Kingdom of Tonga. There is a long history of contact between China and Oceania; hence the connections between them have deep cultural and historical roots. Some scholars argue that the first settlers in eastern and northern parts of Oceania were part of a wider proto-Austronesian culture, which encompassed a group of languages that had a common origin in Taiwan some 5,000 years ago (Henderson and Reilly 2003). Recent research links the indigenous people of Taiwan to the Polynesian, Micronesian, and Eastern Melanesian peoples of the Pacific.

A more recent and direct link dates from the eighteenth century, when European traders found markets for Pacific Island goods in China. This link expanded during the nineteenth century, when Chinese labor was recruited for work in the Pacific Islands. These laborers were employed in phosphate mines in Nauru; coconut plantations in Samoa, Papua New Guinea, and Fiji; and cotton plantations in French Polynesia. Some of these laborers remained on after their contracts expired, although the number was relatively small (Henderson 2001). As a result, today there are small and usually prominent Chinese communities in most Pacific Island states.

Chinese laborers continue to arrive today, as in the case of Fiji, where Chinese laborers have been brought in to work in the garment industry. Some island residents with Chinese ancestry have become prominent businessmen and political leaders, such as Sir Julius Chan, the former prime minister of Papua New Guinea. Although the Chinese population has never challenged the political dominance of the indigenous people, their success in business has sometimes become a source of resentment. This resentment was apparent in November 2006, when pro-democracy demonstrators rioted in the streets of Nuku'alofa, the capital of Tonga, and many Chinese-owned businesses were burned and looted.

Migration from China to Tonga was noticeable during the 1980s and 1990s when the Tongan government, under the control of the late King Taufa'ahau Tupou IV, made extra money by selling Tongan passports (approximately US$10,000 each or more) to foreigners, mainly Chinese (*BBC News Online* 2001). Many of these new passport holders migrated to Tonga and set up businesses such as restaurants and retail stores. Such sales of Tongan passports caused political controversy in Tonga, and in 1988 the practice was declared unconstitutional and the part of the Nationality Act enabling it was repealed. The problem then was what to do with the foreigners who had paid for citizenship but had not yet been issued naturalization certificates and Tongan passports (James 1998: 8). To resolve this issue, the Tongan government presented three bills in a special session of Parliament to amend the constitution, the Nationality Act, and the Passport Act. In 1991, the king of Tonga gave his consent to amend the constitution and naturalize 426 foreigners to whom passports had been sold. The proceeds from the sale of passports were invested in the Tonga Trust Fund.[1]

In the last two decades, the influx of Chinese to Tonga has continued. This has been further strengthened and encouraged by the diplomatic relations established between Tonga and China in 1998. Before analyzing the factors that influenced the decision to recognize China, it is useful to identify some key demographic and economic characteristics of Tonga, as these have played a critical role in determining Tonga's diplomatic relations with great powers.

Tonga in Brief

The Kingdom of Tonga is an ancient Polynesian state and the only remaining monarchy in the South Pacific. The only country in the South Pacific that has never been formally colonized, it has a constitutional monarchical system. It consists of a group of 170 small islands spread out between latitude 15° and 23° south and longitude 173° and 177° west, which are divided into three main island groups, Tongatapu, Ha'apai, and Vava'u. The last population census, held in 1996, enumerated a total of 97,784 people in the Kingdom. The census also revealed a relatively low net population growth rate of 0.3 percent, a result of high emigration rates to Australia, New Zealand, and the United States of America (Tonga Statistics Department 2006). The economy is open and, as in other small island states, is characterized by a small domestic market, remoteness from larger markets, vulnerability to trade shocks, low levels of economic diversification, a narrow resource base, and scarcity of skilled labor. The economy is heavily dependent on aid and remittances (International Monetary Fund 2001).

Tonga's foreign policy is one of independent "friendship to all," but its practical focus is on the facilitation of foreign development cooperation, including trade. It is a long-standing member of the Commonwealth, the Asian Development Bank, and various UN specialized agencies. Tonga joined the UN in September 1999. It maintains a limited diplomatic presence overseas, with a high commissioner resident in London, an ambassador in Beijing, and a permanent representative at the UN in New York. Tonga also maintains a consulate general in San Francisco, is represented by honorary consul generals in Australia and New Zealand, and has honorary consulates in a number of other countries. It is an active member of the Pacific Islands Forum and the South Pacific Community, as well as other regional organizations such as the South Pacific Regional Environmental Programme, South Pacific Applied Geosciences Commission, and Forum Fisheries Agency. On 27 July 2007, Tonga became the newest and the 151st member of the World Trade Organization.

Tonga's economy is highly dependent on foreign aid and remittances. As stated in the government's latest development plan (Tonga 2006),

> Tonga's long term development achievements can be attributed to the combined impact of the modest domestic economic growth, significant growth in remittances from Tongans working abroad, substantial foreign aid flows... Aid and remittances have been important sources of fairly stable income, offsetting the high vulnerability of the economy to natural disasters, crop diseases and fluctuations in world markets... It was felt that the economy was too dependent on remittances and aid.

In 2004, Australia was the largest single donor, and Australia and New Zealand jointly contributed more than half of the official development assistance received by Tonga (Sodhi 2006). But a new and growing source of funding for Tonga is China. In 1998, Tonga terminated twenty-six years of diplomatic relations with Taiwan and established an embassy in Beijing. The debate is now on between those who are concerned that increased dependency on Chinese aid will facilitate unwanted social, political, and economical influence, and those who are more optimistic about this new relationship.

Following is an analysis of three main factors that may have influenced Tonga's decision to switch its diplomatic relations from Taiwan to China: the personal preferences of key decision makers, external pressures from Western powers, and economic factors such as dependence on foreign aid.

Personal Preferences of Key Decision Makers

Some commentators such as Mahina (2007) and Field (2005) believe that the personal preferences of the key decision makers in Tonga were among the main factors determining the choice to recognize China. Tonga is a constitutional monarchy, and the monarch has traditionally been very conservative and resistant to the democratic changes proposed by the opposition party. According to James (2000), the late King Taufa'ahau Tupou IV, who resisted the pressures of the Tongan pro-democracy movement, was unimpressed by Taiwan's adoption of democracy. As he saw it, governance was "his business," in both senses of the word (Henderson and Reilly 2003: 101). The king considered Taiwan's shift away from authoritarian rule in the 1990s to be a threat to his government, which is likely to have been one of the major reasons why Tonga terminated its diplomatic relations with Taiwan (James 2000).

The business interests of members of the royal family may also have influenced the decision to recognize China. The current king's sister, Princess Pilolevu Tuita, controls the country's only duty-free franchise, an import business, a travel company, Tonga's biggest insurance company, and Tongasat, a company that markets access to Tongan-controlled slots for orbiting satellites (Field 2005). Indeed, the princess's link with Tongasat is viewed by some observers as one major reason for Tonga's recognition of China. According to Professor 'Okusitino Mahina, a Tongan academic at the University of Auckland, the switch from Taiwan to China was initiated by Princess Pilolevu Tuita and sanctioned by her father, the late King Taufa'ahau Tupou IV, specifically to create a larger market for the equatorial satellite slots managed by Tongasat (Interview with Mahina, 2007). The princess has repeatedly denied this allegation, claiming instead that Tonga established relations with Beijing so that Tongan missionaries could spread the message of Christianity in China (Henderson and Reilly 2003: 103; *New Zealand Listener Online* 2005). Nevertheless, in April 2006 the princess negotiated a joint venture between Tongasat and a Chinese satellite company, and talk of launching a satellite into Tongasat's 130° east longitude orbital position continues (*China Daily Online* 2006).[2]

Diplomatic ties were further strengthened by the appointment of Tonga's first ambassador to China, Mrs. 'Emeline Tuita, and the establishment of an embassy in China in July 2004. This occurred after China provided assistance to the Shoreline Electric Company, which at the time was chaired by the then crown prince, who also controlled Tonga's beer company, mobile phone company (Tonfon Ltd), and cable television company, and was also the main beneficiary of sales of Tonga's ".to" Internet domain suffix (*Matangi Tonga Online* 2004).[3] The assistance provided for the Shoreline Electric Company included over T$34 million (US$17 million) in technical assistance from the Bank of China in June 2004. According to Pohiva (2006), this suggests that Tonga's recognition of China was mainly due to the business interests of the major decision makers (Interview with 'Akilisi Pohiva, 2006). It can be argued at least that the shift benefited the business interests of the key decision makers.

External Pressures from Western Powers

In the past, aid donors such as Australia, New Zealand, and Japan have funded major development projects in Tonga (Ministry of Labour, Commerce and Industries 2001). However, in recent years, increasing financial assistance has flowed in from China. Although the total amount of aid provided by Beijing is difficult to assess, Chinese-funded projects have included a soft loan for the refurbishment of Dateline Hotel, an unspecified grant for the construction of a new convention hall, and an agreement to upgrade Fua'amotu International Airport and either extend or relocate the Vava'u airport (Sodhi 2006; *China Daily Online* 2006).[4]

The conditions attached to aid from Western powers were a major factor leading Tonga to recognize Beijing. China provides aid and other assistance to Tonga without any strings attached. Unlike the Western powers, it does not ask for good governance or more democratic practices as preconditions for aid. On a goodwill visit in January 2007, the Fiji-based US ambassador to Tonga stated that Tonga does not qualify for certain sources of funds from the US, such as the Millennium Challenge Corporation Fund, because democratic reforms have not been implemented. In particular, he offered no direct financial assistance to help rebuild the 80 percent of Nuku'alofa's central business district destroyed in the November 2006 rioting (*Television Tonga News* 2007). These sorts of preconditions have pushed Tonga to welcome China's offer of more generous aid, including funds to restore the capital city. Such actions remind long-standing but demanding aid donors that Tonga has other options, and they may even reduce the need for questionable income-generating activities, such as unregulated ship registrations.[5]

Tonga's decision to support China may also have been influenced by the fact that the Western powers have reduced their level of diplomatic engagement in the Pacific as a whole. For example, the UK recently closed three diplomatic posts in the region, including the British High Commission in Tonga (Shie 2006). The 2006 closure suggests to Tongans that the former protectorate power is losing interest in Tonga. In contrast, China has shown increasing interest in the region, recently opening new embassies in various Pacific Island states, including Tonga. China has further encouraged its ties with Tonga through extensive use of "visit diplomacy." In the past few years, China has hosted leaders of Tonga, such as the late King Taufa'ahau Tupou IV and the prime minister. In 2006 alone, top officials of the Chinese government, including Vice Minister for Tourism Zhang Xigin and Foreign Minister Li Zhaoxing, visited Tonga (*Matangi Tonga Online* 2006b). China has also promoted friendly military exchanges with the Tongan Ministry of Defence, further strengthening its ties to Tonga (*People's Daily Online* 2001).

The extent of this "visit diplomacy" means that Tongan leaders now have much closer personal contact with the Chinese leaders than they do with senior officials in the United States, and perhaps even in Australia or New Zealand. The Chinese are apparently aware of the importance of maintaining personal contacts with Tongan leaders, especially since decisions are made by only a few key individuals. As correctly noted by Henderson and Reilly (2003), skillful diplomacy can enable an external power to gain influence over vast areas through the acquiescence of very few people.

Other aid donors have also attempted to improve their relations with Pacific leaders, perhaps at least partly in response to China's increased activity in Oceania. For example, Japan announced a significant increase in its aid to the region at a summit meeting with Pacific leaders in Okinawa in May 2006, and the next month island leaders met with French President Jacques Chirac in Paris (Keith-Reid and Pareti 2006).

Dependence on Foreign Aid

A major determining factor for Tonga's recognition of China is the fact that the economy is highly dependent on remittances and aid. For thirty years, the Pacific region has been the recipient of some of the world's highest per capita aid flows. Between 1970 and 2005, Tonga received the highest average annual aid per capita in the Pacific, and traditionally, Australia and New Zealand have been the primary sources of support for Tonga (Sodhi 2006). Foreign aid has helped sustain a large public sector that dominates the formal labor market, and government services account for about 16 percent of GDP. Aid donors have assisted Tonga in funding major development projects, and along with remittances, aid has provided an important source of fairly stable income, offsetting the high vulnerability of the economy to natural disasters, crop diseases, and fluctuations in world markets (Ministry of Labour, Commerce and Industries 2001; SDP8 2006).

On the other hand, aid flows have not contributed to higher growth because, as a source of unearned economic rent, aid (along with remittances) artificially appreciates the currency, making exports and domestic import substitution less competitive (Sodhi 2006). In addition, aid flows draw resources away from the private and into the public sector, providing funding for increases in public wages and benefiting the ruling elites, thereby reinforcing the status quo. This suggests that the dependency of the Tongan economy on aid requires attention. However, the evolving Tonga-China relationship may have further encouraged the country's reliance on foreign aid. Significantly, there are social, political, and economic implications involved; these are explored in the next section.

Social, Political and Economic Implications

The influx of Chinese immigrants to Tonga has been further encouraged by closer Tonga-China diplomatic relations. The Chinese population in Tonga is a small minority ethnic group, but it continues to grow. In 2006, there were approximately 500 Chinese in Tonga, compared to only 55 recorded in the 1996 census (*China Daily Online* 2006, Matangi Tonga Online 2006a). Despite small numbers, the Chinese have become very successful in the business arena, which seems to be a source of resentment. Chinese immigrants to Tonga have become the major competitors of small local businesses in Tonga. Today, there is a Chinese-owned store in almost every village in Tongatapu, and some have appeared in outer islands such as Vava'u.

In the traditional social structure, the king (*Tu'i*) was at the top of the sociopolitical pyramid, followed by the nobles (*Hou'eiki*); the rest of the population were classified as commoners (*tu'a*). The reforms introduced by the late King Taufa'ahau Tupou IV in 1966 opened the doors for Tonga to interact with the outside world. The reforms included developments in telecommunications, investment, migration, and higher education. Since the 1960s, international migration has enabled Tongans to improve their standard of living, not only in host countries such as New Zealand and Australia, but also in the homeland. Some of these migrants seek work opportunities in the host countries, save their income, and then return to Tonga to invest their earnings, putting them in direct competition with Chinese immigrant businesses. By investing in businesses, these returning migrants increase their economic power (*ivilahi*). As a result, they become influential in the society, not only in the basic social institutions such as the family (*famili*), but also in larger institutions such as the church (*siasi*) and the state (*pule'anga*). Their economic power also enables them to improve their status in the society and thus has led to the emergence of a new social class, the businesspeople, or *kau pisinisi*. Through this process, the traditional social structure has been transformed to include the *kau pisinisi*. The king remains at the apex, then the nobles, followed by the businesspeople. The commoners remain at the base of the pyramid.

The Chinese have one advantage over local entrepreneurs. As members of an outsider "middlemen" minority (Bonacich 1973), they are not bound by the traditional values that constitute the core of Tongan culture, such as notions of love (*'ofa*), respect (*faka'apa'apa*), cooperation (*fetokoni'aki*), loyalty (*mateaki*), unquestioned obedience (*taliangi*), humility (*loto to*), or maintaining a close relationship based on love and cooperation (*tauhi vaha'a*). The basic values such as sharing and giving, which make it difficult for many local people to accumulate and invest capital, do not apply to them, nor is there so much pressure to contribute a large proportion of their income to social institutions such as the church. It is a Tongan social custom to request things from relatives, neighbors, or anyone who has what one needs. This is not based on the ethic of economic exchange but on the social principle of generalized reciprocity (Helu 1999). When a person requests (*kole*) something from relatives or friends, it is not noted that he or she owes something to these people. Rather, there is an understanding that society, in the normal course of events, will present an opportunity to reciprocate.

Chinese, on the other hand, maintain social ties within the wider community of overseas Chinese, who constitute a source of loans, capital, information, and expertise that tends to help, rather than hinder, accumulation and investment. Despite their small numbers, by 2006 Chinese had become an important presence in Tonga's main commercial centers, particularly in the capital city. Like middleman minorities elsewhere, this made them a tempting potential target in the event of breakdowns in law and order.

Tonga is faced with increased political instability and a precarious economic future, and even the relatively small involvement of a large power can have a major impact on domestic politics. It can be argued that the political instability in Tonga has presented an opportunity for China to increase its involvement there. Two recent events highlight the increasing internal conflicts and political instability in the Kingdom. In July 2005, the majority of the civil servants went on strike due to dissatisfaction with a performance-based pay system proposed by the government. The strikers demanded more pay because of the huge gap between those at the top and those in the lower echelons of the civil service. The strike continued for six weeks and almost brought the country to a standstill.

The second, and more sudden, event was the rioting on 16 November 2006.[6] This began with a demonstration demanding more democratic changes in government, including the need for a fully elected parliament (Mahina 2006). When the government decided to close Parliament for the year without finalizing the issue, the pro-democracy demonstration turned violent. The factors that led to violent rioting included discontent over the state of play in the reform negotiations; discontent over the economic role of the royal family; and the alienation of youth, linked in turn to the failure of the traditional methods of social control, such as the class system, the family, and the church, to control these elements. Discontent over the increasing prominence of Chinese businesses was also a factor. The subsequent rioting destroyed 80 percent of the central business district in the capital city of Nuku'alofa (*Matangi Tonga Online* 2007a). Significantly, most of the businesses targeted by the rioters were owned by Chinese (*Radio Australia* 2006).

According to Minister of Labour, Commerce and Industries Lisiate 'Akolo, the total amount of money that Tonga needed for a complete reconstruction program was about T$400 million (US$196 million). According to 'Akolo, the Chinese government seemed to be the only possible source for this kind of capital (*Matangi Tonga Online* 2007a). Even though the Chinese community was the hardest hit in November riots, China is still willing to fund the reconstruction of the capital. In May 2007, Beijing authorized a soft loan of T$100 million (US$49 million) to assist with the rebuilding of Nuku'alofa. This loan was approved during the prime minister's first official visit to China, which also yielded a T$10 million (US$4.9 million) grant to mark the occasion (*Matangi Tonga Online* 2007b). These developments also show that political instability can facilitate China's efforts to cultivate Tonga's support. A relatively small investment in Tonga can have a major political payoff for China. Tonga may be small in terms of population, but the number of votes counts more than population in some forums, such as the United Nations.

As mentioned earlier, Tonga is highly dependent on foreign aid. China's generous aid to Tonga may help to strengthen its weak economy so that aid will no longer be necessary in the future. However, Tonga needs to ensure that it improves its trade structure so that it earns more from its exports to donor countries than it pays for imported goods from these countries. This would avoid the problem of a cycle in which aid recipients become systematically dependent on the aid donors for their development needs (Laufa 2005: 6).

Also potentially problematic is the manner in which China is providing aid to Tonga. After the China-Pacific summit in April 2006, China agreed to provide nearly US$6 million as part of a new aid package to balance Tonga's budget (*Taimi o Tonga Online* 2006). This sort of transfer may encourage overspending in government as well as lack of accountability. According to Professor Ian Campbell of the University of the South Pacific, the approach "is very inflationary. It increases the spending power of a government without increasing its productivity so you end up with the classic inflationary scenario of too much money chasing too few goods and that causes rapid domestic inflation as well as encouraging trade deficits or a balance of payments deficit" (*Taimi o Tonga Online* 2006).

On the other hand, the diplomatic relations between Tonga and China have assisted the influx of Chinese investors to the country. This has supported Tonga's economy by developing the private sector, creating job opportunities, encouraging business competition, and providing cheaper goods and services to the people. Although many Chinese entrepreneurs left Tonga after the 2006 rioting, some have returned to reestablish their businesses. An example is the Fung Shing Group, who are now rebuilding a new 1,600–square meter double-story building in Nuku'alofa that may cost as much as T$3 million (US$1.47 million).

In December 2005, after ten years of negotiations, Tonga successfully completed the accession requirements to join the World Trade Organization (WTO). It is generally believed that the Western powers and China strongly influenced Tonga's decision to join the organization. From China's point of view, Tonga's accession to the WTO would further strengthen the trade relations between the two countries by opening up new markets for China to conduct business investments in Tonga. This would cater to the commercial interests of China. Meanwhile, the people of Tonga in general are likely to be the ones to suffer any consequences.

Tonga's accession to the WTO raises concerns, particularly in view of the terms and conditions that Tonga has to abide by. As reported by Oxfam Australia, "the terms of Tonga's accession package are appalling as Tonga will have to fix its tariffs at levels lower than any other country in the history of WTO. Tonga will be allowed tariffs of no more than 20 percent on any product" (Hewett 2005). Such low tariffs threaten to wipe out Tonga's vulnerable farmers and small businesses. Furthermore, since Tonga's main revenue comes from trade taxes, tariff cuts may lead to a financial crisis. By joining the WTO, Tonga agrees to open many of its vital services to foreign companies, including education, hospitals, and telecommunications. This means not only that access to essential services for the poor might become difficult, but also that foreign companies would have access to hospitals and schools, so that Tonga could possibly lose control over its essential services. As noted by Barry Coates of Oxfam New Zealand, Tonga has to change over thirty laws and put in place new administrative and reporting systems (*Oxfam New Zealand Online* 2005). These changes are for the benefit of foreign companies, giving them the right to challenge Tongan laws that may not be to their advantage.

Tonga has much less to gain from joining the WTO than do most other nations, owing to factors like the wide dispersal of its population and the great distance to markets. However, it seems that the major powers have used negotiations over membership in the WTO as a way of pressuring poor countries to open up their economies for the benefit of foreign exporters and aid donors such as China. In a way, Tonga has to comply with the wishes of these aid donors because of its high dependency on foreign aid. Again, this emphasizes the influence of major powers such as China on Tonga. Perhaps this could be reduced if Tonga attempted to reduce its dependency on foreign aid.

Conclusion

China and Taiwan use their aid to the Pacific Islands as a way to gain diplomatic recognition. This can be detrimental to the Pacific Island nations, given that their financial capacity is limited, they are highly dependent on foreign aid, and there are only a few key decision makers in government. China and Taiwan can easily buy the support of these key decision makers, and as a result government systems may become distorted and even dysfunctional. Chinese activities in Tonga may be aimed at sidelining Taiwan, but they have the effect of undermining Tonga's ties with Western powers such as the United States, Australia, and New Zealand. China understands that the US has political dominance, so it considers it important to develop a network of stable international relations with independent states in the region, including Tonga.

The first factor influencing Tonga's decision to develop close relations with China concerns the business interests of key decision makers in Tonga. In particular, Tonga's link with China was established primarily to ensure a ready market for renting satellite slots. In 2006 the current king announced that he would dispose of all of his commercial interests, so perhaps future economic benefits from the relationship with China will be shared more widely than they have been in the past. However, it is yet to be confirmed exactly how the king will divest himself of his business interests.

The preconditions set by Western powers for giving aid to Tonga have also helped foster the relationship with China, which is prepared to provide generous aid without such ties. Western powers attach conditions to their aid in order to control corruption and promote efficiency. However, Tongan leaders see this as interfering with the domestic operations and policies of the country and find the untied aid from China attractive.

A third factor influencing Tonga's new foreign policy emphasis is the traditional regional powers' declining interest in the country. While Western powers have reduced their direct engagement in the kingdom, China has nurtured its ties with Tonga through extensive use of visit diplomacy. China's approach is particularly significant in Tonga, since much political and economic power resides with only a few key decision makers. Perhaps other donors can emulate China's more personal approach.

The last factor that plays a crucial role in the relationship with China is Tonga's high dependence on foreign aid. Aid dependency makes Tonga receptive to China's overtures, but the resulting resource transfers may serve to further encourage Tonga's reliance on foreign assistance. As mentioned earlier, aid flows can fail to contribute to higher growth because of their impact on the value of the currency, on exports, and on import substitution programs. In order to break out of the dependency trap, Tonga needs to encourage relationships and programs that help develop the private sector and promote foreign direct investment.

Evolving diplomatic relations between Tonga and China have social, political, and economic implications. The traditional social structure may be further transformed by a new emerging class, the businesspeople or *kau pisinisi,* which in the future may include Chinese entrepreneurs. This raises the possibilities of Chinese influence in Tonga's political affairs and potential conflicts with the indigenous people. The political instability in Tonga that led to the riots in 2006 affected the majority of the Chinese-owned business community. Although the Chinese government continues to provide aid for Tonga, it is possible that Chinese investors will shy away from Tonga in the near future because of what happened in 2006. This emphasizes Tonga's need for a stable political environment in order to attract foreign business investors to help the development of the private sector.

The relationship with China has helped diversify Tonga's international links and sources of funding. It may give Tonga more leverage in aid negotiations with traditional donors, and perhaps even force those donors to reduce their aid-related demands. However, it is important that rivalry amongst the great powers be avoided and peace maintained. It is also worth remembering that the new relationship with China is introducing unavoidable forces of change into Tongan society, further transforming its social, political, and economic institutions.

Notes

I am very grateful to my doctoral supervisor, Dr Jeremy Seymour Eades, Professor at Ritsumeikan Asia Pacific University, who edited an earlier version of this chapter and provided critical comments on its content and structure.

1. Until mid 2001, the government drew on the Tonga Trust Fund to cover unbudgeted expenditure. The fund, established in 1988 at the Bank of America, and consisted almost entirely of offshore investments. In 1999, on the advice of Mr. Jesse Bogdonoff, a former employee of the Bank of America appointed by the king as his official court jester, the US$20 million investment was withdrawn from Bank of America and invested in Millennium Asset Management, another US-based corporation (*BBC News Online* 2004). By June 2000 the fund was reportedly valued at US$37 million, but two years later it had fallen to US$3 million (Asian Development Bank 2005). At the end of 2002, the government confirmed that Millennium no longer existed and that the Tonga Trust Fund money was gone (*BBC News Online* 2004). The trustees of the fund, including two Tongan cabinet ministers, were held responsible for the bad investment decision and were forced to resign, although it was unclear what personal or political responsibility they had for the financial loss.

2. Tongasat offers a number of services to its clients to support their satellite network orbit and spectrum needs (see the Tongasat Web site at http://www.Tongasat.com). According to Mendosa (1994), Tongasat sells for profit access to orbital slots allocated to Tonga as a sovereign state. In 1999, Tongasat had four orbital slots that covered the Asia Pacific region and China had become the key market for these slots (see also *China Matters,* 28 November 2006 at http://chinamatters.blogspot .com/2006/11/china-as-collateral-damage-in-tongan.html).

3. When then Crown Prince Tupouto'a acceded to the throne in September 2006, he announced that he would dispose of all his commercial business interests in conformity with the obligations and demands of the high office.
4. Other assistance was provided in the form of scholarships. In 2006 alone, the Chinese government offered some twenty scholarships for students to study in China. This was an increase from the four scholarships sponsored by the Chinese government in 2003–2004 (Ministry of Foreign Affairs of the People's Republic of China Online 2003).
5. In 2002, the Israeli navy seized the Tongan-flagged *KarineA,* which was carrying 50 tons of weapons and munitions that Israel claimed were destined for the Palestinian Authority in Gaza. In 2003, three vessels flying the Tongan flag were caught in the Mediterranean moving weapons, explosives, and men for al-Qaeda. In the same year, US officials investigated a shipping company named Nova, incorporated in Delaware and Romania, after two of its Tongan-flagged vessels were used to smuggle suspected al-Qaeda operatives (Stringer 2006).
6. Some observers refer to the 16 November 2006 event as "Black Thursday" (*Matangi Tonga Online* 2007a).

References

Asian Development Bank. 2005. *Program Completion Report – Economic and Public Sector Reform Program in Tonga* (Loan 1904-TON [SF]). Tonga, 14 September.

BBC News Online. 2001. "Tonga's Jester Has Last Laugh." 6 October. Accessed 15 August 2009 at http://www.bbc.co.uk/

———. 2004. "Tonga Court Jester to Pay $1m." 19 February. Accessed 15 August 2009 at http://www.bbc.co.uk/

Bonacich Edna. 1973. "A Theory of Middlemen Minorities." *American Sociological Review* 38 (October): 583–594.

China Daily Online. 2006. "Tonga Seeks $60m Loan from China to Buy Back Assets." 27 April. Accessed 21 April 2007 at http://www.chinadaily.com.cn/bizchina/2006-04/27/content_585992.htm

Field, Michael. 2005. "New South Pacific Crisis Looming as Tonga's Aging King Near Death." *The Dominion Post,* 15 June, 3.

Helu, I. F. 1999. *Critical Essays: Cultural Perspectives from the South Seas.* Canberra: Australian National University Printing Service.

Henderson, John. 2001. "China, Taiwan and the Changing Strategic Significance of Oceania." In *Contemporary Challenges in the Pacific: Toward a New Consensus,* vol. 1, ed. Stephen Levine and Tyves-Louis Sage, 143–155. *Revue Juridique Polynesienne.* Accessed online 14 August 2008 at http://www.upf.pf/recherche/IRIDIP/RJP/RJP_HS01/09_Henderson.doc

Henderson, John, and Benjamin Reilly. 2003. "Dragon in Paradise: China's Rising Star in Oceania." *The National Interest* 72 (summer): 94–104.

Herr, Richard. 2007. "Sovereignty and Responsibility: Some Issues in Chinese/Taiwanese Rivalry in the Pacific." *Fijian Studies* 4 (2): 111–125.

Hewett, Andrew. 2005. "Tonga Set to Join WTO Today on Worst Terms Ever." Oxfam Australia, 15 December. Accessed on 18 August 2009 at http://www.oxfam.org.au/media/article.php?id=187

International Monetary Fund. 2001. *Tonga: Recent Economic Developments.* IMF Staff Country Report No.01/02. Washington, D.C: International Monetary Fund.

James, Kerry. 1998. *Pacific Islands Stakeholders Participation in Development: Tonga.* Pacific Island Discussion Paper Series No.4, East Asia and Pacific Region, Papua New Guinea and Pacific Island Country Management Unit. Washington, D.C.: World Bank.

———. 2000. "Polynesia in Review: Tonga." *The Contemporary Pacific* 12 (1): 252–253.

Keith-Reid, Robert, and S. Pareti. 2006. "China Stirs the Pot of Divided Pacific Loyalties." *Islands Business,* March, 14–15.

Laufa T. M. 2005. "Aid Effectiveness in the Pacific Region under Globalization-Understanding Its Dynamics." Proceedings of the "Pacific Conference on Growth and Development: Building Better Pacific Economies" held 12–14 October. Port Moresby: University of Papua New Guinea.

Mahina, 'Okusitino. 2006. *Tonga in Crisis: Some Reflections on the 16/11.* Panel Discussion, Fale Pasifika Centre for Pacific Studies, University of Auckland, December. Accessed online 12 August 2007 at http://planet-tonga.com/beta/2006/12/21/tonga-in-crisis-some-reflections-on-the-1611.

Matangi Tonga Online. 2004. "Tonga Appoints First Ambassador to China." 26 July. Accessed 18 August 2009 at http://www.matangitonga.to/scripts/artman/exec/view.cgi?archive=2&num=174

———. 2006a. "Tonga Becoming Chinese Tourist Destination." 12 April. Accessed 18 August 2009 at http://www.matangitonga.to/scripts/artman/exec/view.cgi?archive=5&num=1731

———. 2006b. "Chinese Foreign Minister Jets into Tonga." 1 August. Accessed 18 August 2009 at http://www.matangitonga.to/scripts/artman/exec/view.cgi?archive=5&num=2025

———. 2007a. "Tonga Unable to Fund Recovery." 10 January. Accessed 18 August 2009 at http://www.matangitonga.to/scripts/artman/exec/view.cgi?archive=7&num=2559

———. 2007b. "Fung Shing Opens for Christmas." 20 December. Accessed 18 August 2009 at http://www.matangitonga.to/scripts/artman/exec/view.cgi?archive=7&num=3584

Mendosa, David. 1994. "Tonga's Flawed Genius." Accessed 18 August 2009 at http://www.mendosa.com/tongasat.html

Ministry of Labour, Commerce and Industries. 2001. *Annual Report.* Nuku'alofa: Government of Tonga, Ministry of Labour, Commerce and Industries.

New Zealand Listener Online. 2005. "The Not So Friendly Isles." March 19–25, vol.198. Accessed online 25 January 2008 at http://www.listener.co.nz/issue/3384/features/3644/the_not-so-friendly_isles.html

People's Daily Online. 2001. "PLA Chief of General Staff Meets Tonga Military Officer." 15 May. Accessed online 18 October 2008 at http://english.peopledaily.com.cn/english/200105/15/eng20010515_70035.html

Radio Australia. 2006. 16 December. Accessed online at http://www.abc.net.au

————. 2007. "The Pacific Proxy: China vs. Taiwan." 7 February. Accessed online 15 October 2008 at http://www.radioaustralia.net.au/news/infocus/s1842245.html

Shie, T. 2006. "China Woos the South Pacific." *PacNet,* 17 March. Pacific Forum, Center for Strategic and International Studies, Honolulu, Hawai'i. Accessed online 18 July 2009 at http://csis.org/files/media/csis/pubs/pac0610a.pdf

Sodhi, Gurav. 2006. "Time for a Change in Tonga: From Monarchy to Modernity." *Issue Analysis,* no.77. St. Leonards: The Centre for Independent Study. Accessed online 23 November 2007 at http://www.cis.org.au/IssueAnalysis/IA%2077/ia77.pdf

Stringer, K. 2006. "The Pacific Microstates and U.S. Security." *Foreign Service Journal* (November): 39–44.

Taimi o Tonga Online. 2006. 2 May. "China Offers Aid." Accessed online 14 May 2008 at http://www.taimiotonga.com

Television Tonga News. 2007. "Visit of US Ambassador." 19 January. Accessed online 8 June 2008 at http://www.tonga-now.to

Tonga. 2006. "Strategic Development Plan Eight 2006/7-2008/9: Looking to the Future, Building on the Past." 14 July. Accessed on 18 August 2009 at http://www.pmo.gov.to/index.php/Strategic-Development-Plan-Eight-2006/7-2008/9-Looking-to-the-Future-Building-on-the-Past.html

Tonga Statistics Department. 2006. *Annual Report.* Nuku'alofa: Government of Tonga, Statistics Department.

Personal Interviews

Dr. Okusitino Mahina. 2007. Auckland, New Zealand.
Mr. 'Akilisi Pohiva. 2006. Nuku'alofa, Tonga.

CHAPTER 11

Changing Attitudes and the Two Chinas in the Republic of Palau

Takashi Mita

Introduction

The Republic of Palau[1] established an official diplomatic relationship with the Republic of China (ROC, or Taiwan) in 1999. Since then, official development assistance from the Taiwanese government has become an integral part of Palau's economic development. However, even before the official tie came into effect, tourists, investors, and technical missions had already come to Palau from Taiwan.

On the other hand, although Palau has no official diplomatic tie with the People's Republic of China (PRC, or China), the presence of Chinese nationals, including guest workers and investors, has risen in recent years. More recently, an influential Chinese developer, Shimao Group, has approached the government wanting to invest in a large-scale resort complex in Palau (Abrau 2006b). On another front, a notable Palauan businessman who ran for president in 2004 has voiced his strong desire that Palau strengthen its relationship with the PRC (Basilius 2004: 3). Recent activities of Palauan legislators indicate that Palauan people may hold deeper interests in China. Some of them have shown their pro-China position explicitly. Palau has had constant exposure to China, although until recently China's presence was overshadowed by Palau's official tie with Taiwan.

This chapter explores recent trends and activities involving Chinese and Taiwanese in Palau, focusing on their socioeconomic influences and international relations with the country.[2] I begin by reviewing the historical development of Palau's relations with China and Taiwan. I then turn to the major political and economic activities conducted by Chinese and Taiwanese in Palau. I will also discuss Palauans' reactions to these activities, along with the political and economic significance of their interrelationships within the international context. Finally, I will examine the views of Palauans extracted through my interviews with various individuals.

The Development of Palau's Relations with Taiwan and China

Interactions between Palauans and Chinese began during the time of the early traders. During the 1860s, fifty Chinese laborers were brought to Palau as cotton plantation workers, but when they did not get along with Palauans, Ibedul (the high chief of Koror) sent them back home (Rechebei and McPhetres 1997: 104). After the German administration began phosphate mining on Angaur Island in 1909, about 100 Chinese laborers were imported for the operation (Rechebei and McPhetres 1997: 126–127). Despite these early interactions with Chinese, it was not until the Trust Territory period that China and Taiwan became important in Palau's economics and politics, so I will not linger on this earlier history.

It was Kuniwo Nakamura, the president of the Republic of Palau from 1992 to 2000, who decided to conclude an official diplomatic agreement with Taiwan. However, a precursor of that decision occurred during the earlier administration of President Ngiratkel Etpison. According to President Etpison's chief of staff, Bonifacio Basilius (2007), the PRC government invited Etpison to Beijing in the early 1990s. He met with high officials of the Chinese Communist Party and the Shanghai municipality. Basilius states that PRC officials demanded nothing, and their attitude was highly diplomatic.

Several months later, the Taiwanese government invited Etpison to Taipei. There he met with Taiwan's President Lee Teng-hui, and due to their common experience with the past Japanese administration of their respective countries, they were able to communicate fluently in Japanese. Basilius observed that the two leaders seemed to share a congenial spirit and that they even ventured out into Taipei by themselves. Etpison and Taiwan's foreign minister wanted to conclude diplomatic relations at that time, but this did not occur because Palau was still a Trust Territory administered by the United States. Nonetheless, Etpison promised that Palau would recognize Taiwan if and when it became independent (B. Basilius 2007). Etpison's visit was a significant step toward official diplomatic relations. The actual negotiations to establish Palau's diplomatic relations with Taiwan had to wait until 1994, when Palau gained political independence as a sovereign state in free association with the United States. Subsequently, many countries approached Palau, among them the PRC and Taiwan (Sayson 2001: 80).

Like President Etpison, in 1997 President Nakamura was invited to visit by the PRC government. Upon his return to Palau he found waiting for him a similar invitation from Taiwan, which he accepted (Nakamura 2007). It took over a year for him to establish official diplomatic relations with Taiwan, since the proposal had detractors. He gradually released news about his Taiwan visit to the media to let the world know that Palau and Taiwan might establish a relationship. Nakamura states there was neither a threat from the PRC nor guidance from the United States on this matter, and that he made the decision as head of state of a sovereign nation with no obstacles. In December 1999 ties were officially established.

According to Nakamura in our interview, he established ties with Taiwan because (1) Taiwan is a democratic country, (2) it is an island nation, (3) it shares cultural similarities with Palau, and (4) it is a good potential partner for economic cooperation. According to Nakamura, a relationship with Taiwan is more manageable than one with the PRC because Taiwan shares the aforementioned common characteristics and values with Palau. Nakamura asserts that if Palau had instead concluded diplomatic relations with the PRC, it might now be filled with some 20,000 Chinese, which would be unmanageable. He also believes that he could not have established a relation with a communist country.[3] Nakamura believed the decision to link with Taiwan was in the best interests of Palau, and he has not changed this view.[4] He states it was an act of sovereignty, within his powers as president. He continues to say that conditions have changed little, and he would still choose Taiwan today.

In March 2000, Taiwan opened its embassy in the WCTC (Western Caroline Trading Company), the biggest shopping center in Koror. Clark K. H. Chen became Taiwan's first ambassador, and the next year President Tommy E. Remengesau, Jr., appointed Johnson Toribiong, a well-known attorney, to be Palau's first ambassador to the ROC.

Taiwanese and Chinese Activities in Palau

Since Palau and Taiwan established diplomatic ties, the two have worked to further develop the relationship. Taiwan has made an intensive effort to collaborate with Palau's development in the fields of "infrastructure construction, agriculture, fisheries, tourism, aviation, investment, trade, medicare, vocational training, education, culture, and in international organizations" (Lee 2007: 1).

The Taiwanese government's primary tool for securing and enhancing its ties with Palau is official development assistance. It has become one of the largest contributors of economic assistance, along with the United States and Japan.[5] In a speech to explain the relationship, Matthew S. Lee, Taiwan's current ambassador, spoke first of "government-to-government assistance," indicating the crucial significance of aid in the alliance (Lee 2007: 1).

Taiwan's government offers aid in the form of both grants and loans. It is the only donor nation that offers loans to Palau.[6] Currently, Taiwan guarantees three loan programs, actualized through the International Commercial Bank of China (ICBC, currently Mega International Commercial Bank). For the Capitol Relocation project (Phase II—construction of a new government complex to accommodate Palau's executive, legislative, and judiciary branches), Taiwan offered a US$20 million loan at very low interest, which started in July 2000. The principal and the interest payments will be completed in July 2020, and will cost the Palau government a total of US$28,399,996 (Republic of Palau 2006a).

A second loan was made for the Palau International Airport Improvement Project, originally to renovate the runway of the international airport in Airai. The loan was for US$15 million, but the US Federal Aviation Administration also granted over US$26 million to upgrade the airport facilities and resurface the runway (Republic of Palau 2006b). Therefore, Palau and the ICBC agreed to reprogram the loan, and the government has therefore allocated only US$1.5 million dollars for airport upgrade design (Remengesau 2007). It also decided to use US$7 million to renovate the power plant of the Palau Public Utilities Corporation to cope with the nationwide power crisis that Palau suffered in 2006 (*Tia Belau* 2006, 1).[7]

In January 2007, Taiwan offered Palau a third loan of US$3.3 million, interest-free, to alleviate a national economic crisis incurred by the bankruptcy of the Pacific Savings Bank (PSB), a local institution (Gerundio 2007). This has been used for payouts to those who have deposits of $2,000 and less, as well as state governments, educational institutes, and community organizations that had PSB accounts.[8] Taiwan's grant aid usually targets projects, but in the case of PSB, President Chen Shui-Bian, responding to President Remengesau's request, decided to give extraordinary humanitarian assistance.

Taiwan's grant aid projects range from the construction of public facilities and water systems to road maintenance and small-scale renovations. Some notable projects are the construction of Ngarachamayong Cultural Center (US$2.5 million) and the building of the new Belau National Museum (US$2.6 million), both in Koror. The construction of the spectators' stand at the National Track and Field helped Palau host the Ninth Festival of Pacific Arts, the region's premier cultural event, in 2004. Other significant grant aid projects have contributed to the completion of work on the new capital complex and the construction of roads in the states of Ngarchelong, Peleliu, Airai, and Koror. Taiwan's donation of thirty-one patrol vehicles for the Ministry of Justice has significantly enhanced police patrol capacity. Various renovation projects for schools, docks, and other public facilities have also received grants. The Economic Stimulus Packages scheme helps each state address its needs.

Most of Taiwan's grant aid projects are small in scale but rapid, flexible, and responsive to the community needs. The estimated amount of annual grant aid from Taiwan until 2005 was roughly US$4 to 6 million, which is approximately the same as the grant aid received from Japan.[9] Needless to say, no grants or other forms of assistance are received from the PRC.

Taiwan's technical cooperation program encompasses the fields of education, agriculture, aquaculture, and medicine. The most notable and tangible cooperative activities are found in the agricultural technical mission conducted by the International Cooperation and Development Fund (ICDF), Taiwan's overseas cooperation agency. Its stated mission is to help the Palauan people to achieve self-sufficiency (International Cooperation and Development Fund 2007). The agricultural technical mission was established in 1985, first in the state of Koror. The mission's facilities include a farm that was later moved to a vast site in Nekken in the state of Aimeliik.[10] The farm is designed to give Palauans agricultural education and training. The mission is led by four Taiwanese officers and staff, assisted by twenty staff members from Palau and Asian countries such as the Philippines and Bangladesh. The mission first introduced and demonstrated food crops and horticulture techniques, then trained farmers and state officers. It then began extending educational programs to elementary schools, high schools, and the community college.

The mission's more recent goal, in addition to continued demonstration and training, is to establish a model for an agro-tourism business facility (Hseu 2007). It has been constructing summer houses, pedestrian paths, and other facilities at Nekken Farm for the convenience of the tourists. In February 2007, the mission demonstrated the Agro-Tourism Project to local tour agencies and some state governors (Rodriguez 2007b). The mission's leader, Hseu Ming-Lii, emphasizes that Nekken Farm now serves as a demonstration facility for agro-tourism (Hseu 2007). The hope is that eventually all the states in Palau can learn from the Nekken Farm model for their own self-sustaining tourism operations.

On 5 April 2006, Chinese Premier Wen Jiabao visited Fiji for the first meeting of the China–Pacific Island Countries Economic Development and Cooperation Forum. He met with leaders of the Pacific Island states that recognize the PRC, namely Fiji, Samoa, Papua New Guinea, Vanuatu, Federated States of Micronesia, Tonga, the Cook Islands, and Niue (Foreign Affairs China 2006; see Appendix for the forum's communiqué). The Chinese leader reportedly promised US$375 million in economic assistance (Hwang 2006: 18; Radio Taiwan International 2006). Japan has a history of hosting summits with regional leaders: since 1997, Japan–Pacific Islands Forum Summit Meetings have been conducted every three years in Japan, with all the Pacific Islands independent and self-governing entities invited. But this was the first time China had organized a similar regional summit for the Pacific Islands. Obviously, China now has a strong political interest in demonstrating its presence in the region.

Five months after the Chinese allies summit, Taiwan's President Chen visited Palau and held the first Taiwan–Pacific Allies Summit from 3 to 4 September. Leaders from Nauru, the Marshall Islands, Kiribati, Tuvalu, the Solomon Islands, and Palau participated (see Appendix for the forum's communiqué). It is no coincidence that both China and Taiwan initiated exclusive summits with their respective allies in the same year. These events underscored the competition between China and Taiwan over the support of Pacific Island states. Through the summit's subtitle, "Strengthening Oceanic Democratic Alliances and Realizing Comprehensive Partnership," Taiwan emphasized its dissimilarity with China and stressed commonalities in democracy and mutual connections to Oceania. Chen's flight to Palau on the ROC's "Air Force One" was his first trip abroad on the new plane (Hwang 2006: 18). This must have impressed upon the people of Taiwan that Palau was one of Taiwan's strongest allies. On the day of the summit, the flags of Taiwan and six Pacific states were hoisted not only in front of the summit venue in Koror but also on the nation's largest bridge, which connects Koror and Babeldaob. It was an opportunity for even ordinary Palauans to recognize Taiwan's involvement, and to know its allies.

The summit leaders adopted a communiqué labeled the Palau Declaration, which was signed on 4 September (see Appendix). It included acknowledgment that participants and the host country were pursuing goals to achieve economic growth, sustainable development, good governance, and security, as emphasized in the Pacific Plan; acknowledgment of various forms of support to the Pacific allies from President Chen and the Taiwanese people; an expression of support for democratization and economic development in Taiwan; and acknowledgment of Taiwan as a sovereign state with the right to participate in international organizations such as the United Nations and World Health Organization. It also initiated cooperation in economic development and capacity building to strengthen friendly relations, based on ideals of democracy, in the fields of law enforcement training, digital government, tourism, health care, protection of natural resources, development of domestic and renewable energy, economic partnerships, agriculture and fisheries, and cultural preservation (Office of the President Palau 2007).[11] Unlike the PRC at its event, Chen made no promises of concrete financial assistance, perhaps to avoid the appearance of "checkbook diplomacy" (Carreon 2006: 1).

Foreign direct investment indicates the strength of the international economic relations between Palau and foreign countries. Data compiled by the Foreign Investment Board (2007) show that Taiwan is the third largest investor, after Japan and the United States, while China has few investments. Japanese investments are the largest, at $58.3 million in total from thirty companies. The second largest investor, the United States, has $22 million of total investment involving fifty-three companies. The third largest is Taiwan, with $17.6 million involving twenty-one firms. Only one investment from the PRC, valued at $700,000, is active today.

Taiwanese businesses certified to invest in Palau include hotels and resorts (nine companies), and one company each in the fields of agriculture, construction, rock quarrying, airlines, scrap metal, freight forwarding service, mobile phone roaming, tuna processing, and garment manufacture (currently not in operation) (Foreign Investment Board Palau 2007). The majority of the investments in the hotel and resort industry are from Taiwan. Two of Palau's major hotels—the Palasia Hotel and Palau Royal Resort—were developed by Taiwanese. Taiwanese companies also own two middle-range hotels, the Papago Hotel and Airai View Hotel, both in Airai. Several more hotels are being constructed in the Koror area through Taiwanese investments.

In addition to the activities of corporations registered through the Foreign Investment Board, a significant number of small business firms involving Taiwanese investments are registered under Palauan names. These are called "front businesses" because Palauan owners are virtually lending their names to register the companies as Palauan firms, even though most of the money and management expertise is foreign. They involve a wide range of activities, including tour guide businesses, restaurants, retail stores, car dealerships, car repair shops, trading companies, and karaoke pubs.

Another notable Taiwanese endeavor is the Palau branch of the long-established First Commercial Bank.[12] It opened in Koror in November 1998, one year prior to establishment of Palau-Taiwan diplomatic relations.[13] Soong Jin-Yinn, the vice president and general manager of the branch, states that the bank's mission in Palau is to help the economy grow (Soong 2007). He says most businesspeople from Taiwan and even Chinese workers use the First Commercial Bank to remit money to their home countries or for foreign exchange purposes. Soong notes that Palau's economy is gradually growing and foresees a positive future ahead with the expanding tourism sector (Soong 2007). Although the bank's direct investment is only US$1 million, the presence of Taiwan's major bank, considering its primary role as an economic leader, has significant connotations for economic relations between Palau and Taiwan.

Taiwanese tourists are another significant feature in Palau. The number of Taiwanese visitors fluctuates,[14] but Taiwan has been the largest market for Palau's tourist industry over the past decade. Visitor arrivals from Taiwan were less than 1,000 people annually until 1991. The figure gradually increased during the first half of 1990s, but inauguration in 1995 of a direct flight service between Taiwan and Palau led to a sharp increase until 1997, when the figure reached 30,000, or 47 percent of the market. The number dropped in 1998 and continued to fall, to one third of the 1997 level in 1999. This may have reflected the Asian economic crisis, and the 1997 China Airlines crash in Taiwan. More Taiwanese tourists came in 2002, and the trend entered another boom until 2004.[15] The figure dropped again in 2005 and 2006, but Taiwanese still made up 35 percent of the market share in 2006 (calculated from Palau Visitors Authority 2007). Although the number fluctuates, there are signs of further developments that target the Taiwan market.

By comparison, there are few tourists from Mainland China. In 2006, 378 came (Palau Visitors Authority 2007). This was just 0.5 percent of the market share, and Chinese ranked tenth in the list. According to statistics technician Lanny Ngedebuu (2007) of the Palau Visitors Authority, most Chinese used Continental Airlines, coming via either Manila or Guam. Chinese visitor numbers were higher between 1998 and 2002 than in recent years, totaling more than 800 people each year.

Many Pacific Islanders share a common Austronesian cultural heritage with the indigenous peoples of Taiwan. The Taiwan government has emphasized this

Austronesian connection in various cultural events. In the Ninth Festival of Pacific Arts held in Palau in 2004, Amis and four other indigenous tribes of Taiwan participated as special guests representing Taiwan. At the opening of the new Belau National Museum building in September 2005, Taiwan launched a special exhibit on the indigenous peoples of Taiwan. The museum building itself was funded by the Taiwanese government. The exhibition theme was periods of Palau's colonial history. Taiwan had nothing to do with the colonial administrations of Palau, but a special exhibit room was assigned for the Taiwanese exhibit, prepared by the Shung Ye Museum of Formosan Aborigines. The exhibit highlighted commonalities shared by indigenous peoples of Taiwan and Pacific Islanders, based on their Austronesian heritage.

China's presence remains small compared to Taiwan's, but its significance has increased in recent years. Although the PRC government has no official presence, a May 2006 visit by Ji Peiding, vice chairman of the Foreign Affairs Committee of the National People's Congress, opened the door to the PRC for some Palauan lawmakers. Ji met Palauan legislators of both the Senate and the House of Delegates (Abrau 2006a). He did not represent the Chinese government, but his visit was intended to establish relationships with members of Palau's legislature, inspired by a vision of future economic relations (Abrau 2006a). The visit led to a further development of relations between some Palauan legislators and China in 2007.

Certain trends regarding Chinese activities in the private sector deserve mention. The first is an increased involvement in small businesses such as retail shops and restaurants in Koror. Most of these are "front businesses." A second trend is an increase in the number of Chinese guest workers who serve in various sectors of Palau's economy. More than 1,000 Chinese workers now work in Palau. The third and most influential trend has been the emergence in Palau of a large-scale company from China. In 2005, one of China's top developers, Shimao Group, led by Hui Wing Mau, proposed a US$400 million resort complex to be built in the state of Melekeok.[16] Shimao's proposal generated controversy because it demanded an extension of Palau's land-leasing period from fifty to ninety-nine years (Shuster 2006: 119–120). According to the Foreign Investment Board, the Shimao Group has visited the Board to learn the procedure for applying for certificates for foreign investors. The Compact Review Commission of Palau invited the Shimao Group and other large-scale investors to the National Economic Symposium in Koror in 2007,[17] but no Shimao representative attended (Uyehara 2007). Some Palauans suspect Shimao's proposal is yet another of the many investment plans that will never be carried through, but since Shimao seems to be preparing to apply, they may be wrong.

Few corporations from China operate in Palau. The Palau Construction Bank is one case. The bank, established in 2000, is located in the hamlet of Meyuns in Koror. Its main business is small-scale short-term loans for Palauans, and some Chinese workers use the bank to remit money home (Tellei 2007).

According to the Division of Labor of the Ministry of Commerce and Trade, the number of work permits issued to Chinese nationals was 1,296 in 2002—8.6 percent of the guest workers in the private sector (Division of Labor Palau 2006). The estimated number of the Chinese nationals in 2005 was still around 1,300.[18] Chinese guest workers are employed in construction, hotels, agriculture, fisheries, restaurants, and retail stores.

Perspectives on Palau's Relationships with Taiwan and China

Palau's government under President Remengesau, which succeeded the Nakamura administration, has strengthened its official ties with Taiwan. Remengesau has displayed Palau's alliance with Taiwan and its strong and constant support of Taiwan to the international community in various contexts, such as at the UN General Assembly. During a January 2007 trip to Taipei, he not only secured aid to alleviate problems associated with a collapsed bank, but also received Taiwan's most honorable decoration from its president, Chen Shui-Bian. On his return, Remengesau remarked, "Taiwan has been an important development partner of Palau for many years" (*Island Times* 2007b).

There have been several high-level visits: Remengesau visited Taiwan in 2000, 2002, 2004, and 2007 (Office of the President Taiwan 2007), and Chen visited Palau twice, for Palau's 2005 presidential inauguration and for the 2006 Taiwan–Pacific Allies Summit. Taiwan's vice president visited Palau for the opening of the Palau Royal Resort in 2005 (Shuster 2006: 117).

There have been no official approaches from the PRC government regarding Palau's international relations or domestic matters. The only contact between Palau and the PRC occurred in 2003, when the Palau government needed to cope with stranded Chinese workers of the bankrupt Orientex garment factory.[19] Working with the government of the Federated States of Micronesia, the president's office got the 218 Chinese safely home. The PRC embassy in the Federated States of Micronesia arranged for two PRC commercial airplanes to transport them, and Palau permitted them to land.

Palau's ambassador to Taiwan, Johnson Toribiong, appears to favor more flexibility concerning China over the long-term. Although Toribiong, a well-known and influential lawyer, serves under the president, he is one of the most prominent political figures in Palau. He was a 2000 presidential candidate and also declared his candidacy for the 2008 race. Remengesau appointed him ambassador to Taiwan in February 2001.

Ambassador Toribiong (2007) states that it is most important for Palau to maintain and nurture the close relationship with the ROC through mutual cooperation and understanding. He emphasizes that Palau has supported Taiwan's efforts to join international organizations such as the UN and World Health

Organization. Toribiong reiterates that Taiwan has been one of the primary donors to Palau's economic and infrastructure development, and he also considers Taiwan important to private-sector development because Taiwan is the largest source of tourists. The ambassador asserts that having diplomatic ties with Taiwan is advantageous to Palau because Taiwan (1) is a relatively a small country, (2) is democratic, (3) upholds human rights, and (4) is a leading economic power of the region. He says the PRC is "too big and too busy with dealing with other large nations of the world."

When I asked about a visit to China by some Palauan lawmakers, Toribiong said there was no need to worry about that because Palau sees both Taiwan and China as sovereign states, and visiting China is virtually the same as visiting the United States. He referred to deepening economic relations between Taiwan and China, especially through Taiwanese investment in China, and ventured that the political problems of the cross-strait relationship will be resolved by the future promotion of economic activities in Taiwan and China (Toribiong 2007).

Palau is the closest nation to Taiwan to recognize it as an independent state. Taiwan's government demonstrated its full courtesy to Palau by awarding President Remengesau the Order of Brilliant Jade with Grand Cordon (*Island Times* 2007a: 1, 18). In the acknowledgment letter to Remengesau, President Chen noted that Palau and Taiwan share both "rich traditions and culture"and "democracy, freedom, and human rights." He described Remengesau as "a great statesman of profound vision and competence" and praised his visit to Taiwan for promoting their bilateral relationship (Chen 2007). The award, Taiwan's highest presidential decoration, indicates that Chen considers Palau a most important country. The gesture from President Chen shows that Taiwan wants friendly relations to continue into the future. Remengesau was the fourteenth head of state to receive this award from Chen Shui-Bian.

Even though the official government position is to promote an exclusive relationship with Taiwan, politicians are emerging who lean toward opening a relationship with the PRC. President Remengesau's opponent during the 2004 presidential election, Polycarp Basilius (2004), clearly asserted this during his campaign. Basilius, a retired businessman who served as Palau's representative in the Congress of Micronesia during the Trust Territory period, became well known as a supporter of establishing relations with China. When Basilius first came to know China during the 1970s, Palau still had Trust Territory status and was administered by the United States. Because Palau was not a sovereign state it had no right to establish diplomatic relations with other countries. Representing Palau's congress, Basilius went to China and was overwhelmed by the numbers of people walking Beijing's streets. He was impressed by China's scale, and felt it could potentially become a great partner for future development (P. Basilius 2007).

At the end of 2004, another significant movement was initiated by a group called the People's Free Associated Party, with more than twenty members. According to Tadao Ngotel, president of the group and then speaker of the Ngarche-long State Legislature, they aimed to develop an economic relationship with the PRC. The members met in early 2005 with a Chinese diplomat based at the PRC embassy in the FSM. Ngotel states that the group exchanged ideas with the diplomat regarding possible future economic relations between Palau and China. However, the party discontinued its activities because it failed to register as a chartered organization. According to Ngotel, the Palauan president explained to him Palau's diplomatic relations with Taiwan and courteously asked him to understand the situation. As a consequence, the party has since become virtually inactive (Ngotel 2007).

In June 2005, five members of the House of Delegates, including Lucio Ngi-raiwet and Kalistus Ngirturong, along with a senator, went to China to promote Palau as a "tourist destination and as a stable place to invest." The delegation met with Hui Ming Mau, the leader of the Shimao Group referred to above (Abrau 2005).

Senator Alan Seid also seeks opportunities in Mainland China. He first visited the PRC as an official guest with other congressmen in the mid 1990s, when Palau had no diplomatic tie with Taiwan. Like Polycarp Basilius, Seid was impressed by China's scale. He became still more impressed during a second visit in November 2006, when he traveled with Senator Alfonso Diaz in response to an invitation from the Chinese government (*Tia Belau* 2006: 1, 15). Seid stated that this second visit allowed him to compare the recent development of China with that of twelve years ago, and he was impressed and overwhelmed. Everything he observed was new and large, and the cities were well planned. He was awed by China's rapid development and the emergence of a large number of wealthy people. Seid sees China as a potential source for Palauan economic growth. Seid made a third visit to China in February 2007, but this was a private trip to promote his *noni* (morinda citrifolia) business. As a businessman, Seid would like to tap into the large Chinese market. Regarding Palau's future relations with China and Taiwan, he has not called for radical transition of the current diplomatic arrangement, but he does foresee new economic opportunities with China (Seid 2007).

At about the same time that Seid took his most recent trip to China, PRC legislators also invited other Palauan legislators: Senator Joshua Koshiba, Delegate Toribiong, and Delegate Yamada visited China in February 2007 (*Tia Belau* 2007b). They were invited by Ji Peiding, vice chairman of the Foreign Affairs Committee for the National People's Congress. Koshiba does not see China's communist regime as a threat, but he does see China's political system as unique, like Japanese business circumstances. He feels it is more important to consider the economic development that China has experienced and argues that Palau should not ignore China simply because of Palau's diplomatic ties with Taiwan (Koshiba 2007a). He wants Palauans to keep their sights on future benefits. In his remarks at an economic symposium held in February 2007 in Palau, Koshiba asserted that Palau must "cement its relationship" with China (2007b: 2). He also opines that since China will soon become one of the two largest economic and military superpowers, the other being the United States, and so Palau should establish friendly relations (Koshiba 2007a, 2007b). Koshiba asserts that, for the future of its children, Palau must not ignore China. During his unsuccessful campaign for president in 2008 he pledged that, if elected, he would open a dialog with the PRC; however, like Seid, he promised not to alter Palau's policy of recognition (Koshiba 2007a).

In March 2007, another politician expressed his pro-China position. Kerai Mariur, a member of the House of Delegates of the Palau National Congress, not only endorsed Koshiba's pro-China position but also criticized Taiwan's aid activities. According to newspaper reports, Mariur planned to file a joint resolution criticizing Taiwan's "dollar diplomacy" (*Tia Belau* 2007a: 1, 19; Rodriguez 2007a: 1, 13). Mariur says "Palau should respect and honor" UN member countries rather than keeping ties with Taiwan, which is a "province of China" (*Tia Belau* 2007a, 1). Mariur's logic is that Palau should recognize China because "China has endorsed Palau's membership to the UN" (*Tia Belau* 2007a: 19). Taiwan's ambassador Matthew Lee argued against the "dollar diplomacy" criticism and pointed out that Taiwan's economic miracle had been attained through US assistance (*Tia Belau* 2007a: 19).

In sum, the legislative branch is not in concert with the executive branch regarding Palau's exclusive diplomatic relations with Taiwan. This split among Palauan politicians has been an important emerging trend in recent years.

A representative of Palau's business community, Ken Uyehara, president of the Chamber of Commerce of Palau, says there is a certain degree of influx of small Chinese businesses into the already saturated domestic market of Palau, including restaurants and retail stores. He says the chamber recognizes the investment proposal suggested by the Shimao Group because they visited Palau accompanied by PRC officials and contacted the chamber and some member companies to talk about the possible investment. Since then, no investors from China have contacted the chamber, except one that wanted to develop a garment factory. Uyehara supposes that one reason Chinese investors are interested in Palau is that they see Palau as an opportunity to get into the US dollar economy (Uyehara 2007).

Uyehara (2007) also states that Chinese businesses do not threaten Palauan businesses as long as they abide by the country's laws and compete fairly. However, he warns that some unfair and illegal practices, such as smuggling products without paying tax and duty, are apparent among Chinese businesses, and these are unacceptable. If Taiwanese investors engage in such behaviors, the Taiwanese embassy can assist in solving problems, but this is not the case with the PRC government. If a Chinese company or investor is involved in a dishonest transaction, it can only be addressed through the judiciary. This means Palauans have less flexibility in dealing with any problems with Chinese investors.

When foreigners invest in Palau, they must apply for a Foreign Investment Approval Certificate from the Foreign Investment Board (Foreign Investment Board n.d.: 10). The board approves or rejects their applications, and the Chamber of Commerce also reviews them and can advise the board. The board has no policy to shut out investors from countries with no diplomatic ties with Palau, and theoretically any investor may invest and develop business there regardless of nationality. Uyehara (2007) concludes that if Palau becomes a Chinese tourist destination it will provide new business opportunities, but without diplomatic ties with China, it will be risky.

The general public of Palau has very little interest in the political intricacies of China-Taiwan relations. They are generally ignorant of the structural perspective, and their views are based on their daily interactions with tourists, businesspeople, and workers from Taiwan and China. Based on my interviews, Palauans' image of Taiwanese tourists is not necessarily favorable. Three views are often heard. First, Palauans have a negative impression of "mass tourists." The majority of Taiwanese tourists come in group tours, and large numbers occupy the streets or shops at one time; naturally, large groups take up space and often become noisy. Traditionally, Palauans see those who are reserved in the public space as virtuous. They dislike foreign tourists who speak loudly there, and some criticize them as rude.

A second criticism is that tourists do not care for the natural environment while in the sea or at the beach. Some tourists carelessly step on live corals while snorkeling or swimming, and people accuse some of them of collecting jellyfish or other sea creatures. Some in Koror say that Taiwanese or Chinese residents collect seashells and have depleted them, though as yet there has been no scientific investigation of this. A third criticism from ordinary Palauans is that Taiwanese tourists contribute little to Palau's economy while there. People often claim that when they shop or eat they spend less money than do Japanese or European tourists. However, statistical data contradicts this. According to a 2001 exit survey conducted by Palau Visitors Authority, the average daily expenditure of Taiwanese tourists was US$287 per person, while among Japanese it was $239, Americans $177, and Europeans between $150 and $160 (Palau Visitors Authority 2002: 28). That is, Taiwanese tourists spend more money than any other nationality. However, most Taiwanese tourists prepurchase a package tour before they depart. These packages include airfare, accommodation, Rock Islands boat tours, airport-to-hotel transfers, guided city tours, and even meals. Most providers of these services are dominated by Taiwanese capital. Thus most Palauans feel that Taiwan's tourists generate little for Palau's economy.

Another type of ethnic Chinese that Palauans often see comprises guest workers from the PRC. Some of them only attract the public's attention if they become involved in criminal affairs or incidents. Palauans have a clear memory of the marches and barricades set up in 2003 by the stranded Chinese garment workers referred to earlier. In September 2003, a group of twenty-three Chinese nationals tried to enter Palau without labor permits. They had been told they could obtain Palauan citizenship after three years of working there and could then immigrate to the United States (Radway 2003). In another case, reported in 2007, nine Chinese workers complained that they were hired to work as waitresses at a restaurant/karaoke bar but were forced into prostitution (Villaflor 2007: 2). These criminal cases, among others, have promoted negative images of Chinese nationals.

Although ordinary people often have negative perceptions of Taiwanese and Chinese nationals, educated Palauans and entrepreneurs have a more practical take on Palau's future relations with China and Taiwan, based mainly on their business interests, as in the case of Senator Seid. Some, including Bonifacio Basilius, have argued that Palau should get along with all foreigners regardless of their nationalities, and thus treat Taiwanese and Chinese equally. The educated public sees political problems as having little to do with their daily interactions or their business partnerships. They think political matters between Taiwan and China will someday be resolved, and they enjoy doing business with both Taiwanese and Chinese partners simultaneously.

Conclusion

This chapter has outlined recent trends regarding Palau's international relations with China and Taiwan. I began by reviewing how Palau established an official diplomatic tie with Taiwan, and then turned to contemporary Chinese and Taiwanese activities in Palau. I concluded by summarizing various Palauan perspectives, including significant signs that Palauans are interested in forming new relationships with China. The governments of Palau and China have no official relations, and Palau's executive leader has strengthened Palau's relations with Taiwan throughout the period following establishment of diplomatic relations in 1999. However, some members of Palau's legislative branch, politicians, and people in the private sector hold hopes and expectations regarding possible relations with China. The trend has shifted from an exclusive relationship with Taiwan toward an emergence of pro-China views.

In Palau there was once little discussion of choosing between Taiwan and China, but as we have seen, this has been changing of late. The intensification of the aggressive diplomacy both by China and Taiwan, displayed by the summits each conducted in 2006, may have triggered recent debates among the people. The Shimao Group's proposed project also has influenced people to give more consideration to China. Under these circumstances, debates on China and Taiwan will continue, and will probably escalate during the 2008 election campaign.

Discussions of controversial diplomatic issues are healthy for Palau as a democratic nation. However, the emergence of two antagonistic axes—pro-Taiwan and pro-China—is undesirable for such a small society. Palau will not benefit if it is simply played with by foreign powers. Moreover, if Palau simply switches the diplomatic ties between Taiwan and China, as have Nauru and Kiribati, it would lose some international standing and credibility, and possibly deter investors who fear political instability.

As of now, Palau's economy has not shut China out. The Foreign Investment Board and the immigration and labor offices have an open policy toward any nationality. Except for inconveniences caused by the lack of appropriate Chinese government representation in Palau, there are no obstacles for Chinese companies or laborers. The creation of an antagonistic structure between pro-Taiwan and pro-China camps is unnecessary and avoidable. It is wise to refer to other countries' situations carefully. For example, Japan, China, and Taiwan have all promoted economic exchanges, and each has been separately promoted as a tourist destination. Moreover, the PRC and Taiwan enjoy intensive economic exchanges between themselves. Given these facts, there is no reason not to engage in "economic" exchanges with China.

Palau has been exposed to waves of modernization and globalization, regardless of Palauans' wishes. Palau secures its economic development and the government's financial base from foreign aid, foreign investment, international tourists, and guest workers. These are some of the forces of globalization that have penetrated Pacific Island societies. If Palau pursues its development by promoting further interactions with foreigners, it must be careful not to be swallowed up by the foreign, more powerful actors. We must recognize that if Palau's international relations continue to be initiated by the foreign forces, Palau will not become self-reliant and instead may be incorporated as one tiny player in a global competition. To prevent such disadvantageous consequences, Palau, as a stable sovereign state, can strengthen its international relations with foreign governments based on steady trust and clear, shared visions. The Palauan people can maximize their capacity to learn the cultures, languages, and business practices of other countries, including Taiwan and China. Or, Palau may choose to make unsparing efforts to promote to foreigners its own culture, practices, and vision for Palau's future.

Notes

1. The Republic of Palau is located in the western part of the Pacific Islands region. Geographically, it is an archipelago with at least nine inhabited islands and some 300 uninhabited ones. Politically, Palau enjoys sovereignty in the international community, except for rights of defense that it has ceded to the United States based on the Compact of Free Association concluded in 1994. Palau's political system

is a mixture of modern and traditional structures. The constitutional government separates power between three branches and coexists with the traditional leadership system. The capital relocated from Koror to Melekeok in October 2006, but Koror remains the largest city and commercial center. Palau's population is 19,907, including some 6,000 guest workers from Asian countries. Ethnically, Palauans are Pacific Islanders. The official languages are Palauan and English.

2. In this chapter, "Chinese" and "Taiwanese" refer to nationalities, regardless of people's ethnicity, unless specified.

3. During the process of decolonization, pro-compact advocates repeatedly told Palauans that communists would invade the Pacific region if Palau did not establish strong US ties. Therefore, Palauans were very anti-communist. Nakamura (2007) says that people then were afraid of China, so Taiwan was a taboo topic.

4. Nakamura is proud to have opened the door to Taiwan in the Pacific region, since previously few countries had diplomatic ties with Taiwan.

5. The United States is the most significant country for Palau's diplomatic relations because of the Compact of Free Association. The United States began to govern Palau after World War II as the administering authority of the UN Trust Territory of Pacific Islands. Japan began its official development assistance to Palau in 1981 when Palau became self-governing as the Republic of Palau. Since then, Japan as a donor has been second only to the United States.

6. Other donor governments offer grant aid only, so that Palau will not take on the financial burden of loans.

7. The crisis, in August and September, involved a breakdown of generators of the Palau Public Utilities Corporation. The majority of Koror and Babeldaob residents had to cope twice daily with four-hour outages, over a month. The cause was inadequate maintenance of the generators.

8. As a consequence of this, some 6,000 depositors will be saved.

9. It is Taiwan's policy not to disclose comprehensive information on grant aid projects, so as to prevent unnecessary competition among recipient countries.

10. The place name Nekken derives from Nettai Sangyo Kenkyujo (tropical industries research institute) of Nanyocho (South Seas Government of Japan) during the Japanese administration. One reason that Palau government allocated Nekken for the mission is that the place has been known as ideal agricultural land since the Japanese administration period.

11. The political leaders who signed the agreement were President of the Republic of Palau Tommy E. Remengesau, Jr., President of the Republic of China (Taiwan) Chen Shui-bian, President of the Marshall Islands Kessai H. Note, President of the Republic of Kiribati Anote Tong, President of the Republic of Nauru Ludwig Scotty, Prime Minister of the Solomon Islands Manasseh Sogavare, and Prime Minister of Tuvalu Apisai Ilelemia.

12. The Taiwanese government holds 37 percent of the stock in the First Commercial Bank (Soong 2007).

13. The First Commercial Bank established a branch in Palau despite its small population. The bank has overseas branches in London, New York, Los Angeles, Hong Kong, Tokyo, Guam, Singapore, Palau, and Phnom Penh, and representative offices in Bangkok and Ho Chi Minh City (First Bank 2007).

14. The tourist arrival record here is calculated from the visitors' arrival data sheet provided by the Palau Visitors Authority.
15. The Ninth Festival of Pacific Arts undoubtedly increased visitor arrivals.
16. The proposal includes 300 hotel rooms, a casino, golf course, aquarium, yacht club, and shopping center, and 1,000 housing units for foreigners (Shuster 2006: 119–120).
17. The symposium, held from 19 to 23 February, was organized by the Compact Review Commission, whose purpose is to review the Compact of Free Association.
18. In 2002, 6,962 permits were issued (including 1,296 Chinese and 65 Taiwanese); in 2003, 6,190 (801 Chinese, 84 Taiwanese); in 2004, 4,149 (687 Chinese, 79 Taiwanese); in 2005, 3,691 (659 Chinese, 90 Taiwanese). In 2003, the length of permit was extended from one to two years, and because of this, the number issued for foreigners dropped by half.
19. The Orientex Company was built with Taiwanese capital, but most of its laborers were from the PRC. They were unable to buy tickets home because the factory owner had fled Palau without paying them.

References

Abrau, Agnes M. 2005. "Palau Lawmakers Mum on China Trip Funds." *Palau Horizon,* 15 June. Accessed 12 February 2007 at *Pacific Islands Report,* http://archives.pireport .org/archive/2005/june/06-16-06.htm.

———. 2006a. "Chinese Official Meets with Palau Lawmakers." *Palau Horizon,* 25 May. Accessed 11 February 2007 at *Pacific Islands Report,* http://archives.pireport .org/archive/2006/may/05-25-16.htm.

———. 2006b. "Palau Chief Supports Major Resort Project." *Palau Horizon,* 20 September. Accessed 3 February 2007 at Pacific Islands Report, http://archives.pireport .org/archive/2006/september/09-20-04.htm.

Basilius, Bonifacio. 2007. Interview by author. Koror, Palau, 10 January.

Basilius, Polycarp. 2004. Campaign advertisement by Polycarp Basilius. Published in *Tia Belau.* 25 June, 3.

———. 2007. Interview by author. Koror, Palau, 11 January.

Carreon, Bernadette H. 2006. "Cooperative Projects Forged between Taiwan, Pacific Allies." *Palau Horizon,* 5 September, 1–2.

Chen, Shui-bian. 2007. Acknowledgement Letter Sent to Tommy E. Remengesau, Jr., the President of the Republic of Palau on the Occasion of Presentation of the Order of Brilliant Jade with Grand Cordon. English Translation.

Division of Labor Palau. 2006. *Foreign Workers with Permit by Sex and Nationality: 2001 to 2005.* Koror: Division of Labor, Ministry of Commerce and Trade.

First Bank. 2007. "About Us. Introduction. History." Accessed 25 January 2007 at http:// www.firstbank.com.tw/eportal/cmsweb/templatelib/contentViewer.jsp;jsessionid= AEMLKNNDAJBJKQRAQAQ-B?oid=50936&ctName=T1.

Foreign Affairs China. 2006. "Wen Jiabao Attends the First Ministerial Meeting of China–Pacific Island Countries Economic Development and Cooperation Forum." Accessed 10 February 2007 at http://www.chineseembassy.org/eng/wjb/zzjg/bmdyzs/ zwlb/t244801.

Foreign Investment Board Palau. n.d. (ca. 2000). *Palau: The Foreign Investor's Guide.* Koror: Foreign Investment Board of the Republic of Palau.

———. 2007. Excel data on the list of foreign investors in Palau. Obtained 19 January. Koror: Foreign Investment Board of the Republic of Palau.

Gerundio, Aurea A. 2007. "Taiwan Gov't lends $3.3M to Pay Out PSB Depositors." *Island Times,* 25 January, 1, 18.

Hseu, Ming-Lii. 2007. Interview by author. Aimeliik, Palau, 12 March.

Hwang, Jim. 2006. "What Really Counts: Taiwan Denounces Dollar Diplomacy and Consolidates Natural Affinities with Its Pacific Allies." *Taiwan Review* 56 (12) (December): 18–21.

International Cooperation and Development Fund Taiwan. 2007. *Country Situation, Palau, Asia Pacific, Country Programs.* Taipei: International Cooperation and Development Fund. Accessed on 10 March 2007 at, http://www.icdf.org.tw/english/e_co_contect.asp?coarea=02&country=12.

Island Times. 2007a. "Remengesau Receives Award from Taiwan Government." *Island Times,* 25 January, 1, 18.

———. 2007b. "Taiwan Gov't Vows to Support More Infra Projects in Palau." *Island Times,* 25 January, 3.

Koshiba, Joshua. 2007a. Interview by author. Koror, Palau, 1 March.

———. 2007b. Remarks. At the National Economic Symposium, Compact Review Commission, Republic of Palau. 19 February. Koror, Palau.

Lee, Matthew S. 2007. Remarks. At the National Economic Symposium: A Step Towards a Brighter Future. Koror, Palau, 23 February.

Nakamura, Kuniwo. 2007. Interview by author. Koror, Palau, 1 March.

Ngedebuu, Lanny. 2007. Interview by author. Koror, Palau, 7 March.

Ngotel, Tadao. 2007. Interview by author. Koror, Palau, 18 January.

Office of the President Palau. 2007. *The First Taiwan-Pacific Allies Summit Palau Declaration: Strengthening Oceanic Democratic Alliances and Realizing Comprehensive Partnership.* Koror, Palau.

Office of the President Taiwan. 2007. *President Chen's Remarks at a State Banquet in Honor of Palau President Tommy E. Remengesau.* Retrieved 15 March 2007 from Office of the President, Republic of China (Taiwan) website: http://www.president.gov.tw/en/prog/news_release/document_content.php?id=1105499351&pre_id=1105499351&g_category_number=145&category_number_2=145.

Palau Visitors Authority. 2002. *Palau Visitors Authority Comprehensive Exit Survey 2001 Analysis Report.* Koror: Palau Visitors Authority.

———. 2007. *2005–2006 Visitors for Each Market Group by Residency: Comparison between Monthly Arrivals, Comparison Market Share and Comparison YTD Percentage.* Koror: Palau Visitors Authority.

Radio Taiwan International. 2006. "China Offers Sweeping Aid to South Pacific." *Radio Taiwan International,* 5 April. Accessed 8 March 2007 at http://english.rti.org.tw/Content/GetSingleNews.aspx?ContentID=11917.

Radway, Scott. 2003. "Chinese Group Turned Away in Palau Scam." *Pacific Daily News,* 14 October. Accessed 7 January 2007 at *Pacific Islands Report,* http://achives.pireport.org/acrchive/2003/october/10-14-12.htm.

Rechebei, Elizabeth Diaz, and Samuel F. McPhetres. 1997. *History of Palau: Heritage of an Emerging Nation*. Koror: Ministry of Education.

Remengesau, Casmir. 2007. Phone interview by author, 14 March.

Republic of Palau. 2006a. "Republic of Palau: Debt Service Schedule, Capitol Relocation Project." Document attached to the proposed budget bill for Fiscal Year 2007 submitted to the Senate President, dated 12 June. Koror: Office of the President.

———. 2006b. "Republic of Palau: U.S. FAA PIA Improvement Project Grants, 2004–07." Document attached to the proposed budget bill for Fiscal Year 2007 submitted to the Senate President, dated 12 June. Koror: Office of the President.

Rodriguez Jr., Nazario. 2007a. "Mariur Hits Taiwan for 'Dollar Diplomacy.'" *Palau Horizon,* 9 March, 1, 13.

———. 2007b. "Palau Governors Back Taiwan Agro-Tourism Project." *Marianas Variety,* 13 February. Accessed 12 March 2007 at *Pacific Islands Report,* http://archives.pireport.org/archive/2007/february/02-13-15.htm.

Sayson, Malou L. 2001. *Kuniwo Nakamura from the Grassroots: Looking Back at Thirty-one Years of Public Service*. Koror: Kuniwo Nakamura.

Seid, Alan. 2007. Interview by author. Koror, Palau, 7 March.

Shuster, Donald R. 2006. "Republic of Palau, Micronesia in Review: Issues and Events, 1 July 2004 to 30 June 2005." *The Contemporary Pacific* 18: 114–126.

Soong, Jing-Ying. 2007. Interview by author. Koror, Palau, 1 February.

Tellei, Lucia. 2007. Interview by author. Koror, Palau, 28 February.

Tia Belau. 2006. "Seid, Diaz in China." *Tia Belau,* 27 October, 1, 15.

———. 2007a. "Diplomatic Battle: Congressmen Push for Change in China-Taiwan Relations." *Tia Belau,* 9 March, 1, 19.

———. 2007b. "Four Lawmakers Are in China." *Tia Belau,* 9 February, 1, 19.

Toribiong, Johnson. 2007. Interview by author. Koror, Palau, 8 February.

Uyehara, Ken. 2007. Interview by author. Koror, Palau, 26 February.

Villaflor, Salome O. 2007. "Prostitution Case Set to Go on Trial." *Tia Belau,* 9 February, 2.

APPENDIX

China and Taiwan in Oceania

Selected Documents

DOCUMENT 1

Keynote address by Chinese Premier Wen Jiabao, delivered at the opening of the First Ministerial Conference of the China–Pacific Island Countries Economic Development and Cooperation Forum, Nadi, Fiji Islands, 5 April 2006.

Win-Win Cooperation for Common Development

Dear Prime Minister Laisenia Qarase, dear Prime Minister Michael Somare, President of the Pacific Islands Forum, heads of state and government, heads of the delegations, ministers and ambassadors, friends from the business community of China and the Pacific island countries, ladies and gentlemen.

It gives me a great pleasure today to meet you at the opening of the First Ministerial Conference of the China–Pacific Island Countries Economic Development and Cooperation Forum to discuss ways of promoting cooperation and development. On behalf of the Chinese Government, I wish to extend warm congratulations on the opening of the First Ministerial Conference and a warm welcome to all the state leaders and participants. I also wish to thank the Fiji Government and the Secretariat of the Pacific Islands Forum for all they have done for the opening of this conference.

The world we live in today is undergoing complex and profound changes. Steady economic growth, rapid progress in science and technology, the accelerated relocation of industries and the movement of production factors world-wide have created valuable opportunities for all countries to develop their economies. However, the widening gap between the North and the South and between the rich and the poor underscores the increasing imbalance in global development. The growing non-traditional security threats such as terrorism, transnational crimes, environmental degradation and communicable diseases present a daunting challenge for the sustainable development of developing countries, including the Pacific island countries. We must therefore work together to cope with the risks by pooling our wisdom.

China and the Pacific island countries, both being developing countries in the Asia Pacific region, are engaged in economic revitalization and social development. People in the region, facing a new international environment and increasing economic globalization, ardently hope to seize the opportunity, meet the challenge and keep abreast with the advance of the times. It is against this general backdrop that the China–Pacific Island Countries Economic Development and Cooperation Forum is being held, with the goal of "strengthening cooperation and realizing common development" to improve the well-being of people in our respective countries. I am confident that this Forum, a landmark event in the relations between China and the Pacific island countries, will set a new model for South-South cooperation.

China firmly adheres to the path of peaceful development and pursues a policy of peace, development and cooperation in international affairs. China is committed to "promoting peace and development through cooperation," and will continue to strengthen its friendship and cooperation with the Pacific island countries on the basis of the Five Principles of Peaceful Coexistence.

Politically, China maintains that all countries, whether big or small, strong or weak, rich or poor, are equal members of the international community and should treat each other as such. We respect the social systems of the Pacific island countries and the development strategy they have adopted based on their national conditions and their efforts in safeguarding sovereignty and independence and preserving peace and stability in the region.

Economically, China shares the joy over the achievements of the Pacific island countries and is keenly aware of the difficulties they face in their development endeavor. We are committed to implementing the UN Millennium Development Goals and helping the Pacific island countries improve capacity for self-development. China is not rich. Still, we are ready to provide assistance without any political strings attached to the Pacific island countries to the best of our ability.

In international affairs, China strives to uphold the rights and interests of the developing countries, including the Pacific island countries. As a permanent member of the UN Security Council, China supports the Pacific island countries in pursuing their legitimate interests regarding maritime resources exploration and protection, climate change and other issues and their right to equal participation in regional and international affairs.

As a Chinese saying puts it, "Just as distance tests a horse's strength, time will show a person's sincerity." As far as China is concerned, to foster friendship and cooperation with the Pacific island countries is not a diplomatic expediency. Rather, it is a strategic decision. China has proved and will continue to prove itself to be a sincere, trustworthy and reliable friend and partner of the Pacific island countries forever.

China's relations with the Pacific island countries have registered good progress in recent years, and our common interests have expanded. As a dialogue partner of the Pacific Islands Forum (PIF), China has set up the China-PIF Cooperation Fund to help finance the Pacific Plan designed to promote regional cooperation. The China–Pacific Island Countries Economic Development and Cooperation Guiding Framework that we are going to sign today is another significant step we take to enrich our cooperation. To deepen friendship and cooperation between China and the Pacific island countries is the shared desire of our peoples. It serves the fundamental and long-term interests of each side and will strengthen peace and prosperity of the region. With this goal in mind, I propose that China and the Pacific island countries work together in the following fields: conduct regular exchanges between governments, parliaments, political parties and non-governmental sectors to enhance mutual trust and understanding; strengthen consultation and coordination on major international and regional issues; accommodate each other's interests and reinforce mutual support; and establish a new economic and trade relationship of mutual benefit that meets the needs of the island countries.

Economic ties are an integral part of the relationship between China and the Pacific island countries. Our respective economies are mutually complementary. China has funding and technical expertise. The island countries are rich in natural resources. Herein lie huge potentials for bilateral cooperation. Following the principle of "looking to the future, advancing steadily and working for mutual benefit and common development", we can certainly make new progress in our economic cooperation and trade ties. To meet the current need of economic development of the Pacific island countries, China has decided to take the following steps:

1) To strengthen cooperation between the business communities of China and the Pacific island countries, China will provide RMB 3 billion yuan of preferential loans in the next three years to boost cooperation in resources development, agriculture, forestry, fishery, tourism, textiles and consumer products manufacturing, telecommunications and aviation and ocean shipping. The Chinese Government will also set up a special fund to encourage Chinese companies to invest in the Pacific island countries.

2) To support the Pacific island countries in developing their economy and ease their debt burden, China will give zero-tariff treatment to the majority of exports to China from the least developed countries in the region that have diplomatic ties with China. China will cancel their debts that became mature at the end of 2005 and extend by ten years the payment of debts contracted by other island countries that became mature at the end of 2005.

3) China will provide free anti-malaria medicines to the island countries affected by the disease in the next three years to help them treat malaria. China will con-

tinue to send medical teams to the island countries and conduct annual training courses for health officials, hospital managers and medical researchers of these countries. China is also ready to exchange information on bird flu prevention and control, and cooperate with the island countries in various ways in this field.

4) China will provide training to 2,000 government officials and technical staff from the island countries over the next three years to assist them in capacity building.

5) To accelerate the development of tourism of the Pacific island countries, China has decided to formally approve Papua New Guinea, Samoa, and the Federated States of Micronesia as destinations for Chinese tourists. Thus, all the seven island countries having diplomatic ties with China are now approved tourist destinations for Chinese citizens.

6) China will provide assistance in building an earthquake or tsunami early warning and monitoring network in light of the need of the island countries to improve their capability of managing earthquakes, tsunamis and other natural disasters.

It is here in the Pacific island countries that the world sees the first ray of the sun. Your people are warm and hospitable and you have a great potential for economic development. The bond between China and the Pacific island countries, just like the rising sun, has a bright future. We share a common vision for the future. Let's work together to strengthen peace, stability and prosperity in the region.

In conclusion, I wish the First Ministerial Conference of China–Pacific Island Countries Economic Development and Cooperation Forum every success.

Thank you all!

DOCUMENT 2

Speech by Prime Minister of Papua New Guinea and Chair of the Pacific Islands Forum Sir Michael Somare, delivered at the opening of the First Ministerial Conference of the China–Pacific Island Countries Economic Development and Cooperation Forum, Nadi, Fiji Islands, 5 April 2006.

Your Excellency Premier Wen Jiabao, Pacific Leaders and Heads of Delegation, distinguished guests, ladies and gentlemen. Welcome to the inaugural meeting of the China–Pacific Island Countries Economic Cooperation Development Forum.

May I first of all, as Chair of the Pacific Islands Forum, say how deeply honored we are by the presence of Premier Wen Jiabao for this important meeting. Your participation this morning, Your Excellency, is greatly appreciated and reinforces the high value that China places on its good relations with the Pacific region. Our Leaders here today have signaled a desire to see that our partnership grows even stronger into the future.

China has a long and proud history in our region and the contribution of Chinese communities in the development of Pacific Island countries has been immense. These communities are integrated into the social and economic fabric of our societies and we value their commitment to the future of our islands.

Your Excellency, China is obviously an Asian power, but it is also a Pacific power, and we welcome the interest that you and your government have in the concerns of island states. Part of this lies in the fact that China is also a developing country, with similar development challenges although on a far bigger scale. There is much we can learn from one another, and we look forward to sharing our experiences and to also increase our trade and investment, and people exchanges.

I am confident that our meeting will further strengthen trade and economic cooperation relations between China and the region, especially in the context of the Pacific Plan endorsed by Pacific Islands Forum Leaders in October 2005 in Port Moresby, Papua New Guinea.

I wish to say a few words about the Pacific Plan which aims to strengthen regional cooperation and integration. Our Leaders have recognized that the Pacific is in a new era which requires fresh approaches to some of the challenges we face. The Pacific Plan outlines a range of initiatives under the four goals of economic growth, sustainable development, good governance and security. The Pacific Plan is based on the belief that regional approaches may be a better option in many cases where our members seek to advance their national priorities. The work of regional organizations will continue to be based on delivery of services, and not the policymaking itself which remains a responsibility of the member states. This delegation of services, to regional mechanisms such as the Forum, means the member states can focus on key priorities rather than spending scarce resources on costly, duplicated services.

The Pacific Plan has the potential to serve as a framework for activity by development partners such as China, and we will continue to consult with your government and the rest of our partners on ways in which your assistance might usefully follow the aims of the Plan. We also wish to hear from our development partners on ways to ensure better ownership of development interventions, and how best to align them with national and regional priorities.

China is a Forum Dialogue Partner and it maintains an extensive bilateral and multilateral program in the region. At the 2005 Post Forum Dialogues in October in Papua New Guinea, China pledged an additional sum to the China-PIF Cooperation Fund, in support of projects under the Pacific Plan over the next five years, to the value of USD 2 million. This is in addition to other support provided by China for a range of Forum-related activities including its welcome support for the Pacific Islands Forum Trade Office in Beijing. For this, our region is truly grateful.

This week we are considering an initiative to establish a high-level consultation to enhance economic and trade cooperation between China and Pacific Island Countries. This will assist the region to develop a structured relationship that carries a number of potential benefits, while respecting and supporting current and future bilateral commitments and initiatives.

Economic cooperation between China and the Forum Island Countries has grown tremendously over the last four years as a result of concerted efforts to deepen understanding, heighten exchanges and broaden cooperation from both Governments and private sectors, of the two regions.

Trade

Total trade between China and the Forum Island Countries totaled USD 288 million by December 2002, which grew to USD 500 million by December 2003, highlighting a growth factor of some 74%. The leading island states that contributed to trade volume in 2002 included Papua New Guinea, Fiji, the Solomon Islands, and the Republic of the Marshall Islands.

In 2002, Papua New Guinea demonstrated strong export performance to China with a trade surplus of USD 132 million – which was boosted by exports of timber, natural gas, and metals. In the same year, the Solomon Islands also registered a trade surplus of USD 17.15 million – which was boosted by timber and fishery products to China.

In 2003, total reciprocal trade volume between China and the 14 Forum Island Countries reached USD 500 million, demonstrating a 74% increase in import and exports between the two regions. A notable performance was demonstrated by Papua New Guinea with a trade surplus of USD 100.3 million by August 2003.

In 2004, total reciprocal trade between China and the Forum Island Countries reached USD 629 million, in favor of China, as more and more island states began sourcing imports from China, overtaking island exports to China.

In 2005, total reciprocal trade between China and Oceania (including Australia and New Zealand) reached nearly USD 31 billion, with increases of 35% in exports to China; and 26.7% in exports to Oceania. The total reciprocal trade between China and the smaller 14 FICs surpassed the USD 850 million mark, beating analyst targets of USD 786.25 million.

It is estimated that total reciprocal trade between China and the 14 FICs will exceed USD 1 billion by December 2006, in favor of exports from China to the Pacific Islands. The proposed China–Pacific Island Countries Economic Cooperation and Development Guiding Framework, to which I will refer shortly, will provide the impetus to boost greater trade between the two regions, with an emphasis on stronger export performance from the Forum Island Countries to China. This will be via the implementation of new bilateral agreements and corresponding trade facilitation measures designed to fast-track the export process from Pacific Island states to China.

Investments

Over the last four years, Chinese investments into the Pacific Islands have been driven by State-Owned Corporations in search of commodities to feed China's growing domestic consumption. Total Chinese investment into the Pacific Islands was estimated at USD 113 million in 2004; increasing to USD 135.6 million in 2005. It is expected to reach USD 176.3 million by December 2006 as a result of greater exchanges by Governments and private sectors of the two regions.

Investments by Chinese State-Owned Corporations will continue to dominate the investment sources; however, a growing number of Chinese small and medium sized enterprises are expected to invest in the Forum Island Countries as the business relationship grows and this is a most welcome development.

Tourism

Tourism has grown steadily over the last four years with China departures estimated at 35,000 in 2004, of which 78% traveled to Fiji. The China National Tourism Administration confirmed Approved Destination Status in 2004 and 2005 for four Pacific states, the Cook Islands, Fiji, Tonga and Vanuatu, with additional approvals announced this year for French Polynesia and New Caledonia.

China departures to the 14 smaller FICs are expected to grow by 15% per year to reach an estimated 46,000 by December 2006. Tourism industry exchanges by Government and private sectors of the two regions are expected to expand throughout 2006 and 2007 which should result in more Forum Island Countries receiving Approved Destination Status, which will provide a positive net impact on China departures to the Pacific islands region.

These activities provide a valuable foundation for the work we will be conducting at this meeting here in Nadi.

We will shortly be signing the China–Pacific Island Countries Economic Development and Cooperation Guiding Framework. That document marks an historic milestone in the further strengthening of relations between the People's Republic of China and countries of this region. While this is not an international treaty, the Guiding Framework embodies the firm commitment of all signatories to establish a partnership of economic and trade cooperation between them, for their mutual benefit and based on a number of fundamental principles.

In working to establish that partnership, the Pacific Island Countries are pleased that China recognizes their unique characteristics, especially their small economies. For the partnership to develop and flourish in the years ahead, it will be necessary for that reality to be reflected in all aspects of the relationship between China and the region.

As the Guiding Framework clearly illustrates, and as I indicated earlier, there are many areas in which cooperation can be strengthened between China and countries of this region at both the national and regional levels. Pacific Island Countries have been working to strengthen regional economic integration and this is reflected as a key element of the Pacific Plan. Indeed, the Pacific Island Countries see opportunities for co-operation between the two sides to promote regional economic integration with a view to better enabling them to strengthen their own economic and trade relations with China.

Pacific Island Countries recognize the potential for the continued strengthening of investment and commercial relations between themselves and China and, towards that end, the importance of establishing a legal framework conducive to investment promotion and protection as highlighted in the Guiding Framework. This is another area to which attention might be given in the months ahead in line with a work program agreed between our two sides.

The Guiding Framework also highlights, quite rightly, a number of key sectors where co-operation can take place. These include agriculture and fisheries, tourism and transportation, financial services, engineering and infrastructure, the sustainable development of natural resources and the development of human resources. All of us gathered here today can quickly think of areas where fruitful cooperation can take place in each sector and our ministers will be exploring some of those possibilities later today.

In sum, the Guiding Framework offers exciting prospects for Pacific Island Countries and their future relations with China. However, for those prospects to be realized and the Guiding Framework to truly serve its intended purpose, there must be an effective, regular dialogue established between our two sides at the official level.

Through such a dialogue, a well-designed work program could be formulated and implemented over the months ahead so that when our Ministers next gather in Beijing to review activities undertaken in line with the Guiding Framework they will be able to witness concrete progress in furthering the objectives of that Framework.

Given our past history of growing cooperation, I am sure that we will find a way forward that meets our mutual expectations. Thank you

DOCUMENT 3

The Palau Declaration, delivered at the First Taiwan–Pacific *Allies Summit held in Koror, Republic of Palau, and signed on 4 September 2006 by*

Tommy E. Remengesau, Jr., President of the Republic of Palau
Chen Shui-bian, President of the Republic of China (Taiwan)
Kessai H. Note, President of the Marshall Islands

Anote Tong, President of the Republic of Kiribati
Ludwig Scotty, President of the Republic of Nauru
Manasseh Sogavare, Prime Minister of the Solomon Islands
Apisai Ielemia, Prime Minister of Tuvalu

Strengthening Oceanic Democratic Alliances and Realizing Comprehensive Partnerships

1. We, the Heads of State and Governments representing the Republic of Kiribati, the Republic of the Marshall Islands, the Republic of Nauru, the Republic of Palau, the Solomon Islands, the Republic of China (Taiwan) and Tuvalu, met in Koror, the capital of the Republic of Palau, at the First Taiwan–Pacific Allies Summit. H.E. Tommy Esang Remengesau, Jr., President of the Republic of Palau, and H.E. Chen Shui-bian, President of the Republic of China, co-hosted the Summit.

2. The Leaders engaged in comprehensive discussions on cooperation, development, environmental preservation and other key issues in the Asia-Pacific region. The Leaders all agreed to vigorously pursue the four goals highlighted in the Pacific Plan, as adopted by Leaders at the 36th Pacific Islands Forum held in Papua New Guinea in October 2005; these being economic growth, sustainable development, good governance and security. The leaders acknowledge that strengthening cooperation and partnership between our countries is important to enhancing prospects for our future prosperity. Sincere gratitude was expressed to President Chen Shui-bian and the people and government of Taiwan for assisting its Pacific allies to pursue national and regional goals. The Leaders and their delegations also warmly thanked President Tommy E. Remengesau, Jr., the Republic of Palau and all of its citizens, for their hospitality at this important event.

3. The Leaders of Taiwan's Pacific Allies applaud Taiwan's achievements in political democratization and economic development. Taiwan's Allies acknowledge Taiwan as a sovereign nation whose right to participate in international organizations, such as the United Nations and World Health Organization,

cannot be deprived. Taiwan's Allies committed to continue their firm support of Taiwan's entitlement to undertake full involvement in international and regional organizations and initiatives.

4. In order to strengthen their friendship in line with their mutual democratic ideals, the Leaders recommend enhanced cooperation in the areas of economic development, capacity building and society and culture. Through bi-lateral and regional cooperation in the following areas, the aim to strengthen oceanic democratic alliances and comprehensive partnerships can be achieved:

    A. **Law Enforcement Training:** Additional or expanded programs are needed to detect and prevent money laundering and financing of terrorism, international trafficking of persons, illegal border crossings, people smuggling, and customs irregularities. Cooperation shall be coordinated to improve the practical training of each country's law enforcement or other relevant personnel and administration, relating both to land and sea.

    B. **Digital government:** Taiwan shall assist its Allies to bridge the digital divide, in the private and public sector, through the cultivation of IT talent and the strengthening and modernization of IT infrastructure, through the enhancement of basic IT software and hardware.

    C. **Tourism:** Each of the Allies would profit from enhanced tourism industries. While each Taiwan Ally has different needs and challenges in this area, the Leaders agree to explore means and mechanisms for stimulating tourism, improving tourism alliances and focusing on environmentally friendly and sustainable tourism opportunities.

    D. **Healthcare:** Participating leaders shall strive to fulfill the lofty ideal of health care transcending national borders, as upheld by the World Health Organization. The Leaders therefore affirm the success of the First Pacific Health Forum held in conjunction with this Summit. The Leaders also agree to establish a 'Taiwan-Pacific Medical Alliance' to identify and implement long-term public health projects.

    E. **Protection of Natural Resources, Development of Domestic and Renewable Energy:** Taiwan looks forward to assisting its Allies to respond to escalating fuel prices and environmental degradation by enhancing the development of domestic and renewable energy sources, focusing on biofuel, solar, wind and hydro power, Ocean Thermal Energy Conversion and other domestic energy resources. In addition, Leaders recognize that three of the six Taiwan Allies have already made extraordinary commitments to preserve precious natural resources, through the Micronesian Challenge (Republic of Palau and Republic of the Marshall Islands) and the setting aside by the Republic of Kiribati of the Phoenix Islands, as a marine protected area, the third largest in the world. Leaders agree to launch a Taiwan-Pacific Environmental Ministerial Meeting to discuss relevant issues and solutions, encouraging Taiwan Allies and others who have not done so, to make substantial and specific commitments to the conservation and sustainable management of marine and terrestrial resources, including accessing mechanisms for long-term financing commitments to preserve the environment for future generations.

F. **Economic Partnership:** Leaders agree to establish a business information exchange mechanism and promote bilateral trade and investment between Taiwan and its Allies. To fulfill this commitment, Taiwan shall designate additional commercial staff to the region.

G. **Cooperation on Agriculture and Fishing:** The Taiwan Allies agree that the agriculture and fisheries sectors need to be expanded in order to support tourism industries, enhance balances of trade and improve food security. To support this growing need, Taiwan commits to providing expanded technical assistance in agriculture and fisheries. In the area of agriculture, Taiwan agrees to assist each Ally to establish country agriculture development plans focusing on product development. Taiwan recognizes that the livelihood of its Pacific Allies significantly depends on the ocean and its resources and that Taiwan shall assist in the development of their individual domestic fisheries. In this context, Taiwan agrees to launch the Taiwan-Pacific Forum on Constructive Fishery Partnerships.

H. **Education:** As one of the main keys to the development of a nation, Taiwan shall assist its allies in the area of skills training in both formal and non-formal education to prepare their respective populations to manage change and contribute productively to the achievement of their future development.

I. **Preservation of Culture:** In consideration of the cultural diversity treasured by Taiwan and its Pacific allies, Leaders agree to promote and encourage relevant institutions devoted to the research, preservation, education and innovation of common and diverse indigenous cultures.

5. To implement the various commitments of this Palau Declaration, Leaders agree to adopt the Koror Action Plan. In the future, Leaders shall examine the progress and results of various cooperative projects annually, at the Taiwan/ROC Forum Countries Dialogue, and during each subsequent Taiwan–Pacific Allies Summit.

6. We convey our most heartfelt appreciation to the Republic of the Marshall Islands for agreeing to hold the Second Taiwan–Pacific Allies Summit in 2007 in Majuro.

DOCUMENT 4

The Majuro Declaration, delivered at the Second Taiwan–Pacific Allies Summit, and signed on 12 October 2007 in Majuro, Republic of the Marshall Islands, by

Kessai H. Note, President of the Republic of the Marshall Islands
Chen Shui-bian, President of the Republic of China (Taiwan)
Ludwig Scotty, President of the Republic of Nauru
Tommy E. Remengesau, Jr., President of the Republic of Palau
Manasseh Sogavare, Prime Minister of Solomon Islands
Apisai Ielemia, Prime Minister of Tuvalu
Teima Onorio, Vice President of the Republic of Kiribati

Toward a Healthy, Dynamic and Green Pacific Community

1. The Second Taiwan–Pacific Allies Summit was held in Majuro, the capital of the Republic of the Marshall Islands. The Summit was co-chaired by His Excellency President Kessai H. Note of the Republic of the Marshall Islands and His Excellency President Chen Shui-bian of the Republic of China (Taiwan).

2. The heads of state and government and representatives of the Republic of Kiribati, Marshall Islands, the Republic of Nauru, the Republic of Palau, Solomon Islands, Tuvalu and Taiwan have attended the Summit. The leaders and delegations would like to express their appreciation to His Excellency President Kessai H. Note and the people and government of the Marshall Islands for their dedication to making the Summit a great success.

3. The Pacific countries represented here share the values of democracy, freedom and human rights. The leaders recognize Taiwan's achievements in political reform, democratization and economic development. They also fully support the inalienable rights of Taiwan to join international organizations, such as the United Nations and World Health Organization. In recognition of the fact that Kiribati, Marshall Islands, Nauru, Palau, Solomon Islands and Tuvalu maintain official diplomatic ties with Taiwan, the leaders present today appeal to the other members of the Pacific Islands Forum to invite Taiwan to participate in the dialogues and meetings after the forum on an equal basis. In the meantime, Taiwan's Pacific allies reaffirm their commitments and support of Taiwan's right to be a member of the United Nations, World Health Organization, and other international and regional organizations.

4. The leaders and the delegations appreciate the important role that His Excellency President Chen Shui-bian and the Taiwan–Pacific Allies Summit initiated by him have played in the Pacific region. The leaders have also expressed

their gratitude for the energy infused and the new initiatives introduced into the region for its sustainable development during the First Taiwan–Pacific Allies Summit in Palau last year. Likewise, Taiwan appreciates the cooperation and support of its Pacific allies in implementing related programs.

5. As an important partner for cooperation and development in the Pacific region and the Pacific Islands Forum, Taiwan restates its commitment to assisting its Pacific allies in achieving economic growth, sustainable development, good governance, and security – goals embodied in the 'Pacific Plan.' As a result, Taiwan's Pacific allies are grateful to the people, government and president of Taiwan for initiating eight cooperative programs in the three areas of capacity building, economic development, and society and culture via the Palau Declaration. The leaders are satisfied with the results of such multilateral cooperation and agree to broaden the oceanic democratic alliance and establish comprehensive partnerships to accelerate the realization of regional prosperity.

6. Healthcare, education, vocational, technical and entrepreneurial training, and environmental protection are crucial to the livelihood and wellbeing of Pacific islands people. Therefore, as these issues are key to the region's sustainable development, the leaders gave the Second Taiwan–Pacific Allies Summit the theme "Toward a Healthy, Dynamic and Green Pacific Community." The leaders also reached the following agreements during the summit:

    6.1 Healthcare: The leaders wish to urgently solve the healthcare issue because a sound public health system ensures healthcare for all. In the past 12 months, Taiwan has dispatched 16 mobile medical missions with 170 members to provide over 15,000 free clinical consultations. Taiwan promises to continue the dispatch of mobile medical missions to its Pacific allies to deliver public health and humanitarian relief programs. Also, together with the effort of setting up Taiwan Health Center and dispatching long term based medical teams, Taiwan will provide training courses for medical professionals and improve public health system for Pacific Allies. In addition, Taiwan will promote medical referral system between Taiwan and Pacific Allies to provide alternative clinical medical services. Further, development of telemedicine supporting system will also be planned.

    6.2 Environmental Protection: The leaders are acutely aware of the threat imposed by natural disasters, global climate change and rising sea levels to the existence of people in island nations. They support the consensus reached at the "First Taiwan–Pacific Allies Environmental Ministerial Meeting" on July 26, 2007. The ministers agreed to start cooperation in three areas: establishing a long-term dialogue on environmental protection between the countries; promoting the sharing of experience and exchanges on environmental resource management, marine pollution control, waste management and sustainable development; and capacity building to cope with climate change as well as developing and promoting cooperative programs for adjusting to its impact. They advocated the realization of a World Environment Organization based on these ideals.

6.3 Education and Vocational, Technical and Entrepreneurial Training: To develop human resources, elevate education standards, promote labor mobility and foster experience sharing, Taiwan will continue to train law enforcement personnel for its Pacific allies, cultivate digital technology seed teachers, and train environmental protection law enforcement personnel and human resources for tourism and related industries. Taiwan will also train agriculture and aquaculture experts for its Pacific allies, and dispatch volunteers these countries to alleviate the problem of faculty shortages in primary, middle and trade/technical schools. Taiwan will continue to provide the Taiwan Scholarship to assist elites from its Pacific allies to pursue advanced education in Taiwan.

6.4 Austronesian Cultures: The leaders note that the indigenous peoples of Taiwan and peoples of the Pacific Islands share an Austronesian cultural heritage, and support the establishment of the preparatory office of the Austronesian Forum in Taipei in August 2007. The leaders agreed, with the assistance of Taiwan, to set up headquarters in Palau and branches in the five Pacific allies. The Austronesian Forum will abide by the Convention for the Safeguarding of the Intangible Cultural Heritage adopted by UNESCO in 2003 to cherish Austronesian cultures.

7. Leaders are extremely pleased to have reached the above consensus. Taiwan will continue its close contact and cooperation with its Pacific allies at the decision-making and working levels to ensure that all agreements are carried out.

8. The host country for the Third Taiwan–Pacific Allies Summit will be announced in due course.

About the Contributors

IATI IATI is a consultant and lecturer in political science, University of Canterbury, Christchurch, New Zealand. A 2007 PhD graduate in political science from the University of Hawai'i at Manoa, Iati's dissertation engages popular ideas about civil society and political accountability, using Samoa as the case study. Framed by considerations of the tensions between tradition and modernity, his research interests are civil society, governance, and land issues in the Pacific. Iati was a 2007 Macmillan Brown Center Research Scholar and the 2008 recipient of the Pacific Cooperation Foundation Samoa Treaty of Friendship Fellowship.

TARCISIUS TARA KABUTAULAKA is an Associate Professor in the Center for Pacific Islands Studies, University of Hawai'i at Manoa. His research interests focus on issues of governance, development, conflict, peace-building, post-conflict development, international intervention, and Asia–Pacific Island relations. He has written extensively on the Solomon Islands civil unrest and regional intervention there. He is the co-editor (with Greg Fry) of *Intervention and State-Building in the Pacific: The Legitimacy of 'Cooperative Intervention'* (Manchester University Press, 2008). Kabutaulaka has a PhD in political science and international relations from the Australian National University. He comes from the Weather Coast of Guadalcanal in the Solomon Islands.

KOBAYASHI IZUMI is a professor of political science at Osaka Gakuin University and executive director of the Japan Institute for Pacific Studies. His academic field is international relations, and his publications "Studies for Pacific Island Countries" and "US Confidential Paper and Termination of UN Trusteeship" were awarded the Ohira Masayoshi Memorial Prize in 1994. He has organized many international symposium and exchange programs between the Pacific and Japan.

PALENITINA LANGA`OI holds a B.Sc in mathematics from the University of Auckland, New Zealand, and an MBA from the University of the South Pacific, Fiji. In March 2008 she became the first female PhD graduate from Ritsumeikan Asia Pacific University, Japan. Her doctoral research focused on economic, administrative, and political reform in Tonga. Dr. Langa`oi was a senior official in the office of Tonga's prime minister for five years before joining the Tonga Public Service Commission Office in 2004. In 2008 she was a research fellow in the Asia Pacific Leadership Program of the East-West Center in Honolulu. In August

2009 she was appointed acting chief executive officer for the Tonga Public Service Commission.

HYLAND ("HANK") NEIL NELSON was born in Boort, Victoria, Australia, in 1937 and graduated from Melbourne University. Trained as a teacher, he taught in high schools and at the Royal Melbourne Institute of Technology before joining the staffs of the Administrative College and the University of Papua New Guinea in 1966. On return to Australia in 1972, he became a research fellow and finally a professor of history at the Australian National University. Now professor emeritus, he has retained particular interests in Papua New Guinean and Australian history, World War II, and contemporary regional politics. He has produced books, films, and radio documentaries.

EDGAR A. PORTER serves as dean of academic affairs at Ritsumeikan Asia Pacific University in Beppu, Japan. Previously he served in several capacities in the School of Hawaiian, Asian and Pacific Studies at the University of Hawai`i, including interim dean. He is the author of *The People's Doctor: George Hatem and China's Revolution* (University of Hawai`i Press, 1997), *Foreign Teachers in China: Old Problems for a New Generation* (Greenwood Press, 1990), and editor of the anthology *Journalism from Tiananmen* (Gannett Foundation Fellowship Program in Asian Studies, University of Hawai`i, 1990).

MICHAEL POWLES has headed New Zealand diplomatic posts in the Pacific (as high commissioner in Fiji) and Asia (as ambassador in Indonesia and then China). He was deputy secretary of New Zealand's Ministry of Foreign Affairs and Trade and then ambassador to the United Nations. He writes and lectures on international affairs. He edited *Pacific Futures* (Pandanus Books, Canberra, 2006) and is currently completing a book called *China's Rise: A Pacific View*. He is currently an adjunct research fellow at the Institute of International Studies, Fudan University, Shanghai, visiting fellow at the New Zealand Asia Institute, and senior fellow at the New Zealand Centre for Research Studies.

TAKASHI MITA is a researcher at Osaka University's Global Collaboration Center, Japan. His research interests focus on issues of state-making, globalization, and social changes in the Pacific Islands. He served as researcher/advisor at the Embassy of Japan in Palau as well as associate professor of social sciences at Palau Community College. Mita has a master's degree in Pacific Islands Studies from the University of Hawai`i at Manoa and recently completed a PhD in political science at the same university.

SANDRA TARTE is associate professor and the head of the School of Social Sciences, University of the South Pacific, Fiji. She specializes in the international politics of the Pacific Islands region and is the author of *Japan's Aid Diplomacy and the Pacific Islands* (1998). She has written widely on regional cooperation in the Pacific, with a focus on fisheries management and conservation. She has also consulted for the South Pacific Forum Fisheries Agency, the South Pacific Regional Environment Program, the International Development Centre, Tokyo, and Greenpeace Pacific.

TERENCE WESLEY-SMITH is associate professor and graduate chair in the Center for Pacific Islands Studies at the University of Hawai`i at Manoa. A political scientist with degrees from Victoria University of Wellington and the University of Hawai`i, he is editor of *The Contemporary Pacific: A Journal of Island Affairs*. He directed the Ford-Funded *Moving Cultures* research and teaching initiative at the University of Hawai`i from 1997 to 2002. His recent journal articles have addressed conceptual issues associated with self-determination and "failed states" in Oceania, and he is co-editor (with Jon Goss) of *Remaking Area Studies: New Perspectives on Learning Asia Pacific* (University of Hawai`i Press, forthcoming).

BILL WILLMOTT was born and raised in Chengdu, China, where his parents were educational missionaries. He completed a BA and MA at McGill University and earned his PhD in social anthropology at the London School of Economics based on research among the Chinese in Cambodia. He taught at the University of British Columbia in Vancouver, then at the University of Canterbury in New Zealand, where he is now an emeritus professor. He retired in 1998 to become a research associate at the Macmillan Brown Centre for Pacific Studies, University of Canterbury. His academic research has focused on Chinese overseas communities, most recently in the Pacific Islands.

YONGJIN ZHANG is a professor of international politics at the University of Bristol. He has previously held teaching and research posts at Oxford University, Australian National University, the University of Auckland, and the Institute of International Politics in Beijing. Professor Zhang's most recent publications include "China and the Emerging Regional Order in the South Pacific" in *Australian Journal of International Affairs* (2007); "Discourses of Security in China—Towards a Critical Turn?" in Anthony Burke and Matt MacDonald, *Critical Security in the Asia-Pacific* (Manchester University Press, 2007); and "Understanding Chinese Views of the Emerging Global Order" in Wang Gungwu and Zheng Yongnian, *China and the New International Order* (Routledge, 2008).

Index